I0866516

BIBLE TRUTH ABOUT WOMEN

BIBLE TRUTH ABOUT WOMEN

What They Don't Tell You

Lydia Grace Kaiser

Carpenter's Son Publishing

Bible Truth About Women: What They Don't Tell You

Published by Carpenter's Son Publishing, Franklin, Tennessee
www.christianbookservices.com

Edited by Ann Tatlock and Darla Solberg

Cover and Interior Layout Design by Suzanne Lawing

ISBN: 978-1-968127-05-3 (print)

Printed in the United States of America, 2P

Notes to Reader:
All scripture is from the NIV unless marked otherwise. Hebrew and Greek transliterations may vary based on quoted sources. Strong's Concordance numbers ("H" for Hebrew, "G" for Greek) identify original words and work with other lexicons. Readers can use BlueLetterBible.com or BibleHub.com study tools, particularly the Inline Interlinear Language Resource, to examine Hebrew and Greek words.

Dedicated to my mother, Ruth,
to my four biological sisters, and
to all my dear sisters in Christ.

With gratitude to my hard-working husband, Don,
who enabled me to homeschool our children
and serve in ministry.

With gratitude and devotion to Jesus
who fulfilled the Scriptures (Luke 4:17-21)

CONTENTS

PART THREE

Women in the Church

PART FOUR

Women in the Home

MISLEADING TACTICS

Real World Examples of Harm

Lorraine had been invited to speak at her church's conference. Due to denominational standards, she was only invited to speak to the women. The men at her workplace did not know that, especially when it was posted on social media. Three of them came to hear her speak and sat near the front to be sure she saw they were present. She was their manager; they respected her, and they were interested in what she had to say. During a break, some church men came and ushered the male guests out. They could have heard the gospel but instead saw what they felt was bigotry against their colleague and they were humiliated by being informed they could not be there.

Rob and Cindy were missionaries to Outer Mongolia for fifteen years. They had worked hard to raise support and have good relationships with the leadership and other missionaries in their sending agency. The mission agency board members elected a woman to the board because they felt her experience would benefit them. Rob felt he and Cindy must resign and find a new sending agency because he had been taught that a woman must never exercise authority over a man, not even as part of a group. It was disruptive to their already difficult work.

Carol had an idea she was excited about and brought it to her husband. He quickly said no and when she tried to answer his objections, he told her that she was pushy, out of line, and unable to take no for an answer. Deflated and frustrated, Carol felt she must accept that her husband had the final say on all decisions, and it was her role to submit, even though she would have yielded to his wishes anyway after a kind discussion. They often missed the opportunity for meaningful, patient, and connecting conversations about life because her husband was taught that he must be a "strong leader" and on the lookout for when his wife might try to "grasp his authority."

Hannah was in her twenties, the second oldest of several children. She helped a lot with the younger kids and housework. Her father approved of which jobs she took and how many hours she worked, making sure she had time for what they wanted done at home. He disapproved of her desire to move out. She wanted to date a young man from a Christian family with a good reputation and job. Her father said no because the young man was not his choice, even though he had no solid concerns. Eventually, Hannah moved out one day while the family was away, leaving her parents a letter of gratitude and the offer to stay in touch if everyone stayed civil. Her parents grieved that their adult daughter's "mind was poisoned" into thinking she could make decisions independent of them. Hannah and her boyfriend attended a conservative church and did premarital counseling with the pastor. They kept the door open to her family. Eventually, they were married and her parents refused to participate in the wedding.

Abby earned her undergraduate degree in speech and her graduate degree in teaching speech and English. She taught speech part-time at a local college and homeschooled her children, teaching them presentation skills that earned them awards. Her husband was a preacher. He did not ask her for help because his conviction was that women were not to teach men. Seeking regular input for his sermons, even occasionally inviting his wife to share in the presentations, could have moved his sermons from good to great, growing the church and helping people relate to and remember the teaching better.

I am personally acquainted with the people in these stories (names changed) except for the first story which was witnessed by one of my sisters at her church. The church people, the missionaries, the married couple, the parents, the preacher—they are all people with excellent character, a high regard for Scripture and a sincere heart to obey God in all things. But what if they were misguided? What if the fallout in each of these stories was avoidable because these good people did not actually need to take that principled stand in order to obey God? What if they received poor instruction about God's heart and character, and about what the Bible teaches, and they missed a greater blessing on their personal lives and ministries?

If you have the courage to ask these questions, come with me through the Bible looking at passages related to women. For all of us who care deeply about the truth of Scripture, this book covers all those "What about this verse?" questions. I trust you picked up this book to learn if there really is Bible truth on this topic that you never learned before. If some of the material in this book goes deeper than you feel like you need, feel free to skim those sections and primarily utilize the "Misleading Tactic" sidebars. Just be aware of the content so you can use the book as a handy reference when you encounter material that you don't know how to answer. Some of the supporting material was too in-depth for this book but can be accessed on my website, LydiaKaiser.com. Here is where we are going.

PART ONE

We will look at the genesis of the world and then the genesis of the church. When God created the world and later birthed the church, they were ideal, with simplicity and focus. We will see how God meant for things to be, before humanity quickly derailed them. We will see some poor translations and interpretations of Genesis chapters 1-3, and what is overlooked in the birth of the church.

PART TWO

We will look at the very best representation of God—Jesus in the flesh. God's heart for people is revealed by looking at the words and actions of Jesus. We will see the context in which Jesus lived, how he confronted those who held power in his day and what he told his followers to do differently than the world. The reader will find themselves drawn to and comforted by Jesus in new ways.

PART THREE

We will look at the epistolic passages (from the epistles/letters to churches) that have problematic translations and interpretations for women in the church. It is these passages which are used day after day to prohibit women, so we must look at what has been done to and with them. Heads up—they are like a house of cards. Each one has translation and interpretive problems, yet they are used to prop up the others, giving the illusion of a strong house. Part 3 also looks at various abuse problems in the church and draws connections between beliefs and abuse.

PART FOUR

We will look at each of the epistolic passages that address women in marriage. Again, closer examination of those passages reveals translation and interpretation problems. You will see an interpretation that clears up the oddities and is consistent with other passages.

The Conclusion recommends a way forward that promotes truth, healing, and unity.

In this book the reader will find that mutualism of the sexes reflects the perfection of creation, the design for the church, the mutualism of the Trinity, and the heart of God for unity. The reader will find that Bible passages which supposedly promote hierarchy are poorly translated or misinterpreted and fail to consider the whole counsel of God throughout Scripture.

My Beliefs and Motives

In case a reader has concerns regarding whether my beliefs are orthodox, I agree with the statement of faith of the Southern Baptist Convention (SBC), "Baptist Faith & Message 2000," with the exception of two sentences under the article regarding church polity. I have additional beliefs as well, as I'm sure most Baptists do. My agreement with the SBC statement is not an endorsement of the denomination, just a reference point for the reader regarding my orthodoxy.

The first question I'm asked when I reveal that I've become egalitarian (I prefer the term mutualist), is "Do you want to preach or be a pastor?" Let me clear the air—no. I don't want to contend for the "right" to stand at a pulpit and teach a mixed crowd. Rather than focus on one ministry, I want to see the church not worried about it. I want to see the hierarchical spirit yield to the vision of Jesus, so women can serve however God leads them without the hesitation that comes with knowing their brothers in Christ question their service due to gender. If I or other women are invited to preach to a mixed crowd or find ourselves leading a mixed group in a missional endeavor, we need to be able to do it with a clear conscience and our brothers need a clear conscience in supporting us. I love the way Kate Wallace Nunneley put it:

> *Both feminism and egalitarianism resist patriarchy as a corrupt and abusive system, but they do so in different ways and for differ-*

ent purposes: where feminism fights for equal rights, egalitarianism advocates for "equal access to servanthood."[1]

I am as conservative as one can be in every part of my life—pro-marriage and family, pro-life, evangelistic, pro-homeschooling, pro-modesty, belief in the inerrancy of the Bible (in original languages), political conservative—you name it. But as soon as I began telling people that I believe God intended mutuality instead of hierarchy, I was told I'm a liberal, progressive, feminist. It is both laughable and offensive, but I understand, because I wouldn't have believed what is in this book if I hadn't carefully studied it for years. (I condensed it for my readers.) This is not a conservative vs. liberal/progressive issue, it's a spiritual truth issue. This book is not about telling women they don't have to submit; it's about how God wants everyone to submit and cooperate equally, not one more than the other. It's about following the example of Jesus to empower others who have less power. I pray it will help men and women who have been harmed by the misuse of Scripture. I believe God is honored with truth.

There are egalitarian claims which I did not include in this book because they are not supported well enough by good scholarship. I consulted with good critics (those who know Hebrew and Greek far better than I) because I don't want to overstate anything. I worked hard to be fair. There are also assertions that get too deep in the weeds for this book and refutations on both sides that couldn't be included due to space. I am confident that most **people who believe in the inerrancy of the Word of God will, by the time they reach the end of this book, be shocked and upset at what has been done to the English text to mislead people.** They may wonder, "Why is it that I grew up in church, but no one ever told me this (historical fact, con-

1 Kate Wallace Nunneley, "Why I am a Feminist and an Egalitarian (And Why They Aren't the Same Thing)," The Junia Project, October 4, 2013, https://juniaproject.com/feminist-and-egalitarian-not-the-same/.

text, language factor, etc.)?" Due to my own experience, I know that it can require multiple readings and examinations of the evidence before the reality of what has happened can sink in, so I want to be patient with people who disagree and pray they actually will examine the evidence.

For those who want to know who I am, some of my origin story is sprinkled throughout the book. For now, I'll simply say how much I appreciate my parents for teaching me to value the Bible. However, as an adult, I need to correct some faulty hermeneutics and learn for myself about the heart of God, just as my children will need to do as a result of my imperfect guidance. I primarily wrote this book for myself, because I needed to resolve the discrepancies I've seen. I believe God instructed me to turn it into a formal book by repeatedly bringing women to my attention whose relationship with God is destroyed for lack of this knowledge.

Complegaliwhat?

Before engaging in any discussion of depth, one must define terms to minimize confusion and ensure everyone is thinking about the same thing. If you are not familiar with any of the terms below, or you wonder how I define them and use them in this book, or what the difference is between, for example, a feminist and an egalitarian or a mutualist, you need to stop here and check out the terms section on my website, LydiaKaiser.com. It is interesting, with a little history for context.

Terms: authoritarian(ism), hierarchy, patriarchy, complementarian(ism), soft complementarian, servant-leadership, egalitarian(ism), mutualist (or mutualism), complegalitarian(ism), feminist (or feminism, with waves one through four), manosphere, incel, tradwife, theobro, fundamentalist, evangelical, and exvangelical.

Just Who Is Bending to the Culture?

When we listen to teaching, we need to discern the difference between one speaker's dependence on original language scholarship, context within the passage and greater canon, and documented history, compared to an another's dependence on tactics of character assassination, simplistic English "plain reading," or traditional interpretations without solid support. Is there consideration for first-century cultural context (Jewish, Roman, Greek, and their many subcultures) or is a modern culture system erroneously projected onto the passage? We are so steeped in our own culture, mindset, and past training that we often fail to recognize our assumptions or the assumptions of those within our "tribe."

Accusations such as "They're just bending to the world and questioning the Word of God" rely more on rhetorical intimidation than biblical integrity. Instead, people should support their own view with scholarship and by answering the textual issues raised instead of acting dismissively.

The secular world has always primarily had men in authority with more social, economic, and legal rights than women. *That* is "the way of the world" or "the world's system." John Calvin would agree that has always been the world's prejudice and he shares it:

> *Women have in all ages been excluded from the public management of affairs. It is the dictate of common sense, that female government is improper and unseemly.*[2] *… On this account all women are born, that they may acknowledge themselves inferior in consequence of the superiority of the male sex.*[3]

---

2 "Calvin's Commentaries," Bible Hub, accessed July 23, 2025, https://biblehub.com/commentaries/calvin/ 1_corinthians/14.htm.

3 "Calvin's Commentaries," Bible Hub, accessed July 23, 2025https://biblehub.com/commentaries/calvin/1_corinthians/11.htm.

God says to do things that are countercultural. That is radical and an opportunity to demonstrate that believers are different and love each other better. The "world" has slowly allowed more rights for women, but it is still very new and definitely not true globally. Women have had the right to vote in the USA for barely over 100 years, and they only gained the right to open their own bank account 50 years ago. Recent laws have helped to protect and empower women in the workplace, but there are still inequalities. Only around 14 countries have full legal and economic rights for women.[4] Globally, women have an average of 76.5% of the rights of men.[5] There are countries, such as Kenya, where a woman dies every 24 hours from gender-based violence. Christians for Biblical Equality International (CBE) receives testimony from indigenous women that missionaries who bring a message of inequality "from God's Word" contribute to the abuse problem. (See my website for more information.)

It is strange that evangelicals will accuse egalitarians of "following the world" or "bending to the culture." People who say or write such accusations are the ones bending to a historically worldly culture that has always oppressed women, so theirs is an incongruent stance. We will also see that their stance fails to distinguish between what the Bible merely observes in culture and what God revealed as his countercultural will.

---

4 Katharina Buchholz, "Only 14 Countries Have Full Equal Rights for Women," Statista, March 9, 2023, https://www.statista.com/chart/17290/countries-with-most-equal-rights-for-women/

5 "Nearly 2.4 Billion Women Globally Don't Have Same Economic Rights as Men," World Bank Group, March 1, 2022, https://www.worldbank.org/en/news/press-release/2022/03/01/nearly-2-4-billion-women-globally-don-t-have-same-economic-rights-as-men.

Translation Versus Interpretation

The reader should distinguish between when I use the words "translation" and "interpretation." To translate is to cross over from one language to another with the meaning of words, whereas to interpret is to further expound on the meaning and often make applications. They are two different activities, but it starts with translation. A translator may claim to not be interpreting, but it's impossible to translate without lending to an interpretation, and then every reader further interprets for themselves. Bible teachers interpret for others. As we go along, I will often distinguish between translation problems and interpretation problems. A translator might do a poor job that leads to misunderstanding or do a good job that interpreters might still misunderstand and teach wrongly.

Translation Challenges

A seminary hermeneutics course opened my eyes to the many challenges translators face. I recommend the book, *How to Choose a Translation for All Its Worth* by Gordon Fee and Mark Strauss (member of the NIV Committee on Bible Translation from 2005 – present). Also, *40 Questions about Bible Translation* by Strauss. The challenges listed below (and many others) are explained in more depth in these books. Translating requires difficult decisions. We owe a tremendous debt to great believers throughout history who have given their lives to laborious study (and even persecution and martyrdom) to provide and preserve the Bible in contemporary languages. The job is not done.

Because of the many challenges of translation, I'm extremely hesitant to accuse translation teams of dishonesty. However, there are cases where translators know they are steering people to certain ideologies without people knowing they are being steered. And there are gender-related passages that have been treated dishonestly—mainly words added that are not indicated in the Greek.

And then there are interpreters (teachers) who do not acknowledge the various possibilities of a word or passage because someone has chosen to limit the information to a certain ideology. Even if a teacher has no intent to mislead, it does not change the fact that misleading happens.

Before I list misleading tactics, I need to acknowledge some translation challenges which are most related to the content of this book. You might be tempted to skip this list, but it is essential for understanding the problems described later and will help open your eyes/mind when you read your English Bible. If you ever wonder why we need new or updated versions of the Bible, this list might help you understand.

- Language keeps moving on us and changing meaning. This challenge is accelerating due to the internet and social media. The common understanding of a word can change in just one year's time, so it is difficult to keep up with a new edition of something as significant as the Bible. One humorous example is Gen Z people saying "sick" when they especially admire something. Granted, this is probably not going to be a lasting language change, but we have to wait and see. (There's an element of meaning that they are so smitten with admiration it makes them ill. Would a reader understand "sick" to be about "admiration" in the distant future?)

- In many languages, it is traditional to default to "he" when gender is not known ("masculine generics"). In English, if there's a group or even one person of unknown gender, we now say "they/them." But in Greek, the default remains masculine unless it's a known fact that only females are present. If there's even one male in a group of women, the default plural word is masculine. Because that is not the way we do it today, people can be misled into thinking that males were intended exclusively. Younger people are increasingly expecting gender to be inclusive unless it is meant to be exclusive, so resistance to discarding masculine generics can lead to misunderstanding. What we should want is "gender accuracy," representing the author's intention and avoiding misrepresenting God's Word. See the book by Strauss, *Distorting Scripture?: The Challenge of Bible Translation & Gender Accuracy* and questions 18-20 in Strauss's *40 Questions about Bible Translation.*

- Different languages have different grammatical rules for things such as word order, tense, voice, how to indicate sentence types, number, and gender, so translations cannot be word for word, or they would be unintelligible in the target language. A translator must have a grasp on what is *meant* in order to communicate someone else's writing, which requires contextual research and decision-making. Therefore, the translator is actually interpreting and paraphrasing as much as translating. The truth is, all translations are paraphrases to some extent, so the idea that one translation is less reliable than another due to being a paraphrase is misleading. There could be greater unreliability or misunderstanding resulting from too minimal paraphrasing.

- Some translations claim to be "literal," but words do not have "literal" meanings. For example, the words "bank" and "field" can have several meanings based on context and part of speech. (Is it agricultural or an area of study, a noun or a verb?) See the article, "The Literal Meaning Fallacy," by translator Dr. Mark Strauss linked on my website. Better is a "dynamic" translation that simply attempts to convey accurate meaning.

- Individual words do not perfectly correspond with words and their meanings in other languages. The meaning will be nuanced differently. That is another reason why a truly word-for-word translation would be awkward, unintelligible, and impossible.

- Idioms can be misunderstood. For example, we think clean teeth is a good thing, but in OT times, "clean teeth" was an idiom for starving. It meant no food, thus, clean teeth. Once scholars understood the idiom, they changed the translation from "clean teeth" to "starving." Do they identify and understand all idioms? Are they updating the Bible when new idioms are discovered in first-century documents?

- Because ancient Hebrew and Greek did not have quotation marks, translators must decide when to use them. We assume they are always used accurately. However, translators cannot always be sure, risking the possibility that we are misunderstanding who said what. Paul often quoted errant thinking and then refuted it. What if an error was not put in quotes? Even Peter (who spoke Greek and was Paul's contemporary) said Paul's writings were difficult to understand (2 Peter 3:15-16). We do not realize just how difficult and subjective translation decisions can be. (Ancient Hebrew also had no quotations marks.) Bible versions differ from each other in the use of quotation marks which greatly affects interpretation.

- Geographic, historical, and cultural context can be missed. Imagine that you are asked to write a letter to a friend and to impart complex and nuanced wisdom. After you write the letter, imagine being told that the letter will be read by people 2,000 years from now, in an entirely different culture, on the other side of the world, and in a different language. Know that they will be frustrated with you for not being clearer, argue with each other about what you really meant, mistreat each other and break fellowship because even among themselves they will have a diverse understanding of their own changing language and culture. I bet you would rip that letter up and say, "I'll pass!" However, we forget these are the very challenges we have when reading the Bible, and we expect everything to be clear.

  We let someone else do the study and tell us what it means without healthy skepticism. We let others berate us with "Can't you accept the clear Word of God?" as if the English translation is perfect. We do not want to let new discoveries affect our understanding for fear of implying that God did not preserve the Word for us (even though it has been revised many times and some of the things we believe are fairly new interpretations).

- Translators must make choices so it's important to have a committee with its members having extensive and varied language experience and contextual knowledge. Some translation committees have been lacking in this regard, having a small number of people, everyone with the same background, and everyone vetted to have the same theological perspective. (Commentaries can also be biased in this way. A good commentary will state various views with their reasons.)

- A world-famous translator explained that translation committees consider what words other translators have chosen in the past with a concern that choosing something different could cause people to lose faith in the Bible. When listening to this interview, I was struck by the admission that trying to manage people's confidence is a large part of the consideration rather than only considering accuracy.

- Every translator cannot do all the work over again. They reasonably rely on the work of past scholars. Also, we will see some places where Reformation scholars commented extensively on their translations and influenced the understanding of millions of people to this day, over 400 years later. *This effectively elevated tradition to the level of Scripture—something evangelicals claim to highly oppose.*

Translators fear trying to correct hundreds of years of misunderstanding, not only due to the fear of shaking people's faith, but due to the fear of others asking, "How dare you change this?" The "Information Age" has begun to break down some of these inhibitions since people can connect with others who share similar concerns and valid research, bolstering support for changes. However, improvements come slowly and cautiously while language changes are accelerating.

Specific Misleading Tactics

I have been horrified to learn that some translators have let their theology and ideology affect their translation choices, instead of letting consistent translation choices affect their theology. One quick example is the Greek word *diakonos* translated into the English word "deacon" in a passage where males are included but then where it relates to a woman, *diakonos* was translated into the English word "servant" (Romans 16:1 ESV). Sadly, there is bias while people are trusting translators to be unbiased.

It is a very serious thing to tout one's fervent belief in the inerrancy of God's Word but then intentionally practice inconsistency, obscure the meaning, or even change the meaning when it benefits one's own status or power. Throughout this book, I will identify different types of obfuscation or misleading translation and interpretation tactics when discussing specific passages.

It is difficult to isolate different types of tactics and distinguish them from others. I have numbered them and will refer to these numbers when identifying them in discussions of particular Bible passages. (Just because I am identifying a certain number of cases cited in this book does not mean there are no additional cases.)

Following is a list of 20 Misleading Tactics. Throughout the remainder of the book, I will refer to these tactics by number. The reader may wish to bookmark the spread with this list in order to reference them.

1. Interpretive arguments that sound good but are illogical (twelve examples)
2. Poor translations that obscure the best meaning (eleven examples)
3. Widely repeated teachings that are not in the Bible (eleven examples)
4. Translation of the feminine word to "wives" instead of "women" (two examples) and a non-gendered singular pronoun into "women" (one example) where it affects theology
5. Cherry picked verses which seem to limit women contrasted to neglected verses which empower women (five examples)
6. Loss of a theological debate among fellow conservatives but leaving the erroneous theology in marriage books and seminary textbooks which impress tens of thousands of Christian lay people and upcoming preachers (one significant example)
7. Addition or omission of a word or phrase which strengthens a restrictive viewpoint for women (ten examples with some involving addition of multiple male pronouns)
8. Negative and uncompassionate assumptions about Bible females that interfere with exegeting good applications from the narratives (nine examples)
9. Interpretation of a NT verse about the creation of man and woman out of context and in isolation from another text which illuminates the topic (two examples)
10. Interpretation of a description as a command (two examples)
11. Section breaks and uninspired headings fragmenting inconvenient truths and misdirecting the reader's focus (two examples)

12. Masculinization of a female leader's name (to disguise her) in spite of extensive historical evidence she was female (two examples)

13. Accurate gender-inclusive translation unless context implies leading or teaching, then switch to masculine generics (three examples)

14. Failure to use quotation marks when there is evidence Paul is quoting those he disagrees with before refuting them, making him appear to endorse opposing views (two significant examples)

15. Obfuscation of the translation when leader language refers to a female (seven examples)

16. Teaching that is inconsistent with Scriptural theology (eighteen examples)

17. Minimization of verses that emphasize spiritual equality or leadership of women (ten examples in addition to #15 which also qualifies as minimization)

18. Uncorrected translation or interpretation of English terms with meanings that have shifted since the first century (two examples in several passages)

19. Interpretive overreach (unfounded extrapolation) from a narrative, typological figure, or phrase (eleven examples)

20. Disregard of good exegesis rules to arrive at a prohibitive interpretation (three examples)

Because of all these tactics, sadly, we cannot take the simple English reading at face value in the gender-related passages. Even a quick comparison between different English translations shows that translators do not always agree, and sometimes we do not realize the significance of a seemingly minor difference.

I've heard and repeated the statement, "We believe in the inerrancy of the Bible in its original languages" but I did not realize just how important that disclaimer is or I would have read my English Bible with a little less confidence in the English. I am grateful for translators who are doing their best to look afresh at the translation work of past scholars as well as considering which language changes are presenting new problems.

Now, away from translators and back again to interpreters and teachers. I believe there are "big names," hailed as the best teachers in the USA and the world, who have distorted God's Word and misrepresented God's character and heart. No doubt, all of us have at various points misrepresented God's character and heart, but those who are recognized as teachers of God's Word accept a greater responsibility according to James 3:1. It is amazing to me that God lets any of us represent him at all, since we often do poorly.

Finally, we need to acknowledge the interpretative factor of each individual reader. Bethel University in St. Paul, Minnesota, has a short and fun video by Dr. Jeannine Brown which demonstrates how each of us has bias factors affecting how we understand various passages: *The Peopled Nature of Interpretation* https://youtu.be/9epTN0b6FP4.

In the last few decades, there have been discoveries of first-century documents/artifacts/inscriptions that have increased the understanding of scholars regarding how certain words or phrases were used and understood at the time of their writing. Discoveries also aid with understanding the culture. In addition, long-time resources are finally digitized and posted online. (See my website for examples.)

Both new discoveries and new access to original documents can show us that we misunderstood something due to inadequate information. If we truly believe that the Bible is inerrant in its original languages, we need to be open to new discoveries and not fear that because my godly grandpa or my wonderful pastor believed "X," I will fall into apostasy if I now learn differently. (I'm not talking about basic, well-supported doctrine like salvation by grace through faith.)

I've been told all my life that we need to understand first-century context, but I did not grasp how very different that context was. After all, we do not know what we do not know. We do not even realize when we are projecting a modern and western construct onto an ancient, eastern culture. So, I do not blame myself or others who do not know, but I do blame us when we have too little curiosity to learn more and are too confident in what we think we know.

The topic of misleading tactics would not be complete without acknowledgment of obstacles encountered by the average pastor to prevent them from objectively considering the evidence for a mutualist interpretation. These obstacles as I see them are listed on my website. Because of them, I do not consider every complementarian teacher to be part of a conspiracy or guilty of the tactics identified in this book. I believe the vast majority of complementarians are sadly misled by a few and unknowingly pass on error.

Some might wonder if all that I shared above shakes my confidence in the accuracy of the Bible. It does not, and if you're curious why, see that topic on my website.

PART ONE

GOD'S ORIGINAL DESIGN

When God first created the world and first birthed his church, we can assume that it was at its best. This is why we study pre-fall creation and the early days of the church. We're looking for how God meant for things to be before we messed it up. We'll look at the genesis of the world first and then the genesis of the church.

Chapter 1:

CREATION - THREE ROADS DIVERGE

While reading numerous authors on the creation narrative, I noticed that their views fit into one of three different frameworks, each taking the believer to a different destination.

One framework believes there was hierarchical authority given to Adam over Eve prior to the fall of mankind. The fall changed nothing except that the hierarchical construct was no longer accepted by the woman, and she began to grasp for the man's position, contrary to God's plan. We will look at two places in Genesis that people with this view would point to as indicating a hierarchy. **I will call this view the Pre-fall Hierarchical Construct.**

A second framework holds that the text indicates a pre-fall, egalitarian construct as the ideal. But this view contends that once sin entered the picture, a post-fall reality required that God prescribe a hierarchical construct so humans can manage life better in our fallen state. **I will call this view the Post-fall Hierarchical Construct.**

A third framework says we know that the primary gender-relations construct throughout history has been hierarchical with the subordination of women, but it was not the ideal will of God for relationships. This framework says that it is important to know about the creation ideal before the fall into sin and we should work to practice it with the help of the Holy Spirit. **I will call this view the Pre-fall Mutualist Construct.**

It is important to determine on which view to build. We will have our answer by the end of Chapter 2. I believe that one's interpretation of Genesis should affect one's interpretation of New Testament (NT) passages more so than the other way around. This would be consistent with many theologians who say that the first mention of something in the Bible is most significant. I am uncertain as to whether that statement is true down to individual words, but I believe it to be true with principles. For example, the doctrine of salvation by atonement starts in Genesis and builds throughout time in the Bible, precept upon precept, culminating in the sacrifice of Jesus, which would not make sense (or would be very difficult to make sense of) without Old Testament (OT) teaching. Jesus repeatedly hearkens back to Genesis to support his teachings. The importance of Genesis cannot be overstated.

God's Purpose for the Creation of Humanity

In Genesis 1:26, the Trinity is talking among themselves and states the purpose of creating humanity.

> *Let us make human beings in our image, in our likeness, **so that they may rule** (emphasis mine) over the fish in the sea and the birds in the sky, over the livestock and all the wild animals, and over all the creatures that move along the ground.*

Then in verse 28, God gives them life instructions.

> *God blessed them and said to them, "Be fruitful and increase in number; fill the earth and subdue it. Rule over the fish in the sea*

> *and the birds in the sky and over every living creature that moves on the ground."*

Notice that the purpose of creating human beings (in two genders) is so that they may rule (together) over every other living creature and the physical matter which makes up the earth. This would have been a good place to state that man is to rule over all, and the woman is to rule under him. For those who believe in a pre-fall hierarchy, this is a stark omission of God's clarity. This is the first of many opportunities for the Scripture to be clear, but a pre-fall hierarchy is not stated in Genesis.

Image Bearers

What does it mean to be created in God's image? Does God have two arms and legs? No, John 4:24 and Colossians 1:15 tell us God is an invisible spirit. Humans have God's communicable attributes—some aspects of God's nature. Those attributes include love, justice, mercy, wisdom, faithfulness, goodness, patience, kindness, truthfulness, creativity, and the potential for holiness, because God has given us a conscience and the ability to make moral decisions. God gave humans dominion over the earth as his representatives, to exercise these divine attributes with the authority God delegated to us.

Ontologically Equal

Since male and female are both created in God's image, complementarians must explain why they believe in hierarchical authority. They explain that men and women are "ontologically equal (in essence) but have different roles." If pressed, they admit "equality in essence" includes spiritual equality but quickly add there are different roles. Then, when those roles are given out, men are always the spiritual authority. How can anyone say the two sexes are spiritually equal but one has spiritual authority over the other? Sorry, but that is not spiritual equality.

> *It is illogical to say that man and woman are spiritually equal but have different roles, and then say one of those roles always has spiritual authority over the other.*
> Misleading Tactic #1

Simple logic (and math) says there is either spiritual equality or there is not spiritual equality. If there is spiritual inequality in any area (such as one being "over" the other), there is not spiritual equality. I'm struck by how easily we accepted such illogic.

The term "complementarian" was coined in 1988 by John Piper, Wayne Grudem, and others, and introduced by them at a meeting of the Council on Biblical Manhood and Womanhood (CBMW). https://cbmw.org/2019/08/01/whats-in-a-name/ It is a new teaching. It was promoted heavily in the evangelical circles of my high school years and onward, so it is all I was aware of during my spiritually formative years, making it seem as old as every other doctrine I was taught. But it is new, and I unwittingly helped to pass a new doctrine on to the next generation. My first clue that this is a new doctrine was when I was in my fifties and began to rub shoulders with women my age who had also grown up in the church but were not familiar with the term.

For a history of how we got here, see chapter three of Terran Williams's book, *How God Sees Women* (2022). He starts with George Knight's book in 1977, Knight's relationship with Piper and Grudem, the development of *The Danvers Statement* and the *Council on Biblical Manhood and Womanhood*, the major marketing and public relations efforts of 1989-1991, books by Wayne Grudem and Southern Baptist seminary professors, Piper and Grudem's involvement in the acquisition of the RSV by Crossway in 1996 and the RSV's revision/renaming into the ESV Study Bible published in 1991, founding of *The Gospel Coalition* by Piper, Carson, and Keller in 2004, help from Crossway

Publishing, etc. He has insightful points on the misrepresentations and creation of a movement that is less than 50 years old.

There is probably no more clear and concise verse related to equality than Galatians 3:28.

> *There is neither Jew nor Gentile, neither slave nor free, nor is there male and female, for you are all one in Christ Jesus.*

This verse covers ethnicity (cultural, genetic, physical background), worldly socio-economic status, and gender (another physical trait with which a person is born, akin to skin color and other features such as athletic propensity). God does not consider any of these things as qualifications. He only considers the "heart" (the soul created in God's image—able to make moral decisions) and that heart's spiritual condition. A popularly quoted verse is 1 Samuel 16:7.

> *The point of Galatians 3:28 is equality. If we are going see men above women then we need to keep seeing Jew above Gentile, and free above slave.*
> Misleading Tactic #1

> *The Lord does not look at the things people look at. People look at the outward appearance, but the Lord looks at the heart.*

The same people who quote that verse look at biological sex (gender) even though that is an outward appearance. We shall see that influential theologians in the past have resolved this dilemma by saying that the heart of the female is more prone to sin. Really, is that what we see? Perhaps complementarians do not

> *It is illogical to claim that God only considers the heart (not the physical) but then claim God considers biological sex.*
> Misleading Tactic #1

realize they are promoting the same erroneous thinking without being so bold as to say it.

Spiritual inequality based on factors such as level of surrender to the Holy Spirit is a godly consideration. Inequality based on physical factors over which a person has no control (such as gender and ethnicity) is not godly. Spiritual equality is also not the same thing as spiritual giftedness. This topic will be explored later in conjunction with the NT passages on the gifts of the Spirit, with the truth that the Holy Spirit gives gifts for ministry without external considerations such as physical anatomy, ethnicity, or socio-economic status.

Roles

Are there gender roles? I would say, "Yes, but very limited." We can learn from nature. The most obvious difference between men and women is physical function. Physical function lends to some physical typical roles. For example, if a job requires brute-force strength and a level of aggressiveness that requires a lot of testosterone, it's a man's job. But perhaps not aspects of the job that do not require physical strength. It was the Israelite men of military age (not the women) who were condemned to die in the wilderness because of their refusal to fight the Canaanites (Deuteronomy 2:14-16). Most men are given a physique to provide for and protect most women who have a physique to birth and nurture children. However, physical function should not be the only consideration when deciding complex roles. We are so much more than our bodies.

The idea that men must always be the sole or primary breadwinner can be taken too far. Jesus accepted the financial support of women when he was in ministry (Luke 8:3). They provided for him out of their own means, so probably their own economic earnings. Roles can change with seasons of life, experience, and what is best for the family or community at any given time. Partnership allows for role flexibility. Men have made unique contributions to social services (female-dominated fields) and women have made unique contributions to male-dominated fields, because, according to the Bible, it is not good for man to be alone—in anything. There were no qualifiers to that statement.

There are many Christian marriage books that try to pigeonhole "his needs" and "her needs." These stereotypes are a desperate attempt to organize things to reduce conflict. It is a legalistic fantasy: "Here's your contract, do the job description and all will be well." The fundamental premise in these books is hierarchy, and his needs often trump hers since she was supposedly created to be his assistant. (For example, the subtitle of one book is "The love she *desires*, and the respect he *needs*.") The fact is, we are all human beings with very similar needs and if we both honor and care for each other instead of being selfish, that is what will reduce conflict. A caution not to lean on stereotypical role assignments can be learned from research-based writings by Sheila Wray Gregoire, her husband, (pediatrician) Dr. Keith Gregoire, and their daughter, Rebecca Lindenbach, a trained statistician and researcher. They are Bible-believing Christians who debunk much of the gender stereotypes and unsubstantiated "research" taught in Christian marriage books. In a discussion about traits distributed by gender on bell curves, they say this:

> *Often, there's more difference within males and within females than there is between the average man and the average woman.*[6]

When the advocates of hierarchy (complementarians) use the word "roles," it is code for gender stereotypes that include hierarchy, obedience, patriarchy, and one-sided spiritual leadership. However, we can acknowledge functional roles that are worked out by each couple and by each ministry or local church, while acknowledging those roles

6 Sheila Wray Gregoire and Dr. Keith Gregoire, *The Marriage You Want* (Grand Rapids, MI: Baker Books, 2025), 22.

have nothing to do with hierarchy and gender. They should have to do with physical/mental ability, gifting, interest, experience, or even just availability. Chapter 8 explores themes connected to the Greek word *proistēmi*, which encompasses leading, managing, caring for, and providing for. This term is applied in the NT to both men and women.

Unity in Diversity

Some complementarians build a straw man and say that the egalitarian view is solely based on Galatians 3:28, and one verse is not enough for all the counter evidence. On the contrary, Galatians 3:28 is just one (excellent) piece of much evidence throughout the Bible that God practices equality and God is interested in unity within diversity.

The Bible recognizes, describes, and condemns the reality of oppression based on slavery, poverty, gender, and nationality/ethnicity. Although the Bible does not condemn this reality in every mention (because it's obviously wrong), the Bible never prescribes it. If there had to be a condemnation for every mention of injustice, the Bible would have to go off track from many other teachings. Instead, it strongly condemns it in many places (like Jeremiah 34:8-22) but not in every mention.

I've never forgotten a sermon I heard at my church's mission conference in the 90s, delivered by guest speaker Bob Sjogren from Unveiling Glory. He expounded on how God obviously loves diversity among people because he made so much diversity in our genes, our languages, and our cultures. Sjogren said that when we work together in spite of being different, we bring glory to God.

Up to that point, I had always seen diversity as obstacles to unity, and as catastrophic consequence of the sin at the Tower of Babel. I reasoned that if God did not have to use different languages to drive people into opposite directions to populate the world as instructed, they would not have developed such differences. It was a new paradigm to me that God loves differences, planned for people to scatter and develop differences, and God wants us to go through the struggle of honoring him and one another by working through our differences instead of trying to get everyone to conform. It is a shortcut to put people in a hierarchy to make things easier (for those with the power). We are to be likeminded about the things of God but not be just like each other. Men and women are different individuals, having different strengths and perspectives, so cooperation in partnership honors God as we honor and celebrate each other.

In some areas of the country where there is less ethnic and economic diversity, if one considers a typical local church, it is a group of believers who largely share the same culture, heritage, language, and socio-economic status. In these spaces, one of the few remaining diversity options left (with which to bring glory to God) is gender.

God's Appeal to Conscience

Throughout history, God's people have helped the oppressed in various situations (i.e. Christians protected Jews during the Holocaust, Christian missionaries fought to make sati illegal in India, and Christians fought against slavery). However, God's people have also twisted the Bible to support oppression. One example would be early American preachers using the Bible to teach slaves to submit, citing passages such as Ephesians 6:5-9. This passage acknowledged a cultural situation (rampant slavery) without endorsing it. Endorsing it made perfect sense to some Americans at that time, and now we are indignant about how wrong they were. Could we be just as blind now on the gender issue?

> *Ephesians 6:5-9*
>
> *Slaves, obey your earthly masters with respect and fear, and with sincerity of heart, just as you would obey Christ. Obey them not only to win their favor when their eye is on you, but as slaves of Christ, doing the will of God from your heart. Serve wholeheartedly, as if you were serving the Lord, not people, because you*

know that the Lord will reward each one for whatever good they do, whether they are slave or free. And masters, treat your slaves in the same way. Do not threaten them, since you know that he who is both their Master and yours is in heaven, and there is no favoritism with him.

This passage appeals to the conscience of the slave owner that God is master to them both and has no favorites. Meanwhile, 1 Timothy 1:10 condemned kidnapping people and enslaving them.

I want to be clear that the injustices against Blacks were far worse than the injustices against women. I'm only making a parallel regarding the blindness of Christians in the matter of gender hierarchy. If someone today wanted to claim that the Bible supports slavery or hierarchy based on ethnicity, they would have far more Scripture passages to support their position (using mere mention without condemnation) than the number of passages that could be used to support gender hierarchy. Yet our consciences have informed us that ethnic hierarchy is wicked, and the Bible was merely reporting the realities of the day.

Similarly, we will see that some Scripture passages which seem to support gender hierarchy are merely acknowledging the realities of the times (some being subversive to those realities). Other passages are specific situation prohibitions, and others are affirmations of mutuality. While in the recent past, Christendom ignored 1 Timothy 1:10 to do with slave trading, much of Christendom still ignores Galatians 3:28 and other affirmations.

First Peter 3:7 says to respect the wife as a weaker vessel (physically, a metaphor for the body, see Chapter 18) and "heirs with you of the gracious gift of life." I believe passages such as this are appealing to the husband's conscience in a patriarchal society, the same as Ephesians 6:5-9 was appealing to the slave owner's conscience and Galatians 3:28 was appealing to everyone's conscience. The apostles were not calling for slaves and women to riot for justice or demand it at all costs. They told slaves, servants, and wives to submit with reverence for God, but then called for God's people to have a conscience and do the right thing as a witness to the world.

It is my prayer that books such as this which point out the weakness of the arguments for gender hierarchy will give space for our collective Christian conscience to do the same work that was done to abandon ethnic hierarchy.

Creation Order

A lot of weight has been given to the fact that Adam was created first, then Eve. Some assume it gave Adam more authority. I accepted creation order as proof of hierarchy when I was told it was so, but after giving myself permission to question it, I'm not sure this argument is even logical. Animals came first before man—does that give them more authority? No, because God was working from the foundation of matter, to living beings, to the apex of the creature who would be created in his own image. Therefore, one could also say that since woman came last, she was the apex or crowning achievement. "Since man came first, he has more authority" is one of those ideas that has been repeated so often that we just accept it, even though the Bible does not actually say it.

> *"Man was created before woman, therefore, he had more authority than woman" has been taught so many times that it is assumed to be in the Bible somewhere, even though it is not.*
> Misleading Tactic #3

The narrative in Genesis 2 gives some clues as to why God chose to create Adam and then Eve instead of creating them at the same time, and then 1 Corinthians 11 spells out the reason.

Clue One: God had Adam observe all the animals and then conclude he was missing a counterpart. God stated (in 2:18) that it was "not good for *adam* to be alone." Then, apparently, God knew Adam needed to discover this truth for himself. We who are teachers know this is the best way to learn something—experience it. After Adam surveyed and named the animals and saw there was no one for him, then God created Eve. God went to great lengths to make sure man knew it was not good to be without woman, which strongly implies Adam would think he did not need her (or even view her as a competitor?) without the lesson. Complementarians say that naming the animals was proof of headship. It was certainly domination over the animals but says nothing about domination over another human. The passage tells us the purpose of surveying and naming the animals (to recognize his need), so to come up with a headship purpose over woman is pure speculation and ignores the giving of dominion over the animals to the both of them.

Clue Two: God created Adam from the ground and then created Eve from Adam's side. God could have chosen to create them both from the ground. Notice that Adam said, "bone of my bone and flesh of my flesh." This was an illustration of their one-flesh unity. If they had both been created from another material, it would not be the same as "bone of my bone and flesh of my flesh."

Clue Three: The material taken from Adam was from his torso, not his head or foot. This seems to be a picture that she is to be by his side, not above or under him.

Clue Four: When Eve gave birth to a son, it was evident that man is born from woman. This biological fact would give some people the idea that woman is superior. When we look at the NT passages, we will see how this letter to Timothy addresses numerous problems related to cults in Ephesus and we will examine every sentence in 1 Timothy 2:11-15, including *"For Adam was formed first, then Eve."* This verse, in the context of countering Gnostic heresy, is primarily why people put a hierarchical significance on Adam being created first – a hierarchy that was not mentioned in Genesis.

For now, while in Genesis, we will leave it with the point that God brought woman out of man so it can be said that both get their origin from the other, demonstrating interdependence, not superiority.

This is explained in 1 Corinthians 11:11-12.

> *Nevertheless, in the Lord, woman is not independent of man, nor is man independent of woman. For as woman came from man, so also man is born of woman. But everything comes from God.*

"Woman came from man, therefore he has more authority" is one of those ideas that has been said so many times that it is assumed to be in the Bible somewhere. The Bible actually says they both came from each other.
Misleading Tactic #3

I believe that 1 Corinthians 11:11-12 is similar to Galatians 3:28, both affirming equality in God's kingdom. One says, "in the Lord" there is no difference regarding independence or origin, and the other says "you are all one in Christ Jesus" without regard to gender.

> *There is neither Jew nor Greek, there is neither slave nor free, nor is there male and female, for you are all one in Christ Jesus.*

Notice the words "one in Christ Jesus." The emphasis is equality and unity. If we are going to continue to insist that male is over female, then we must also give hierarchy to Jew over Greek and to free over slave.

When you hear complementarians say "creation order" or "divine order," they are referring to their

The phrase "creation order" is not found in the Bible. However, it is repeated so often by complementarians that one would think it is all throughout the Bible.
Misleading Tactic #3

belief that man was ordered above woman, that because man was created first, that's "the natural order of creation" in their belief system. But in God's kingdom, everything is upside down. God uses the weak, the younger son, the child, the woman, the man with a speech impediment, etc., and he even lowered himself to "the Son of Man." So, it makes no sense to keep appealing to a "created order" of hierarchy as if that's how God does things. This is a made-up term that is not found in the Bible.

Garden Keepers

Husband

Some Bible teachers will take the English word "husband" and its etymology from "husbandry" as it relates to taking care of plants and extrapolate that idea to the man taking care of his wife, as if watering, pruning, and weeding her, to help her grow (spiritually). I have heard complementarian teaching that God gave the man extra responsibility to steward and manage his wife, similar to or as an extension of caring for the garden. They make it sound very nice as if this is a great act of service, but that extra control is simply not in the biblical text.

According to Etymonline.com, the word "husband" came into English from a Norse word in the ninth century, which means to manage agriculture. It gradually began to include management of the home and became a word for a married man in the thirteenth to fifteenth centuries, replacing the English word for man, *wer*. We need to be careful to not take the etymology of an English word and put it back onto a Hebrew or Greek text; in this case, the Hebrew word (*adam*) that simply means "human." Translators avoid considering etymology because all the focus needs to be on the understanding of the original language word by the recipient of that time, the context in which it was being used, and the understanding of the English word at this time. (For example, "understand" does not mean "to stand under.") When one hears teaching based on the etymology of either the original language word or the English word, they should run. Because there are places where it makes sense to translate *adam* into "husband" for modern contextualization, Misleading Tactic #16 is more about bad interpretation and teaching than about translation.

"Husband" instead of "human" was chosen by translators for modern understanding. Errant interpretation gives the impression the man should function as manager for the wife per English etymology.
Misleading Tactic #16

Working, Keeping, Guarding

Before woman's creation, God put man in the garden and commanded him to work it and take care of it—or keep it (Genesis 2:15). Some say these words have a "priestly flair," similar to worship.

Did man have additional responsibility, job description, or role, to care for this place, different from the command to "dominate" or "subdue" which comes later to both of them (Genesis 1:28)? It is not clear there is extra responsibility. There is no separate, later command recorded to the woman not to eat of the tree, yet she is expected not to eat of it, so the command was simply appropriated to her. Why would we not assume the same appropriation with the command to "keep" the garden, especially considering her inclusion in the "Dominion Mandate"?

Assuming extra responsibility for the man, to then build a case for hierarchy, is an extremely weak argument for a very significant conclusion. Would we build any other doctrine on such weak footing?

The idea that man was given greater responsibility than woman for caring for the garden is not in the text and is countered by the "Dominion Mandate."
Misleading Tactic #3

Some will claim that since the man was told about care of the garden first, he was responsible to communicate instructions to the woman, making her subordinate. In Genesis 3 the man and woman recognized the sound of God walking in the garden, inferring that the two of them were accustomed to walking with God. There was plenty of opportunity for God to instruct them both. There is no indication of a chain of communication from God to man and from man to woman. It sounds plausible, but as people who are careful not to add to Scripture, we should not add here either.

> *An instruction related to hierarchy or subordination is not recorded anywhere in Genesis. The idea is spoken of as factual so often that one would assume it is in Genesis.*
> Misleading Tactic #3

Anywhere to this point, God could have been clear that there was a hierarchy with a command such as, "Man, you must instruct the woman" or "Man, you must lead the woman" or "Woman, you must follow the man" or "Woman, you must submit to the man." God commanded the man to take care of the garden, to not eat of the tree, to name the animals (chapter 2), and told him and the woman (together) to fill the earth and to subdue it (1:28), so it is not like God was sparing commands. The absence of something (such as a command to lead the woman) is not a solid argument from silence, nor is it solid logic to assume something that is not there. It is more logical to assume that all commands were appropriated to the woman, and there was another reason man was created first and given some instructions first, as explained above.

Some complementarians claim that since God gave the man a "priestly service" in the garden, he became the priest of the woman or, something I heard many times, "the priest of the home." That's a huge leap. Another person is not a garden. After he was given the (priestly?)

duty to keep the garden, it was stated that it was not good he was alone; therefore, she was essential. This "priest of the home" claim is a major case of adding to Scripture and assuming things that are not there. There is no place in the Bible where the husband is called the priest of the wife or the priest of the home. First Timothy 2:5-6 reads:

> *For there is one God and one mediator between God and mankind, the man Christ Jesus, who gave himself as a ransom for all people.*

This Scripture says only Jesus is priest for all humans. Furthermore, there is a common teaching described as "the priesthood of the believer" which applies to men and women (1 Peter 2:5-9, Revelation 1:6, 20:6).

The husband as priest assumption might have been influenced by the fact that OT priests were always men. The explanation for that is the purity laws which forbid anyone with a discharge to enter the Temple (including men). Since women have a monthly flow of blood and have random bleeding after giving birth (ceremonially "unclean" for 40 days after giving birth), they were relieved from the requirement of sacrificial duties and the husband could represent the household if she was not able to come. Priests were also limited to a certain tribe and family lineage so this was not all about gender. If we give special status to men today because all priests were men, we should give special status to Levites. Regarding family sacrifices, Bible passages and historical records indicate that women sometimes brought sacrifices. The fact that men often took care of the household in this matter should not be extrapolated to him being the priest of the home when the Bible does not say so,

> The teaching that the husband is a priest for his wife is not anywhere in the Bible and it contradicts 1 Timothy 2:5.
> Misleading Tactic #2, 3

> *Logically, if we give special status to men today because all priests were male, then we should give special status to Levites today.*
> Misleading Tactic #1

with plenty of opportunity to say so.

In God's instructions regarding the Tabernacle and then the Temple, there was no barrier beyond which women could not pass along with non-priest men. It was not until Herod's Temple was built (18 BC – AD 64) that a special extra courtyard was made and designated Court of the Women beyond which women could not pass. Beyond it was the Court of Israel where men could be present and then the Court of Priests. This segregation was man's sexist idea, not God's, and it made it seem that women could not be as close to God as men. Traditions like this affect the subconsciousness of Judeo-Christian thought.

The OT priesthood was abolished by direct access in the New Covenant. When Jesus took our sin upon him, the veil in the Temple was torn and those who believe were now clothed in his righteousness with no separation from God. First Peter 2:5 became true of all of us who believe, not just men or Jews. All believers became "a holy priesthood, offering spiritual sacrifices acceptable to God through Jesus Christ." Do we truly believe this?

> *Sexist traditions (such as the Court of Women) which were not part of the Torah, add to a subconscious perspective that God favors men.*
> Misleading Tactic #16

Dominion Partners

Genesis 1:28 has what is called the "Creation Dominion Mandate." It is the granting of dominion over the earth and everything in it to both the man and woman together. Some versions use the words "have dominion over" and others use the words "rule over." There is also "subdue it."

> *God blessed them and said to them, "Be fruitful and increase in number; fill the earth and subdue it. Rule over the fish in the sea and the birds in the sky and over every living creature that moves on the ground."*

In chapter 2, before God made Eve, he gave the command only to Adam not to eat the fruit from the tree. God could have given Adam the dominion mandate as well, but instead, God waited for Eve. Dominion together is the ideal. A complementarian book I read misrepresented the Bible and said the command to have dominion was given to Adam before Eve was created. This misconception feeds into the idea that man is meant to rule his wife instead of ruling with her.

Multiply and Rule Are Not Separate Roles

There is a deeply grounded bias from the influence of Reformation leaders. Martin Luther and John Calvin made extensive commentaries as if God's commands to multiply and to rule were separate to the genders and they had different roles. Although acknowledging spiritual equality, Luther taught that women must be subordinate to their husbands to suppress sin.

Even though modern, conservative theologians discuss agreement and disagreement with the Reformers on other doctrinal issues, this particular influence seems to be one where we are oblivious to the water in which we swim. With the separate roles advised by Luther, men take a back seat in the raising of children which is a terrible loss, just as women taking a back seat in the dominion of the earth is a terrible loss. We know that before the industrial revolution, families worked together in "cottage industries" which benefitted families greatly. Men were present and available to train children and women contributed their resourcefulness to the family business. During the

> *The teaching that the dominion mandate was given only to the man or that the roles or responsibilities given in the dominion mandate were gender specific, is not in the text.*
> Misleading Tactic #3

COVID pandemic, families were forced back together, and some learned the benefits of togetherness. A whole new cottage industry and homesteading movement began in the USA.

God gave both genders quite the expansive authority between the commands to "rule," "have dominion," and "subdue." When I think of the extent of the authority given to them in Genesis 1:28, and the huge job that it is, it seems petty and grasping to say one gender has more authority than the other.

Strong Ally

God says it's not good for man to be alone so he will have a partner. Two Hebrew words are used for this partner, *ēzer* (Strong's H5828) and *kénegdô* (H5048). They are translated into two English words in various versions: "suitable helper" and "help meet." Neither of these translations comes close to being a good interpretation. We'll look at these two words one at a time, starting with *ēzer*.

The Hebrew word, *ēzer*, for "help" (as opposed to other words for help which could have been used) is used 21 times in the OT:

Ezer is used two times for "woman" in Genesis.

Ezer is used three times for armies that Israel appealed to for help due to them being stronger than Israel.

Ezer is used sixteen times for God, as in, "Yahweh is our help (*ēzer*) and rescue." Two examples of Yahweh as *ēzer* are King David's strong defender and deliverer (Psalm 70:5) and Israel's shield and helper (Deuteronomy 33:29).

Scholars agree that *ēzer* is not a word which expresses subordination, but rather expresses strength and rescue. However, John Calvin described the woman as man's accessory (bold emphasis added below).

> *Yet St. Paul has an eye here to the beginning of the creation, where it was said that it was not good for the man to be alone, and that he needed someone at hand who would always be ready to help. Since God was thinking of the man, it certainly follows that* ***the woman is only an accessory****. And why? Because she was only created for the sake of man, and she must therefore direct her whole life toward him. She must confess, "I am not supposed to be without direction here, not knowing my purpose and station. Rather, I am obliged by God, if I am married, to serve my husband, and render him honor and reverence. And, if I am not married, I am bound to walk in all soberness and modesty, cognizant that men have the higher rank, and that they must rule, and that the woman who disregards this forgets the law of nature and perverts what should be observed as God commands." This then is the place to which St. Paul brings back women.*[7]

Would any of us refer to God as our accessory? We should all agree that would be blasphemous. So, complementarians have agreed to call the woman "a strong helper" which retains the subordinate idea but condescends to admit she is strong (while the man is stronger—too strong to need rescue). This avoids the fact that the "rescuer, strength" meaning negates the subordinate idea, and that God is not subordinate when he helps as our *ēzer*.

It would be interesting to conduct a survey regarding how people understand the word "helper." The question would be this: "When you hear the word 'helper,' do you imagine that the helper is weaker than

---

7 John Calvin, *Men, Women, and Order in the Church: Three Sermons* (Dallas: Presbyterian Heritage, 1992), 36#.

> *The poor translation of ézer into "suitable helper" and "help meet" rather than a word that conveys strength has led to the subordination of women instead of recognition of partnership.*
> Misleading Tactic #2

the one being helped or stronger than the one being helped?" If the great majority of people believe the helper is weaker, then that is not the biblical meaning, and translators should choose a different word because, for accuracy, they should be concerned with how people currently perceive a word.

We do not want to view the woman as superior to the man any more than we want the man to be viewed as superior to the woman. Carolyn Custis James describes the woman as a "strong ally." It connotes neither subordination nor superiority.

> *I love how Victor Hamilton puts it: "[Kenegdo] suggests that what God creates for Adam will correspond to him. Thus, the new creation will be neither a superior nor an inferior, but an equal. The creation of this helper will form one-half of a polarity and will be to man as the South Pole is to the North Pole." She will be his strongest ally in pursuing God's purposes and his first roadblock when he veers off course.*[8]

We rely on God, and we cannot manage without him. Eve was not just a nice add-on to the self-sufficient man God created—she was essential (and not just for procreation). Each of them is created in the image of God and together they reflect the interdependence and cooperation of the trinitarian God (more on that later).

---

8 Carolyn Custis James, *Half the Church: Recapturing God's Global Vision for Women* (Grand Rapids, MI: Zondervan, 2015), 112.

The fact that *ēzer* is used for the woman and for God is another demonstration that some of God's nature is represented specifically by the woman. Use of the word *ēzer* shows us that God did not intend for us to view women as weak. There is one verse in the NT which refers to the woman as "the weaker vessel" (physically, because a vessel was a metaphor for the body). That verse has been emphasized while *ēzer*, which is referring to more important human functions than the physical, has been de-emphasized and even obfuscated.

> *The NT verse referring to a woman's physical weakness was cherry picked and emphasized to generalize women as weak while the creation description of strength was de-emphasized and obfuscated.*
> Misleading Tactic #5

While we women admire a physically strong man, even more, we appreciate his being strong in character, disciplined, and dependable. Mature men should also admire a woman who is strong in these ways and receive her alliance with appreciation.

Equally Corresponding, Counterpart

Now, we will look at *kenegdô*. This key word that greatly influences the understanding of the relationship of the genders is found nowhere else in the entire Bible! Therefore, rather than guessing, or using our theology to influence our translating, we need to look at the Hebrew, other Hebraic writings, and how it was translated in the Septuagint (LXX) hundreds of years before Christ.

Of all the things I've read with the same explanation, Marg Mowczko's article gathers the most scholarly research and presents it most concisely. https://margmowczko.com/kenegdo-meet-subordinate-suitable-or-similar/ Mowczko shows through Rabbinic texts and from the Greek Septuagint that *kenegdô* means "similar" or "corresponding." The Brown-Driver-Briggs (BDB) lexicon (one of the most authoritative and widely used resources for biblical Hebrew and Aramaic) translates Genesis 2:18 as "I will make him a help corresponding to him (i.e. equal and adequate to) himself." With *ēzer* as "strength" and *kenegdô* as "equally corresponding," put together, they make the most sense as "equally corresponding strength."

It is odd to me that even some complementarian preachers will use the words "corresponding to him" when reading this passage but still conclude a subordinate role. Why do theologians make such a significant assumption of subordination when it simply is not there? This is a case of letting theology influence their understanding of the text instead of letting the text influence their theology.

I like the way a friend described this to me as if the man and woman are facing each other, so "opposite" but not in an adversarial way. They both see what is between them. But they also both see each other and what is behind the other—things the other cannot see, or at least not as well or in the same way. I would call this a "together perspective" and "a unique angle perspective." One is not "right" and the other "wrong."

I think about the times I tackled a project or problem in life with another person and our differences were a great help to each other. This has often been true in my marriage and my workplaces, as I partnered with an opposite personality. Another fun example is when my son was 21 and I was 56 and we went on a ten-day adventure in California. We are very different, but our common sense of adventure gave us a similar goal to see as much as we could of San Francisco, Highway 1, and three national parks. The old saying is,

> *The poor translation of kenegdo into "suitable helper" or "help meet" rather than a word that conveys similarity and counterpart has led to the subordination of women instead of partnership.*
> Misleading Tactic #2

"two heads are better than one." But it's not just the "two heads." It's the different perspectives that come from different gender, life experience, age, personality, physical ability, observation, and giftings. We saved each other from scrapes of all kinds. (A few times I half joked that with there being two of us, if one of us died, at least someone would know where to look for the body!)

This is the gift God gave to the first humans—the realization that they were different, yet similar, and that they desperately needed each other. If this special union of marriage is carried out with respect for both individuals and a healthy interdependence, they each become a great gift to the other. This is the ideal of creation. Proposing stereotypes, such as one needs more respect and the other needs more love, is misguided.

Even though people might give a nod to the fact that a wife is not just for support but is essential, how much do they flesh this out in real life? Do complementarian husbands consider their wives' input essential or do most consider it optional? (This is a rhetorical question.) Even the word "input" has come to imply secondary contribution in complementarian circles. The attitude is, "I'll listen to your input and decide whether to accept it." A true partnership would consider the input of both to be essential and not take action that is contrary to that input. The definition of male leadership in these circles is that he has ultimate responsibility for all decisions but especially he has "the final say" or "the tie breaker vote" when there is a disagreement. Where is this in the Bible? The NT tells both husbands and wives to submit or cooperate.

As an informal survey, I have asked self-described complementarian marriages how they work. Those marriages where the husband feels that all final decisions rest with him (even minor ones) and he has the "option" to receive his wife's input are not nearly as satisfactory to either of them as those in which the husband feels that her input holds the same value, and he must make the decision only in highly rare, urgent occasions. The men in the latter group seem to feel less pressure to perform well, and they seem to be more secure in their self-esteem, possibly because they are not constantly defending their decisions to themselves and their wives. Sharing decision-making has the sense that they are truly "in this together." Sheila Wray Gregoire has fascinating stats regarding marital satisfaction from scientific studies of tens of thousands of individual men and women and of couples in her 2025 book, *The Marriage You Want.*

In one of my interviews of a couple married for 43 years (happily, after a rough start), they described how they tabled decisions until they both agreed. However, if a decision needs to be made quickly and they don't agree, the person whom the decision most affects makes the decision and must agree to take full responsibility for the outcomes. This avoids resentment and blame.

One of the couples I interviewed had just come through a difficult time at their church and had left. The husband told how they had led the children's ministry, but their input was repeatedly disregarded by the elders. The attitude of the elders was, "We are the elders, so what we say goes" even though this man and his wife had "boots on the ground" experience in the children's ministry for many years. The elders should have either submitted to this worker couple or done the honoring work of helping this couple buy into the reasons for doing things differently, perhaps with compromise. This man said to me, "For the first time in my life, I finally understood what it felt like to be my wife for all these years. She had boots on the ground at home with schooling the kids and all sorts of things, and I made decisions like those elders did."

Shared decision-making is also a check on running ahead of, or behind, God's will. My husband and I had purchased land to build our house, but the house we were living in was not selling. We waited nearly two years and then we both, separately, had the conviction that it was time to start building. We had a conversation and agreed God was telling us to do it. Three months into the construction, a buyer came but had the stipulation we had to close in a month. We were able to move all our furniture into the garage of the new house and the kids and I stayed with friends a few weeks while my husband finished enough for us to move in. No double move, no double mortgage payment—it was perfect! This would have been a risky endeavor if God was not in it, but both of us hearing from God was the guidance and confidence we needed.

Interdependent Individuals

Psychologists have pointed out that men feel they are maturing when they become more independent, and women feel they are maturing when they become more connected. One is not more correct; they are both correct and need to balance the other. Without the balance, the wife (who is supposedly to follow) would not be essential, just always wrong, and more of a hindrance than a help. We need to figure out how to honor both genders and not become swallowed up in one person's identity and perspective to the point of losing the God-given individuality of the other.

The phrase "one flesh" is sometimes used as if the two must be like one person instead of two individuals. But that would be uniformity rather than unity. The Bible celebrates unity in diversity (1 Corinthians 12:12-27), not uniform conformity. This is an important, ongoing conversation for couples to have. If it's not a safe topic, one of them is too dominating. Both should be happy to identify how the other completes them.

When the man is commanded to leave his parents and cling to his wife, this is indication that he has a new identity with her, rather than absorbing her into his identity (including his family of origin's identity). This command to the man has always been a radical, countercultural concept, in a world with historically systemic patriarchy. I have yet to find a good explanation written by a complementarian author as to why God commanded the man to leave his father and mother and cleave to his wife rather than commanding that the woman leave her family and join his. If it were the other way around, I dare say the complementarians would have made a lot of hay with it. But as it is, they are quiet on why the command was specifically given to the man rather than the woman. Some believe God was telling the man to establish his own identity, but the context is clinging to her. I believe it was because God knew how dominating men would be, so this command needed to be specified, like God knew man needed an illustration in the Garden of Eden of how he needs woman.

Although there is no place in Genesis that says God gave Adam more authority than Eve, it did not take long for Adam and other men to notice they had superior physical strength. Also, when the woman is pregnant, gives birth, is nursing babies and caring for children, she is physically vulnerable. The man's strength was meant to be used to take care of the woman as she used her unique physique to give birth to and nurture children. But instead, in keeping with human nature to exploit others for selfish gain, men throughout history generally used their strength to oppress women.

> *The complementarian instruction for the woman to focus entirely on supporting the man's identity is incongruent with the Scriptural mandate for the man to leave his former identity and create a new one with his wife.*
> Misleading Tactic #16

If men and women had equal physical strength, it could give men an excuse to run off on their own instead of recognizing that they are essential to the survival of this other human (to whom he is also physically attracted). Likewise, the woman needed to understand that she needed her partner, so she was given a body that could nourish children but was generally not able to lift even her own body weight. While she is the source of sustenance for children, the man is her source of sustenance. I do not believe the strength differential was meant to encourage men to dominate women; I believe it was meant to encourage the two sexes to depend on each other and form an interdependent partnership with intimate unity.

Following is a biblical example of servant stewardship which can be applied to marriage. Jesus told a parable about some men who dominated where they had no business dominating (Mark 12:1-12). A man (representing God) left tenants (religious leaders) to care for a vineyard (Israel). The tenants acted like they owned the vineyard. They would not relinquish the vineyard or the profits from it to the owner's son (Jesus). The NT says that wives are "co-heirs" with their husbands of the grace of God (1 Peter 3:7). Husbands need to relinquish control and ownership of their wives to the rightful owner (God) and serve only as a faithful servant/tenant to help the women in their lives to flourish for the kingdom and not their own profit. Women also should help men to flourish for the kingdom because women are a tenant of the master's vineyard in the husband's life.

A believing man I know who was led by God to repent of mistreating his wife heard God say to him, "Take your hands off my inheritance." He did not physically abuse his wife but was in the habit of not letting his believing wife speak freely and he was in the habit of harshness. These habits caused emotional turmoil and did not allow her to thrive and exercise co-heir partnership. In the parable above, God's people need spiritual leadership. In a marriage, both believing individuals can develop spiritually in a way that provides spiritual leadership to the other. If a husband is controlling or believes he cannot be spiritually outpaced by his wife in any area, he will miss out on her service and fail to flourish.

The Trinity

I've been surprised to learn just how many topics relate to the study of gender in the Bible. One of those related topics is the Trinity. First, a quick review of Genesis 1:26, 27:

> *Let us make mankind in our image, in our likeness... So God created mankind in his own image, in the image of God he created them; male and female he created them.*

God reveals himself as three persons and speaks of himself in the plural with this action. God has relationship among the three persons within the Godhead (speaking among themselves). God helps us understand himself by giving us relationships with others (i.e. friends and family members) and then gives us illustrations about himself using those relationships with limited metaphors.

Some complementarian theologians (primarily Wayne Grudem) said there is hierarchy in the Trinity—God the Father is on top, then below the Father is Jesus, God the Son (because of course, sons are beneath fathers in our world), and then below Jesus is the Holy Spirit. They said that because the Trinity has hierarchy, God shows us that he has given a hierarchical order to the world, and therefore, there is hierarchy with man over woman - or at minimum, husband over wife and church men over church women. This theological position regarding the Trinity was called the "Eternal Submission of the Son" (ESS), then later "Eternal Functional Submission" (EFS) and claims Jesus has always been in submission to the Father.

Is EFS true, or does it do harm to the Trinity? This was a huge debate in early (Nicene) Christianity and then, due to complementarianism, was relitigated again recently. In 2016, the debate intensified and is chronicled in *The Rise and Fall of the Complementarian Doctrine of the Trinity* by Kevin Giles. I read some on each side of the debate, and am most convinced by the position laid out in the book,

The Son Who Learned Obedience by Glenn Butner Jr. The scholarship is far more extensive than the EFS position.

Some in the non-eternal submission camp accuse the eternal submission camp of Arianism (second-century heresy which denied that Father and Son share the same essence). The eternal submission camp vehemently denies Arianism and would like for us to think this is the only argument presented by the non-eternal submission camp. Butner tries to refocus the debate on the single divine will of God, saying that the persons of the Trinity cannot have separate wills while being the same in essence.

Butner shows that EFS advocates adopt a trinitarian theology that is incompatible with their own view of Christology, the atonement, and the divine attributes. EFS is contrary to historic Christian orthodoxy from the Nicene Council and First Council of Constantinople to today. EFS was introduced in the last few decades by Wayne Grudem as support for complementarianism.

Butner is concerned that even though high-profile figures in the complementarian camp such as Grudem, Bruce Ware, and Denny Burk made some concessions and even the *Council for Biblical Manhood and Womanhood (CBMW*—the primary complementarian organization) hosted discussions but did not endorse EFS, some seminary textbooks still contain the teaching. Grudem's 1994 *Systematic Theology* and the *ESV Study Bible* (he was General Editor) are major selling books which teach it. The 2020 edition textbook of *Systematic Theology* doubles down on it. Butner expects it to continue gaining acceptance and thus felt the need to write his book. I summarized four of Butner's most easily understood points on my website.

It has become evident to me that this belief in a hierarchy in the Trinity (and therefore hierarchy in marriage) causes seminary students to believe that if they give up the subordination of wives, they are denying the person of God and the entire Bible. *The Gospel Coalition* published Tim and Kathy Keller's books, *The Meaning of Marriage* and

Jesus, Justice and Gender Roles prior to the 2016 debate and they have not yet been revised. The way that the Keller books correspond the functions of the husband and wife to a hierarchical Trinity is dangerous theological ground because it is not supported in Scripture by even one verse.

However, this correspondence is widely believed in circles influenced by CBMW. I was sitting in Sunday school when a teacher (with no formal theological training) said that hierarchy in the Trinity demonstrates God's will for hierarchy in marriage. I spoke up and said I did not think hierarchy in the Trinity is a historically orthodox doctrine and I was rebuked.

> *In spite of losing the EFS debate, authors have not corrected marriage books and textbooks, leading couples and seminary students to believe that if they reject subordination of wives, they reject solid doctrine on the Trinity.*
> Misleading Tactic #6

It seems as if they think changing the name of the teaching from "Eternal Submission of the Son" to "Eternal *Functional* Subordination" will get them off the hook. Then they use "function" to describe the subordination of women due to "functional roles." So, the word "function" carries far more meaning than one would suspect, just like the word "roles," "divine order," and "creation order" are in their code book.

The news about the reversal of acceptance of EFS by theologians and institutions has not spread as far and wide as the original teaching. Rather than listing which theologians ended up rejecting EFS, I encourage my readers to search for "eternal submission of the son" online and see for themselves that theologians whom they trust have rejected this false teaching.

****

God demonstrates throughout the Bible, but especially in the first two chapters, that he cares more about cooperative relationship than hierarchical authority. Complementarian teaching concedes ontological equality but supports hierarchy with new sophistry and marketing. Therefore, I consider "complementarian" a misnomer. I only use it in this book when I feel that I should use the term they would use, but I use it reluctantly. The more accurate term is "hierarchy."

As we move on, we should recognize that we are moving into complicated areas with sin and cultural considerations. There could be honest debate about whether a NT passage simply reflects culture or agrees with it, but back in Genesis chapters 1 and 2, there was no sin, history, or culture to add context. It was the purest look at a male/female relationship there will ever be, and there was no clear hierarchy; in fact, the woman was described as a powerful ally or corresponding strength. We have answered the big concerns (such as why man was created first). We could pack up and be done, but we will press on and acquiesce to those who have a proof-text that has not been addressed yet.

Chapter 2:

THE FALL AND CURSES - NOT WHAT WE'VE BEEN TAUGHT

Portrayal of the First Sin

The events surrounding the first sin have been used by church fathers to shape an enduring impact on attitudes toward women. In the book *How God Sees Women* by Terran Williams, chapter two is titled "The Inferior Sex." He quotes well-known "church fathers" second through fifth century, medieval and Reformation theologians, and early American revivalists. These quotes are blood-chilling in their vile view of women. Much of the theology is wrong, including that only man and not woman is created in God's image, that Eve was the archetype of the female seductress and contaminated all women, and that all sex is wicked even within marriage. On top of wrong theology are jaw-dropping insults on the morality, character, and mental ability of women. I asked AI to give me original sources of this content and there is seemingly an endless supply of homiletic literature from the early church on, bible commentaries, vernacular storytelling (i.e.

Chaucer), and visual arts. Following is an analysis of particulars in the Genesis narrative from which these historical writers took their ideas which were then propagated for up to 2,000 years.

Were Adam and Eve Together?

As a young adult, I heard interpretations that Eve ate the fruit alone ("away from her husband's protection and covering"), ran to find him, and he, not wanting to be without her, was highly pressured to join her in the sin. This speculation promoted the idea that Eve was a wily seductress. The seductress theme was carried by Medieval, Renaissance, and Reformation theologians with additional themes of female weakness of all kinds, portraying the woman as dangerous and linked to sexual shame. Was Adam with Eve while she was tempted in Genesis 3:1-6? The following is an example of a modern-day teaching:

> *The Hebrew word translated as "with her" (אִתָּהּ, ittah)* can indicate proximity but does not require immediate presence or involvement in the preceding actions.*[9] *[*actual Hebrew word is עִמָּהּ 'im-māh]*

This author admits that the language indicates Adam was with Eve, but the author argues that does not mean Adam was standing in close proximity. However, when Satan says "you" he uses the plural form. So, between the "with her" language and the plural form, it is likely Adam was standing right there. When in a group, whomever the speaker makes eye contact with is who we say the speaker was speaking to, so that is all it took for the serpent to speak "to the woman." All four translation teams for the four versions I am primarily using for this book have decided it is more accurate to indicate Adam was

9 Edward D. Andrews, "GENESIS 3:6: Was Adam Present When Eve Was Tempted by the Serpent?" Christian Publishing House, August 23, 2024, https://www.christianpublishers.org/post/genesis-3-6-was-adam-present-when-eve-was-tempted-by-the-serpent.

there. The woman engages, argues, and becomes persuaded, but the man says nothing. (It seems more likely to me that he would have said something if he were under the impression that he was "in charge.")

When Jerome translated the Latin Vulgate (completed AD 405) from Hebrew to Latin, he left out that the man was with the woman. He may have thought it was ambiguous, so made the decision to leave it out. I suspect it was a biased decision because the evidence leans toward Adam's presence. All major translations now include some variation of "who was with her" but we can see from the article cited above that some interpreters still argue for the most negative scenario. Three lesser-used versions omit the phrase and some, like the NKJV, omit "who was" which makes it unclear.

The characterization of the woman as a seductress and linking her to sexual shame contributed to men and women avoiding each other completely with monastic and/or celibate lifestyles. Not to say women never seduce, but there are limitless examples from Christian literature, even contemporary books, that put more responsibility on the woman, portraying the man as helpless with temptation in her presence. This view, more recently termed "purity culture," gained new traction in the 1990s. It attracted criticism from some evangelicals in 2018 and 2019 as authors and speakers pointed out the guilt it imposed primarily on women. Christians should be sexually pure, but there has been undue pressure on women to feel responsible for the purity of men, as if men are incapable of being honorable.

> *In spite of two indications in the Hebrew that Adam was present with Eve and the serpent, Jerome left it out of the Latin Vulgate, adding to historical bias against women.*
> Misleading Tactic #7

Why Did God Speak to Adam First About His Sin?

Some hold the opinion (I did) that because God spoke to Adam

> *God confronted Adam first. The possibility of more responsibility due to more guilt should not be conflated with more responsibility due to hierarchy.*
> Misleading Tactic #1

first when confronting Adam and Eve about their sin, it was a sign of his being the "head" or "leader." Again, this is not in the text, just an assumption. Following are two alternative possibilities for why God spoke to Adam first:

First, God could have felt Adam's sin was greater because he sinned knowingly rather than being deceived. (I trust no one thinks greater sin is somehow related to greater authority.) I feel like this is the weaker of two possibilities. Second, God knew that someday, redemption of the mess would come through one man, Jesus Christ, representing humanity in righteousness, so Adam would be the one man representing humanity in sinfulness.

Some people think that Paul places more blame on Adam in Romans 5:12-21, thus giving him more responsibility, prominence, or importance. This is because they miss the larger picture of what Paul is doing. Paul is using a literary device to repeatedly compare one sinful man and one righteous man.

We need to not focus so much on Adam as the symbol or type, rather focus on the point, which is that Jesus is able to rescue all of humanity as the representative "Son of Man (Humanity)." I think we evangelicals revere the Word so much that we can sometimes lose the forest for the trees, losing sight of the purpose by focusing on individual words. When there is a "type" (and there are many in the OT—a person, event, institution, or object that foreshadows or prefigures a greater reality later revealed in the NT), one should not force additional meanings or applications. For example, Isaac and Ishmael, Sarah and Hagar were types (Galatians 4:21-31). We focus on the purpose of the Galatians passage and don't unduly focus on and elevate

Sarah, imagining extra authority for her because of God using her in that type. (And she's even a good type!)

Also, Paul uses the word *anthrōpos* for Adam, which is for humanity, not the male person (anēr), even though the English translation says one "man." So, Adam is representative of mankind, not himself. Likewise, the Greek for Jesus's title, Son of "Man" is *anthrōpos*, better translated as "Son of Humanity" (more on that in Chapter 5). See, God gave dominion to mankind, who immediately abdicated rule to Satan and threw the world into chaos with sin. God would not (or could not, because God cannot lie or go back on his word), intervene except to come as a true human with dominion and conquer sin and death. Thus, the "Son of Humanity" undid the curse wrought by "*adam*" the first *anthrōpos*. This goes back to the topic of "Creation Order," in that God created Adam first and then used him as a single representative of humanity. None of that changes the fact that God gave humans authority over the earth but did not give individuals authority over each other. To interpret "Adam being chosen for the type" as "Adam having hierarchy" is an interpretive overreach.

> *As the one "man" (anthròpos = human) in Romans 5, Adam represents sinful humanity (not himself, a male, anèr), in contrast to Jesus, the one righteous representative for humanity (anthròpos).*
> Misleading Tactic #16

The Blame Game

Instead of humbly owning and confessing his failure, the man protected himself and blamed both God and the woman. God asked him two questions which he answered evasively.

> *"Who told you that you were naked? Have you eaten from the tree that I commanded you not to eat from?"*

"The woman you put here with me—she gave me some fruit from the tree, and I ate it."

The correct answers would have been, "My new enlightenment told me I'm naked" and "Yes, I did." But he resorted to deflection and blame. No doubt, the woman was shocked at this first betrayal ever. Then God turned to the woman and asked,

"What is this you have done?"

After the man had just blamed her, she could have easily pointed back at him and said "He stood there and let me do it" but she did not return his blame. She did deflect to the serpent though. She said,

"The serpent deceived me, and I ate."

The NT tells us she was deceived, so that is true. Acting under deception may seem like it was a mistake and not a sin. However, I believe her choice to believe the serpent over believing God was her sin. So, a more accurate answer that accepted responsibility would have been, "I chose to believe the serpent, and I ate."

The human pattern still today is self-protection and defensiveness which blames others. What would have happened if the man only accepted responsibility for his part and repented with sorrow? Would the woman have followed his example? We will never know, but we do know that if we want to lead others well, humble confession without deflection is a good start. Leading by example and caring for others in a way that builds trust rather than a sense of betrayal will go a long way.

The Curses

Curse on the Ground

Most believers are under the impression that due to sin, God cursed the man and woman as well as the serpent and the ground in Genesis chapter 3. The fact is, the word "curse" was only used for the serpent and the ground. God *described* the consequences of sin for woman and man. All of creation was thrown into chaos, including their own bodies which began to die. Woman and man would suffer great toil in their work of bearing children and working the earth.

> *It has been said so many times that God cursed man and woman, that people believe it, though Scripture does not say so. God was simply describing natural consequences, not giving commands or pronouncing curses on humans.*
> Misleading Tactic #3, 10

I'm clarifying all this about the curses because it goes to the heart of God. God was not angrily and punitively pronouncing dire curses on human beings. No doubt, with great grief, God was simply describing what life would be like for them going forward in this world which God had given them dominion over, but they quickly chose to believe Satan and handed dominion off to Satan and chaos.

Curse on the Serpent

The curse on Satan was that his representative (the serpent) would physically crawl on the earth, but the greater curse was enmity between Satan and the woman. She will have an offspring who will defeat him (most importantly, his power) permanently. So, it stands to reason that Satan wants to get every culture to oppress women because she is his mortal enemy according to God. Man is also Satan's enemy, but there is a peculiar emphasis on the enmity between Satan and woman. I think this is worth noting and returning to as we will see the mind-bending, horrific assaults on the shared dominion and personhood of women by not only the world, but by religious people. Satan loves power. He hates that humans were given power over the earth and does all that he can to usurp it. His first move against humans was to tempt them to sin and I believe his second move was to displace the woman's co-dominion with the man.

Effects on the Woman – Labor, Grief, and Subjugation

Following is Genesis 3:16a compared between the NIV first, then the KJV:

> *To the woman he said, "I will make your pains in childbearing very severe; with painful labor you will give birth to children."*

> *Unto the woman he said, I will greatly multiply thy sorrow and thy conception; in sorrow thou shalt bring forth children.*

Notice how differently this verse is translated. Study of the Hebrew shows the KJV to be a better translation although I would say the same English word "sorrow" should not have been used for two different Hebrew words.

The first "pains" (NIV) or "sorrow" (KJV) for woman is the same word, *issābôn* (H6093), for the labor of man, so it could mean the same toil related to the earth. Or it could be related to motherhood. Or it could be both—agricultural labor and motherhood labor. The "child-bearing" word is better translated as "conception," *hērāyôn* (H2032). "Conception" is the accepted meaning in the family of *hērāyôn* words everywhere else in the OT (occurs 62 times). There are other Hebrew words for giving birth (delivery) which were not used in this passage. The final "painful labor" (NIV) or "sorrow" (KJV) is *ēseb* (H6087), a word for "sorrow" having to do with raising children. Authors Iain Proven and Mark Boda share an important insight:

> *The word* ētseb *is used of emotional pain and the pain involved in work. It can also be used of a more generalized kind of pain. It is never used elsewhere in the Old Testament, however, to refer to [birthing] labor pains or birth pains. Conversely, there's a well-established vocabulary that's routinely used to describe [birthing]*

> *labor pain,* tsrar, khebel, *and* khul. *If we take our lead from the meaning of ētseb elsewhere in the Old Testament, then Genesis 3:16 also refers to the agony, hardship, worry, and anxiety of the circumstances in which children are conceived, born, raised, and in which they die.*[10]

Sure enough, if one looks at the Hebrew words in an interlinear Bible, follows the Strong's Concordance numbers to find other uses, and reads the meanings in those uses, we see that the second sorrow is more of a hurt of words or mind, an offense or grief, rather than a physical pain. Anyone who has raised children knows the emotional pain involved. The difficulty of parenting, heartbreaking concern for their welfare, overwhelming feelings of inadequacy, costly sacrifices, wayward children, unrequited love...all these and more. Only God knows the pain of a parent, especially a mother. When I learned what God was saying here, I burst into tears because I felt God's empathy for all the grief we would experience as parents.

Iain Provan's essay on 1 Chronicles 4:9-10 (Jabez and his mother) explains other reasonable understandings of *ētseb*. He suspects that the heart of the problem with the modern translation regarding emphasis on birthing pains goes back to an opinion from John Chrysostom around AD 400:

> *And she then dragged her husband down with her, she is punished first, receiving that punishment which carries with it lengthy admonition. ...accordingly I impose this curb on you to prevent your further running riot, and I sentence you to painful labor. ...*

---

10 Iain Provan and Mark Boda, eds., *Let Us Go up to Zion: Essays in Honour of H. G. M. Williamson on the Occasion of His Sixty-Fifth Birthday* (Leiden, The Netherlands: Brill Publishing, 2012), 288.

> *you will personally have a reminder, through the distress and pain of each birth, of the magnitude of this sin of disobedience.*[11]

Provan also says this about Chrysostom's contemporary, Jerome:

> *Jerome, whose Latin Vulgate translation speaks of the multiplication of "your toils and your conceptions" and predicts that "in grief you will bear children"* (multiplicabo aerumnas tuas et conceptus tuos in dolore paries filios).[12]

Provan points out that accepting Jerome's translation rather than Chrysostom's interpretation does not depart from church tradition. Provan says there has been plenty of support for the Jerome translation over the Chrysostom opinion all the way through the nineteenth century, especially from doctors who had to become skilled in exegeting this passage to counter those with convictions that women should not receive medical intervention to lessen birthing pain.[13]

I can testify that there has been too much emphasis on the woman's giving birth, as if the pain of birthing babies is a curse on the woman, when the passage is actually rich with meaning about the many labors she will have and the many griefs she will endure in a fallen world due to difficult relationships with her children and husband. It is interesting that both Jerome and Chrysostom gave an interpretation, but Chrysostom's more negative interpretation became more widely accepted. Men don't understand the shame and fear that Christian women feel at the prospect of giving birth when told all her life she

---

11 St. John Chrysostom, Homilies on Genesis 17.30. p. 238, Internet Archive, accessed September 11, 2025. *https://archive.org/details/saint-john-chrysostom-homilies-on-genesis-1-17/page/237/mode/2up.*

12 *Let Us Go Up to Zion,* 294.

13 Linda S. Schearing, *Mother Goose, Mother Jones and Mommie Dearest: Biblical Mothers and Their Children.* Cheryl Kirk-Duggan and Tina Pippin, eds. SBLSymS 61 (Atlanta: Society of Biblical Literature, 2009) 85– 96.

should suffer this pain in her most private area as a result of sin. Some cultures even do things to increase the pain, deny help for it, or make a woman feel she isn't accepting God's will if she focuses on learning to diminish it. Instead, she should be honored for her labor, just as men should be honored for their labor.

> *The poor translations of "issàbôn" and "ètseb" wrongly choose childbirth pain instead of general toil and child rearing, casting God as punitive, especially towards women.*
> Misleading Tactic #2

The next prediction for the woman is in the second half of Genesis 3:16b. We will look at the first phrase and then the second phrase.

Your desire will be for your husband, and he will rule over you.

Her Desire

Many times, this is explained as follows: "Wives will desire to rule over or control their husbands, but husbands will rule, as God meant them to." Everywhere else, we are instructed to first choose the plain reading and meaning of the text. "Desire" means "to yearn for" or "want," as in, "You will want him." The same Hebrew word for desire, *teshuqah*, is used by Solomon as he desires his lover in a romantic way in Song of Solomon 7:10. A small minority of translations have made the choice that *teshuqah* (translated "desire" in English) means to try to control. There is weak reason to interpret it this way. The definition of the word *teshuqah* (noun) (H8669) is "desire, longing" in the lexicons of Brown, Driver, and Briggs (BDB) and Gesenius.

Besides the use of *teshuqah* in the Song of Solomon, it is used just one other time in the OT (a grand total of three times), in the narrative of Cain and Abel in Genesis 4:7.

> *The choice to interpret "desire" negatively rather than positively is biased since there are many reasons that it should not be interpreted negatively.*
> Misleading Tactic #8

If you do what is right, will you not be accepted? But if you do not do what is right, sin is crouching at your door; it desires to have you, but you must rule over it.

Some translators and interpreters teach that this use of desire in Genesis 4:7 is comparable to Eve's desire in Genesis 3:16; therefore, her desire is sinful. I did a lengthy study of this topic and listed some of the many textual reasons why this teaching is wrong. See "Eve's Desire" on my website.

The unjustified idea that the woman is grasping for control is especially promoted by complementarians. In the late 1990s, Crossway (publication house with deep ties to the SBC), received permission from the National Council of Churches to use the 1971 edition of the Revised Standard Version (RSV) as the foundational text for the ESV, a version with their revisions which would be dubbed "the complementarian version." Translation committee members included those affiliated with CBMW. The first edition of the ESV was published in 2001. The 2008 Study Bible edition reinforced complementarianism in the notes in many places. Genesis 3:16 appeared as follows in the 2011 edition:

> *Your desire shall be **for** your husband, and he shall rule over you. [bold emphasis mine]*

However, the word "for" had an added footnote: "Or, *shall be contrary to*." Not too many people pay attention to footnotes or didn't feel it a great offense as long as it was a footnote and not in the text. However, a firestorm took place when the 2016 edition had those reversed; the text included "contrary to" and the footnote included "Or, *for*."

> *Your desire shall be* **contrary to** *your husband, but he shall rule over you. [bold emphasis mine]*

The other widely used translations show their translation teams agree that the desire is **for** or **toward** the husband. No others included the word, "contrary," even in footnotes. The lesser-used NLT and NET say, "you will desire to control your husband," and "you will want to control."

The Hebrew preposition 'ēl can be for many prepositions, but the primary spatial meaning is "to" or "toward." There would need to be good evidence for making it negative. Because the complementarians had to include "to" or "toward" (which is normally considered a positive thing), they added the word "contrary" to make it negative.

> *Your desire will be* ***for*** *(NIV)* ***toward*** *(NASB) your husband, and he will rule over you. [bold emphasis mine]*

In 2025, the ESV announced edits to be phased into the printing of their many types of Bibles over the next several years and one of those changes will be to remove the words "contrary to" and revert back to "for" (with a footnote saying "Or, contrary to"?). That is good, but it has already done great harm. I have personally had it quoted to me by young men who are just starting in ministry. I dare say they will never get that interpretation out of their minds. Around five million print copies with "contrary" were published excluding digital editions which are likely even more widespread. Those five

> *Adding the word "contrary" to impose a negative context is adding to Scripture and likely making the passage say the opposite of its true meaning.*
> Misleading Tactic #2, 7

million copies will continue to be used for another decade or longer, in church auditorium seat pockets and private shelves.

I believe a more accurate interpretation of Genesis 3:16b would be, "You will turn toward him with a healthy desire but instead of having that desire returned, he will dominate or rule over you in an unhealthy way." This is observable all around us in life. How often do abused women feel like they cannot leave their husbands or boyfriends? Women frequently desire a man at any cost.

When there is a power struggle, we do not have to assume the power struggle is because one person is trying to grasp the rightful position of the other. The power struggle could be because both people sinfully want dominance, or it could be because either of the two people is exercising unjust power, and the other is resisting the injustice. Both people need to lay themselves down and consider the other's interests more important than their own. The failure of either or both people to lay themselves down will result in a power struggle.

> *The interpretation that Eve desires to rule or be "over" Adam when the preposition for "over" is only attached to Adam's verb "rule," is to impose a meaning the text does not support (eisegesis) instead of exegesis.*
> Misleading Tactic #16

I cannot even begin to express all the shame that I and other women have felt over being told that the Bible teaches that our true motive is to grasp at and take away the legitimate authority of the man. There are countless times when what wives want is cooperation and teamwork, to feel their contribution is appreciated, that there is togetherness and connection. But assertion toward that end is characterized as this ugly grasping interpretation, and wives are shamed for it and put back in their subordinate lane. My mother was a brilliant woman who graduated *magna cum laude* from a rigorous institution, but she was made to feel like a mindless accessory. My father labeled any female who spoke her mind in front of him as "sassy." A popular book among fundamentalists during his formative years was *Bobbed Hair, Bossy Wives, and Women Preachers* by John R. Rice, reprinted for seven decades starting in the 1940s.

Of course, women can be inappropriately controlling just like men can be. But in Christendom, there is a belief that a controlling woman is far worse than a controlling man, or that a controlling man is legitimately exercising authority. His control has to be extreme and obvious to others in order to be considered sin.

In general, throughout history, men have dominated and controlled women far more than the other way around. The secular world's negative view of women (see revered figures such as Aristotle who taught horribly misogynistic ideas[14]) was baked into the Greco-Roman culture and affected how men viewed women in the early church. The world's framework would also have affected how Jewish leaders viewed women, especially those "Hellenized" with Greek culture. My reading of church history revealed there were always some with a fear-filled, negative view of sex (which eventually contributed to monastic living). When Paul wrote 1 Corinthians chapter 7, he was countering an ascetic element in the church which was teaching that celibacy (even within marriage) made one more holy. These factors considered together would have affected the commentaries of early church fathers all the way through the Reformation.

Following is my theory about why Genesis 3:16 was interpreted as parallel to Genesis 4:7 and given a negative interpretation: When English Bible translators and commentators during the Reformation

---

14 One of Aristotle's teachings was that the developing female body was too cold, so male genitals failed to come out, producing a malformed, female human. He also taught that semen contributed the essence of a human while the woman contributed only brute matter. These views are found in Aristotle's works, Generation of Animals and History of Animals.

looked at the only three uses of *teshuqah* in the Hebrew OT, they felt 1) that the word in Songs was sinful due to the opinion that sexual desire was sinful, 2) that the word "desire" in Genesis 4:7 was evil because it was "sin" doing the desiring (however "woman" is not the embodiment of sin), and 3) that the woman was a wicked temptress. Therefore, the word "desire" in 3:16 must be sinful. Their entire perspective was already negatively biased. Even though the Reformers decided priests could marry, it was a concession and not because of their elevated view of women or sex.

The Reformers continued a negative interpretative tradition from the world's philosophers, the strict rabbis, and ascetic Christians. I believe the outsized influence of these prolific Reformation writers carried down through the centuries along with a sinful nature which takes any opportunity to dominate others under the pretext of being more righteous.

His Rule

It should be an encouragement in this narrative of the fall that the woman would continue to desire and turn toward her husband. Many preachers have grossly twisted this passage away from a plain reading of it. The twisting of it is to their own advantage—that God wants them to rule over their wives.

In the 1990s, my Dallas Theological Seminary-trained pastor told me that the "ruling" in this verse was God's prediction, not God's prescription. (God was not saying what <u>should</u> happen.) But I never heard him teach that from the pulpit in over a decade of sitting under his teaching. The most generous explanation I can think of for why he did not teach it from the pulpit is that perhaps he did not think it important. He greatly underestimated the damage that the misunderstanding of this passage was having on Christian households. Even when he told this to me, I felt he was sharing a secret, possibly an unbiblical perspective, and I did not have the courage to even bring it up to my own husband because of the shame that had been hard-wired into me from childhood. Now, I know it is not a "view" but a solid interpretation.

I've heard preachers say that "Men are supposed to rule over wives, women, etc., just in a nice way, not in an ugly way." There is much discussion about various Hebrew and Greek words for "ruling over" or "exercising authority over," where they appear in the Bible, and which of those words are nicer or not so nice. I was distracted by that for a time until I finally realized it is irrelevant. Here is the bottom line: In Genesis 1:28 when God gave rule of the earth to humans, there was no mandate to rule over other humans. So, any rule over humans is not "nice."

Eventually, God gave the law and judges, and thus government was established to "carry the sword" of justice and help people cooperate. (The phrase "for rulers do not bear the sword for no reason" (Romans 13:4) is widely interpreted to mean that God delegates the authority to enact justice to governing powers, so that individuals are not responsible for taking justice into their own hands.) Ungodly people need the rule of government and God sets up and takes down kings. But those who follow God should manage themselves well enough that if government were to disappear, cooperation would still exist. In God's Kingdom, as described by Jesus, it is forbidden for individuals to rule over each other. We will revisit this topic when we examine the words of Jesus and the apostles in Part Four.

Translators know that rendering Genesis 3:16 from Hebrew into English is problematic, but they cannot ethically add their own text into the sacred text, so study Bibles offer commentary. The ESV Study Bible has lengthy notes that include the complementarian viewpoint as explained and refuted above. It *assumes* "leadership role of the husband ... ordained by God before the fall ..." without specifying how it was ordained. It indicates that the husband's rule will be "domineering" but doesn't indicate that the husband was not told to rule. It points to Ephesians 5:21-32 for "the NT pattern for marriage founded on the redemptive work of Christ." (We will look at Ephesians 5 in Part Four.)

The *Common English Bible (CEB) Study Bible* frames the verse as a description of brokenness, not a divine prescription of hierarchy. It emphasizes that the "rule" is a consequence of sin, not a creation mandate. The N*RSV Updated Edition* with the *Harper Collins Study Bible* notes the distortion of mutuality in marriage due to the fall. It often highlights literary and cultural context without affirming hierarchy. The *NIV Study Bible* provides nuance that can support alternative readings. The *New English Translation (NET) Study Bible* includes multiple interpretive options for *teshuqah* and *mashal* (rule) acknowledging scholarly debate.

At the least, there needs to be a footnote (such as, "This is predictive, not prescriptive"). We will see this again in the NT where Greek sentence construction gives help in distinguishing a simple statement of fact from a command, but the reader is left with the opposite impression.

Remember how Jacob gave blessings and prophesied over his twelve sons on his deathbed (including Joseph's two sons)? Many prophecies were decidedly negative. Should they have taken those predictions as commands and intentionally set out to do the ugly things? Should we assume God wanted his people to act that way or was God simply demonstrating that he is omniscient and knows the evil and foolishness that people will commit?

> *To give an interpretation that God prescribed ruling by men over women rather than described it, is misleading.*
> Misleading Tactic #10

Those of us brought up on the KJV hear the word "rule" in Genesis and immediately remember 1 Timothy 3:4-5 as overseers being instructed to "rule" their home well. (See how well indoctrinated I was?) That poor translation is addressed in the chapter which examines 1 Timothy 3.

"Because You Listened to the Woman"

When God tells Adam the consequences he will endure as the result of sin creating chaos in the world, God prefaces it with, "Because you listened to the woman...." Does that mean men should not listen to women? No, it means that if anyone tells a person something different than what they know for certain God told them, they should not listen. There are many ways we can fear man (Proverbs 29:25) and thus listen to people and want their approval more than we want God's approval. There are many instances in the Bible of people taking bad advice from men and enduring the consequences. To assume this verse meant that in general, for all time, men should not listen to women, or at least be especially cautious of listening to women, would be an extreme extrapolation, especially considering the many Scriptures we will see which include women as those to whom people should listen. (For example, Jesus scolded the eleven remaining disciples for not believing the testimony of the women that he had risen.)

However, church history was totally immersed in this extreme extrapolation that men should not listen to women. In my seminary church history class, we surveyed original documents from church history. Sadly, there is not much preserved writing and teaching by women even though there is testimony that women wrote significant works and commentaries. For example, Jerome and Chrysostom had female correspondents. Those with power chose not to preserve their work. Here is a quote from a prominent theologian in the fourteenth century, John Gerson:

> *All women's teaching, especially formal teaching, by word or by writing, is to be held suspect, unless it has been diligently examined, and much more fully than men's. And why? Because they*

are easily seduced and determined seducers. And because it is not proved that they are witnesses to divine grace.[15]

This opinion has additionally been expressed in various forms by Reformation leaders and more contemporary leaders. I would ask my reader to pause a moment and consider the first sentence in that Gerson quote and ask if you have had a knee-jerk response when a teaching comes from a woman; to be more cautious about it than if it comes from a man. I speculate that if you grew up in the church and are over the age of forty, that is your experience. I am not suggesting that you should feel shame for it; I am suggesting that we are often unaware of the extent to which we have been influenced on a subconscious level.

It cannot be overemphasized that evangelicals have a bad habit of taking one verse and making doctrine (or at least a theological perspective) out of it without considering the full counsel of Scripture. The reader will notice that time and again, this book will consider the full context of the Bible or the Gospels or the epistles when considering verses which trouble people on the topic of women teachers rather than "proof texting" (taking one verse out of full-canon context).

There is a choice of how to interpret, "Because you listened to the woman" as either the woman was intrinsically evil or that people should not act on any teaching that is contrary to God's teaching.
Misleading Tactic #8

Adam Names Eve

God gave Adam and Eve good news and bad news. The good news included that Eve would

15 Henrik Lagerlund, ed., *Encyclopedia of Medieval Philosophy: Philosophy between 500 and 1500,* Springer, Dordrecht. Accessed September 11, 2025, https://doi.org/10.1007/978-94-024-1665-7_269.

have multiplied conception. Adam proceeded to name her. Some commentators point out that naming is the function of pronouncing value, blessing, and future on others. God changed Jacob's name to Israel, and Saul became Paul. The man in the Garden of Eden was given the task to name the animals, demonstrating God's nature in the human. There was a dominance displayed when naming the animals. Therefore, some commentators point to Adam naming Eve as evidence for God-given dominance over her. However, God instructed Adam to name the animals but God did not instruct Adam to name Eve. Other commentators think Adam may have done it as his first act of impulsive domination over the woman.

I would like to have a more generous spirit than that and speculate that Adam was thrilled with the news she would bring forth life so wanted to honor her with a name which means "mother of all life." After all, he had been in the naming mode with the animals so why would he not keep it up? My point is, there is nothing within the text regarding Adam's motive in naming Eve. It could have been good, bad, or neutral—we simply do not know, so we should not use it for evidence either way.

Why All This Matters

First, the man and woman had become sinners, and their children would be sinners, and they would have multiplied labor and grief. However, there was no special curse on either of them personally or ontologically, causing the need for one to dominate the other. The idea of a "curse on woman" and a "curse on man" has resulted in a view of a punitive God instead of a natural consequences view. It affects our relationship with God, our view of ourselves and each other, and how we should act towards each other.

Second, taking the woman's labor from the field exclusively to childbirth supports the idea of completely separate roles with hers in the home and his outside the home. God's perfect plan was to include both in childrearing and both in economic management. Certain seasons of life or situations might cause an emphasis one way or the other, but role rules have impeded flexibility and cooperation in marriage.

Finally, prescriptive "rule over" teaching has been used to limit women and exacerbate the problem of male dominance to the detriment of both genders. Historical Christianity has cast women as especially wicked, more easily tempted (gullible), the conniving temptresses of men, and in need of being ruled over to keep them in line. Tru316 continually makes the point that the mistranslation and misinterpretation of Genesis 3:16 has affected the interpretation of NT Scriptures and limited women unnecessarily. I believe it has undermined God's ideal of unity among believers and has harmed the witness and effectiveness of the church.

The Three Divergent Roads - Creation Constructs

We identified the following three constructs at the beginning of Chapter 1 and can now identify which is most accurate:

The Pre-fall Hierarchical Construct – We saw there is no evidence for a hierarchical construct prior to the fall. There were plenty of opportunities for God to make such a construct clear, but he did not. In fact, he gave man and woman the rule over the earth together, not the rule over people. Subscribers of this view point to creation order as indicating a hierarchy but we saw a good biblical explanation for the order of creation. First Corinthians 11:11-12 explains that neither man nor woman can claim they are superior due to the other coming from them, because they both come from the other.

The Post-fall Hierarchical Construct – We saw that God predicted (not prescribed) that man would rule over woman in an ugly way, contrary to the command for them to have dominion over the earth together (but not dominion over each other). We saw that church history has interpreted the nature of woman in an unfairly negative light, leading to bias and providing an excuse for man to yield to a fleshly desire to rule over.

The Pre-fall Mutualist Construct– We saw that God created an *ezer kenegdo* to be a strong ally and partner (not subordinate helper), that God created both men and women in God's image with spiritual equality, that God cares more about relationship and unity than top-down hierarchy, and that God looks on the heart rather than physical and circumstantial attributes. We will continue to see how the whole Bible fits this construct. The goal for practical equality and mutual respect and concern for the other is not to be "culturally relevant" or to "keep up with the times." The goal is to return to the original ideal of creation and show the world how God intended humans to live in a way that brings glory to God by reflecting God's love and character.

Chapter 3:

CHURCH ORIGIN - THREEFOLD GENDER INCLUSION

When the church was born on the day of Pentecost, it represented God's ideal. Things have gone downhill, but Jesus said the gates of hell will not prevail against the church, so it has been preserved even though sometimes it's hard to recognize. We should look closely at the ideal, just as we looked closely at the ideal in the Garden of Eden before sin. We will start by looking at three passages foundational to the birth of the church.

The Empowerment on Pentecost

The birth of the church occurred during the celebration of Pentecost, 50 days after the death of Christ. The death of Christ happened on Passover. The first Passover was when lambs were killed in Egypt and their blood was put on the doorposts so the death angel "passed over" those homes and the firstborn did not die. Fifty days later, God gave his people the law out in the desert. The giving of the law was thereafter celebrated as Pentecost (meaning 50 days).

Fifty days after Jesus, the Lamb of God, gave his lifeblood on the wooden cross, the Holy Spirit was given on the celebration of Pentecost. The old covenant/testament and law were now fulfilled and replaced by the new covenant/testament and Holy Spirit. Everyone who believes becomes the church, grafted into the promises that were given to God's chosen people of the OT (Romans 11:17).

On the occasion of Pentecost, both men and women were gathered and praying.

> *They all joined together constantly in prayer, along with the women and Mary the mother of Jesus, and with his brothers.* ["Brothers" being the Greek *adelphoi* (offspring of the same womb) should include Jesus's biological half-sisters, *brothers and sisters,* for gender accurate translation.] *(Acts 1:14)*

The Holy Spirit filled "all" of them, who began to speak in tongues and prophesy. Peter explained what was happening to the bewildered crowds.

> *These people are not drunk as you suppose. It's only nine in the morning! No, this is what was spoken by the prophet Joel: In the last days, God says, "I will pour out my Spirit on all people. Your sons and daughters will prophesy, your young men will see visions, your old men [people--presbyterioi] will dream dreams. Even on my servants, both men*

> *Women were present when "all" of them began to speak in tongues and prophecy. Peter included the women of Joel's prophecy. There was no distinction between the empowerment of men and women for ministry.*
> Misleading Tactic #5

and women, I will pour out my Spirit in those days, and they will prophesy. …And everyone who calls on the name of the Lord will be saved." (Acts 2:15-18, 21, emphasis mine)

There was no difference in how God empowered the men versus the women. Also, Peter explained the phenomenon as being the fulfillment of a prophecy which included all people, young and old, sons and daughters, and both men and women. Could it be any clearer that God wanted to empower women equally?

The Great Commission to Make Disciples

This is the second passage that is foundational to the birth of the church.

All authority in heaven and on earth has been given to me. Therefore, go and make disciples of all nations, baptizing them in the name of the Father and of the Son and of the Holy Spirit, teaching them to obey everything I have commanded you. And surely, I am with you always, to the very end of the age. (Matthew 28:18-20)

I am under the impression that most of the church believes this commission is for all believers, male and female. I was surprised to learn that some people believe this command was only for the eleven disciples. The thinking is that verse 16 only specifies The Eleven, which could imply that only the eleven were present. That is a legitimate dilemma. I will explain below why I believe women were present. For those who believe this commission is for everyone, there is one main

> *Jesus told all believers, including women, to make disciples with his authority, teaching and baptizing them. There was no limitation to only teach and baptize one's own gender.*
> Misleading Tactic #5

Greek verb; "make" (disciples), which is elaborated on by three participles, "go," "baptize," and "teach." Women are to make disciples with the authority of Jesus by going, baptizing, and teaching. Jesus did not say, "Go unto your own gender in the world..."

I believe Jesus was not speaking only to men, because of what we read about Jesus's farewell in Acts 1:1b-9:

> *...I wrote about all that Jesus began to do and to teach until the day he was taken up to heaven, after giving instructions through the Holy Spirit to the apostles he had chosen. After his suffering, he presented himself to them and gave many convincing proofs that he was alive. He appeared to them over a period of forty days and spoke about the kingdom of God. On one occasion, while he was eating with them, he gave them this command: "Do not leave Jerusalem, but wait for the gift my Father promised, which you have heard me speak about. For John baptized with water, but in a few days you will be baptized with the Holy Spirit." Then they gathered around him and asked him, "Lord, are you at this time going to restore the kingdom to Israel?" He said to them: "It is not for you to know the times or dates the Father has set by his own authority. But you will receive power when the Holy Spirit comes on you; and you will be my witnesses in Jerusalem, and in all Judea and Samaria, and to the ends of the earth." After he said this, he was taken up before their very eyes, and a cloud hid him from their sight.*

Women also waited for the gift and received power from the Holy Spirit on Pentecost; therefore, they were included in this group to whom Jesus was speaking. A case could be made that they were included in this reference to "the apostles he had chosen," with "apostles" meaning "those who are sent." (This general descriptive word, apostles, was used elsewhere in the NT apart from The Twelve.) Because we can deduce that women were present in the narrative of Acts 1, we can deduce women were present in the narrative of Matthew 28, tagging along with The Eleven just as they had throughout the Gospel narratives, whether or not they were specifically mentioned every time. As close as the women stayed during the death, burial, and resurrection, it is obvious that wild horses could not have kept them away from Jesus post-resurrection.

Recently, I sat at a table where a Christian man spoke derisively about "empowering women." I wish I had thought to say, "Excuse me, but Jesus gave me power and if you try to withhold it, you are working against Jesus!" It is a shame that the world uses the phrase "empower women" but the church does not. I have heard of churches who allow women to speak with the explicit understanding that they "are not speaking with authority." Jesus gave his own authority to women, so who are these people to think they have the authority to give a platform but withhold the spiritual authority or power of Jesus? It might be "their" earthly platform to give, but not the authority and power of Jesus. I have personally experienced the power of the Holy Spirit speaking through me when teaching and witnessing, and experienced supernatural power for other things. Ignoring Scripture which equally empowers women with Jesus's authority is misleading.

> *It is misleading to downplay the fact that Scripture equally gives women Jesus's power and authority.*
> Misleading Tactic #17

The Proclamation of the Gospel

As we think on the basic command to the church to go and share the "gospel" *euangelion* (good news) to others about the facts that Jesus came as God in the flesh, died for our sins, was buried, and rose again, we remember that the very first person to be commissioned to go and share the good news of the resurrection was Mary Magdalene. She was told by Jesus himself to go and tell males. Prior to the resur-

> *It is illogical to agree with the Bible that no one can teach truth except by the Holy Spirit and agree all believers have the same Holy Spirit, yet on the other hand think the Spirit is somehow encumbered by the sexual biology of a human.*
> Misleading Tactic #5

rection, we know that the second person whom Jesus sanctioned to tell people that he was the Messiah was the Samaritan woman, who told a whole city, not just the women. (The first person was John the Baptist.) Someone might say, "He didn't tell her to go, she just went." However, up to that point, every time Jesus healed someone, he said, "Don't tell anyone." This woman was the first person he did not tell to keep his identity a secret.

These first examples were the beginnings of the church, with individuals called to preach (or proclaim) the good news. Jesus was very intentional about everything he did. I have to believe that he was making a point by using these women.

Today's complementarian leaders draw some distinctions here. They say that these women were not told to lead men, just to tell them the gospel. (Although John Piper has a problem with women telling men anything, even directions to the store). So, we would have to remove from our vocabulary that telling someone the gospel is to "lead them to Christ." Sounds like splitting hairs to me—leading vs. telling. Also, if "telling" is okay, women should be able to teach and preach.

Oh, but there is also telling "with authority." The thinking is that some believers have more authority than others or are operating under sanctioned authority and a woman could be sanctioned to do the same thing but "without authority" only because the Bible supposedly forbids it.

Here is a news flash: all believers who speak the Word do so with the only authority there is – the Holy Spirit! It is God's Word, not ours, so that's what has authority, not the human mouth speaking it. First Corinthians 12:3 says that no one can speak the truth about Jesus except by the Holy Spirit. Therefore, people need to be careful not to disparage that teaching (saying it is not authorized) because of the vessel God is using, or they are working against the Holy Spirit! As we know, even vile men living a double life have preached powerfully with genuine results, because it is the Word of God, not them, that will accomplish God's purpose (Isaiah 55:11).

Again, the beginning of the church is the ideal. There were no pulpits, platforms, sanctuaries, seminary degrees, or ordination boards—those are modern-day constructs. People spoke as they were led by the Holy Spirit, not always with carefully prepared sermons cleverly alliterated with the letter "P."

Over the last two hundred years, there have been (and still are) countless USA-sent women on foreign mission fields, both preaching to and teaching large, mixed-gender crowds. Sometimes the teaching was out in the open air rather than delivered standing behind a podium in a building for fear of doing wrong. The mixed crowds were a concern to the women, but they couldn't bear to let the men go to hell because there was no one else to teach them. Lottie Moon (who initially went to China with the Southern Baptist Convention) is just one example.

The big thing missed by people who restrict women is that God dwelt in a building in the OT, but now he dwells in the sanctuary of human believers—men and women. There is no building, platform, or pulpit as sacred as the lowliest believer who ministers as part of the Body of Christ.

Part One Closing Thoughts

What we have seen so far in Genesis and in the birth of the church should be enough. If we weren't putting some misconceptions from the epistles back onto these foundational beginnings, we could see

God's ideal. Therefore, we will go through all the seemingly problematic passages where it is claimed that women were prohibited or claimed that males were given special spiritual office. We will also go through the many neglected permissive passages where women are sanctioned to teach, pray, and prophesy in church gatherings, teach men, and hold "office." I know from personal experience that blindness causes these Scriptures to completely disappear from view (with a lot of help from some misleading tactics). I learned to skim over them and not question what I had been taught. But if we claim to value Scripture, we should be willing to fully consider these words just as carefully as every other passage we have carefully considered over our lifetimes.

First, we need to set the stage for first-century culture and see how Jesus handled the culture. Then we can better understand context in passages when we see that Paul occasionally advises that concessions be made for the culture (not only as it pertained to women but in other matters). We will see that while balancing cultural considerations, Paul encouraged interdependence between men and women, and he commended women with the same co-laborer language, as frequently as he commended men.

PART TWO
THE HEART AND EXAMPLE OF JESUS

Chapter 4:

JUDAISM AND WOMEN

To have a better understanding of what Jesus did, we need to examine the first-century Jewish culture as it relates to women. First, a disclaimer: because we are in a post-Holocaust era and antisemitism is still all around us, I want to make it clear that the following critical analysis of Judaism in the first century is not criticism of Jews in general. The religious leaders of that day added their own legalism, just as modern Christian religious leaders have added their own legalism. I identify errors regarding Jewish treatment of women of that time, not all time. This book includes far more criticism of the modern Christian church which has greater culpability. Also, I do not intend to portray Jesus as a renegade when it comes to legitimate Torah law which honored God and protected his people. Jesus only broke illegitimate law, which I will define. Anyone who comes away from this chapter with a lower view of Jewish people completely misses the point about the example of Jesus which some of the church today is failing to follow.

New Religious Burdens on Women

Around 500 years before Christ, the Jews returned home from their exile in Babylon. Religious leaders believed that the Babylonian exile was due to failure to obey the law, so to do better, they came up with thousands of oral "fence laws" to ensure they never broke any of the 613 actual laws in Torah. Yes, thousands. For example, 39 categories of laws defined what would constitute working on the Sabbath. These additional oral laws were burdensome to all the people. They affected women in areas such as modesty, ritual purity, marriage, work at home, Sabbath observance, and public conduct.

There is some disagreement over how much women were restricted in Jesus's time. How does one reconcile conflicting information? I imagine it was much like today, where opportunity depends on one's wealth, influence, household, and community circle. The more religiously strict the circle, the more restricted the women. The more devout the women, the more susceptible they are to being restricted *in the name of God* (spiritual abuse). Asking what life is like for women in any time or place is much like two blind people describing an elephant while one is holding the tail and the other an ear. I have a friend who is my age, we both grew up near Chicago, and our fathers were both pastors. Her father urged her to let nothing hold her back, and as a missionary he had ordained the first woman in Egypt in his denomination. When I told my friend about my upbringing, she said, "Your lips are moving and I hear sound, but it is not computing." She was totally unaware of the circles I had lived in even though we were both raised in Christian families involved in ministry just a few miles apart.

In first-century Israel, each of the following groups had different family/religious/social circles:

- Pharisees and Scribes -- strictest about the oral law (by varying degrees), believed in the resurrection, spirits, angels, and devotion to God

- Sadducees -- priestly class, wealthy, Hellenized (fond of Greek culture), cooperative with Rome, rejected the oral law, did not believe in the resurrection, spirits, or angels
- Herodians -- observed the Torah but not strictly, rejected the oral law, politically motivated and supportive of the Romans through Herod's dynasty
- Zealots of varying stripes -- primarily concerned about political liberty so did not care for the Sadducees or Herodians, so those who were more religious aligned with Pharisees
- Essenes -- acetic separatists who lived in the desert and rejected the oral law
- Average Israelite family – most seemed to follow the Pharisees

Jesus would have aligned more closely with the Pharisees than any other group because they cared about devotion to God and believed in resurrection. But their obsession with the law caused them to lack compassion and place heavy burdens on the people. They were just as keen as the other groups to wield every possible scrap of power and were jealous for the people to follow them. The focus of this discussion is on the women who were most under the influence of Pharisees.

We know that teaching the Torah to women was discouraged by some rabbis, men were discouraged from speaking with women in public, and women couldn't lead outside the home. Men could initiate divorce, but women could not (Josephus, *Antiquities of the Jews.* 15.7.10 §259), nor could they testify in court (ibid. 4.8.15) because it was said they were dishonorable and unintelligent. In general, young people from poor families had more freedom in choosing their own marriage partner, whereas families with wealth and/or influence chose spouses for their children based on advantage for the family.

After AD 70, the oral tradition/laws began to be written for preservation. At the end of the second century, these writings were compiled into the Mishnah, the first written collection of Jewish oral traditions. The Mishnah is the foundation of rabbinic literature and is a key component of the Talmud. Unlike later rabbinic works, the Mishnah does not provide a single, unified legal code. Instead, it presents disputes between different rabbinic sages. Just like we find variances of worship practices in today's churches, first-century rabbis had different opinions on exactly how to keep the law.

For example, there is a debate where Rabbi Eliezer (lived approximately AD 40–120) asserted that teaching one's daughter Torah was akin to teaching her promiscuity. He opined that "a woman's wisdom is solely in her spinning-wheel . . . let words of Torah burn rather than be transmitted to women" (*Sotah* 3:4). Another rabbi said she should be taught so she understood the consequences of breaking the law. Elsewhere, they debated whether a man may divorce his wife for burning food, or because he wished to marry a more attractive woman, or whether the standard should be higher.

The Talmud (*Sotah* 22b) describes a group known as the "bruised Pharisees"—they would close their eyes or look away when encountering women, sometimes bumping into walls and injuring themselves. Others just avoided eye contact. The legitimate law in Leviticus says that anything a woman sits on when menstruating (the rags that become bloody) are "unclean." In the Mishnah (*Niddah* 2:1) they debated whether to extend the designation of impurity to anything she touched—the perfect way to make women feel like a contagion instead of a valued person. The Mishnah were considered tradition. Practices must be in place for a significant length of time to be considered tradition, so I think it reasonable to assume this was going on during the life of Jesus.

A traditional morning prayer for Jewish men thanks God for not making them a Gentile, slave, or woman. This prayer is included in the Talmud, but it's reasonable to think the oral tradition was much older. In Luke 18, Jesus talks about the self-righteous prayer of the Pharisee, openly thanking God he is not like others.

For a thorough description of Second Temple Era life for women, see *Post-Biblical and Rabbinic Women | Jewish Women's Archive* (https://jwa.org/encyclopedia/article/post-biblical-and-rabbinic-women#pid-16299). This source explains that women may have held some sacred offices in the First Temple period (Solomon's Temple) but not the Second (517 BC to AD 70). The Jewish historian, Flavius Josephus (approximately AD 37 – 100), wrote that women were not allowed to proceed past the women's court in the Jerusalem Temple unless they were bringing a special sacrifice. He also wrote the following in *Against Apion* (Book 2, section 25, published approximately AD 97):

> *The woman, says the Law, is in all things inferior to the man. Let her accordingly be submissive, not for her humiliation, but that she may be directed; for the authority has been given by God to man.*

Does the legitimate law (the Torah) say this? No. So, what "Law" is he referring to? He is Jewish, and he is talking about God, so probably not Roman law. More likely, he is talking about the Jewish, man-made oral law. We will see reference to this illegitimate "law" again in the epistles.

Despite variables, one thing is certain: over time, the Pharisees had increased the restrictions on the women over whom they held influence. Men had more restrictions as well, but the restrictions on women were more dehumanizing. Why did the woman's wisdom over a few hundred years get relegated to the spinning wheel in the minds of some Pharisaical rabbis? Looking back at God's prediction of enmity between Satan and the woman in Genesis, it seems to me like a demonic conspiracy, a specific attack on the woman's personhood that culminated in the time of Christ when the prophecy about her offspring crushing Satan's head is about to be fulfilled.

When the Jerusalem Temple was destroyed in AD 70, the Pharisees transformed into Rabbinic Judaism, and the Sadducees lost their institutional base and power. Worship became less centralized, the local synagogues became more important, and women gradually held some offices and titles over the next few centuries. I wonder if this was partly due to the subversive nature of what took place with Christianity as well as the changes in secular culture.

Jesus Stood Up for Women

Jesus was radical in the way he stood up for women at every turn, even breaking the oral "law" (fence laws) regarding women.

Isaiah's Prophetic Mission

Jesus quoted Isaiah (61:1-2), saying he came to set the captives and oppressed free (Luke 4:18). We interpret that to be spiritual freedom more so than physical freedom. This spiritual interpretation is correct in the context of the spiritual oppression of women. The oppression was led by religious leaders who did it in God's name. This was spiritual abuse. (Note that today, any oppression that is done in God's name is also spiritual abuse.)

Did Jesus Tell Women to "Just Go Lower"?

In case the reader has not encountered it, good Christian teaching encourages believers toward humility, including the phrase "just go lower." Oddly, Jesus never indicated to any individual woman that she should "just go lower" in order to please God with her humility. Jesus frequently encouraged more humility when speaking with men or teaching crowds in general. There are two reasons why it would have made sense for Jesus to tell individual women to "just go lower."

First, Jesus could have told women that submitting to these illegitimate oral laws and accepting lower class status was an opportunity to lay themselves down and be more humble, like himself. Just look at his example according to Philippians chapter 2. He was equal with God but humbled himself and put himself into a human body. Then he patiently endured disrespect and misunderstanding. So, it makes sense that he could call on women and others who are being mistreated to abase themselves as well. After all, according to Jesus, none of us is better than our master, so we should expect mistreatment.

A danger with this teaching is that it can be used to turn a blind eye and become complicit with sinful abuse. Or, if the one committing the mistreatment is the one telling the mistreated that they should go lower on account of Jesus, that is spiritual abuse. I believe Jesus was sensitive to power differentials and that is why we never see him instruct an individual woman or group of women to be humbler, but he does instruct men. In the following passages, I think there were men acting pridefully, so Jesus lectured them on humility or gave them an object lesson. Women could have been present but Jesus would have been speaking to the men due to their conduct. (See Matthew 18:1-4 and parallel passage Mark 10:42-45; Luke 14:7-11; 18:9-14; John 13:1-17.)

I am not saying that the message to simply go lower is wrong—often it is right—but I am sure that sometimes it is wrong, so we need to be cautious. We have been called to do the ministry of reconciliation when people are hurting and sometimes that means helping someone obtain dignity and/or justice. Jesus told a parable about a woman pestering an unjust judge until he helped her get justice only to get her off his back. Then Jesus said,

> *And will not God bring about justice for his chosen ones, who cry out to him day and night? Will he keep putting them off? I tell you; he will see that they get justice, and quickly. (Luke 18:7-8a)*

The message, "always go lower" could go against God's heart in certain situations. Sure, there might be times to advise, "Just be kind to your adversary and see if God does something on your behalf," but if we have the ability or influence to take up the cause of the person who is in front of us, our taking action might be God working through us to encourage them. Perhaps God would have us let them know they are valuable to him, and they can be bold in praying for and pursuing justice. Micah 6:8 tells us to do justice, love mercy, and walk humbly. It might be complicated, but those things are not exclusive since God told us to do all three.

Second, Jesus could have told women to "just go lower" by saying, "All authority that exists is in place because I allowed it, therefore, submit to this authority." He did not say that either. Instead, Jesus defended women and tacitly encouraged them to break the Jewish oral law, not noisily or in a rude way, but definitely boldly and publicly. There is an ungodly way to resist abuse and illegitimate law, and there is a godly way to resist, (more on that in chapter 13) but resistance, especially to spiritual abuse done in God's name, is something Jesus modeled for us.

Fence "Laws" Which Jesus Broke

Following are some illegitimate laws which Jesus broke on behalf of people oppressed by religious leaders.

Teaching Women

Jesus was radical in that he taught women. Martha and Mary called him "Teacher" because it was so important to them that he allowed them to "sit at his feet" with the male disciples. Because it was so unusual, the Gospels say "and the women" when counting crowds. In contrast, today, we would assume women in a group. The women knew that their religious education was against the teaching of some Pharisees, but they did it anyway, with Jesus's encouragement. Another overlooked nuance is that in the first century, when someone "sat at the feet" of a teacher, it was often with the goal of becoming a teacher themselves, not to just sit in adoration.

I have noticed that in the last few decades, women are now allowed into some seminaries where they didn't used to be. Even though they are often denied formal ordination into ministry, they are no longer denied access to advanced teaching as this would be a direct contradiction to the life of Christ. Women are still not always permitted in pastoral or preaching courses.

D.L. Moody was one of the first modern-day evangelicals to encourage women to get advanced theological training for the purpose of ministry. He saw that many women went overseas as missionaries while untrained, because they were not allowed into religious institutions of higher learning. So, after his retirement from (what would become) Moody Memorial Church in Chicago, he started his own school for women on the property of his childhood home in Northfield, Massachusetts. (Also on this property, he started a memorial grove for women who died on the mission field. Their names have been recovered from a buried plaque, and The Moody Center is attempting to discover their stories.)

This illegal, or at least frowned upon, teaching of women by Jesus happened publicly. When the Gospels say, for example, there were "about five thousand men besides women and children," we think the writer is implying that women and children weren't as important since they weren't counted. The opposite emphasis is true. The writers were pointing out that women and children were present because it was so unusual for anyone called "rabbi" to allow it.

Intervening in the stoning of a woman

The Pharisees brought a woman caught in adultery (not the man she was with—did they frame her?) to Jesus because they wanted to trap him. The Torah said she should be stoned. They felt his advocacy for women would be his downfall as he would no doubt defend her in contradiction to the law. Jesus pointed out their hypocrisy and they backed off. Some people speculate that Jesus was writing the

Pharisees' sins in the dirt and only they could read so it was private, but still alarming. That would explain why they de-escalated so fast, dropped this particular strategy, and were so hell-bent on killing him.

Praising a woman who broke fence laws

When the woman with the perpetual flow of blood touched Jesus, she was breaking oral purity "laws." Jesus could have kept quiet, but he made her say what happened in front of everyone, and then he commended her in public as if he wanted to flaunt his approval of her while she was breaking the law. Can you imagine the reaction of a Pharisee if he discovered that a menstruating woman had touched him?

Frequent illegal contact with women

Jesus allowed women to travel with him, even some who didn't have husbands. He spoke to women, healed them, and frequently touched those he healed. When Jesus said to Simon the Pharisee, "Do you see this woman?" he may have been directly challenging Simon's refusal to literally look at and acknowledge a woman. Or he could have been challenging Simon to truly "see" and think about her more deeply. Jesus's interaction with women was not one of mere tolerance but a soul-level attunement and acknowledgment.

Luke 13 tells of a time Jesus was teaching in the synagogue, and he saw a woman who was crippled and bent over. He healed her, placing his hands on her. The synagogue leader was indignant that Jesus healed on the Sabbath. Jesus said, "You lead your donkey to water on the Sabbath, so should not this woman, who is a daughter of Abraham…be set free?" These leaders couldn't have missed seeing this bent over woman for eighteen years, but they didn't see her with value and compassion or they would have rejoiced at her healing. To them, she was worth less than a donkey, but Jesus saw her, touched her, and pronounced value on her as a daughter of Abraham.

Defense of women regarding divorce

Jesus's talk about when divorce is warranted (Matthew 19) was pointed at the men, because women could not divorce their husbands unless the husband granted it, no matter how badly they were treated. Husbands, however, could divorce wives for almost any reason. Men were hoping Jesus would condone this. Jesus told them adultery was the only valid reason for divorce. They argued, saying that was too high of a standard—who could live up to that?! What he said was solely in defense of women, because it wasn't the women who were divorcing for trivial reasons. Today, religious men turn the intentions of Jesus (to protect women) backwards by telling women they may not divorce except for adultery, causing women to suffer all kinds of other abuse with no way out.

If one is willing to see it, Jesus stuck his neck out on behalf of women—repeatedly.

During that time, man-made, oral law was often referred to as "The Law" as if it was legitimate when it really wasn't. Jesus said he didn't come to break the law but to fulfill it. Therefore, every time he broke a "law," he was distinguishing between legitimate law and illegitimate law. When we are told "obey the authority," we can follow Jesus's example. He obeyed legitimate law and disobeyed illegitimate law.* When epistolic passages on this topic of civil authorities are difficult to interpret, the words and life of Jesus should be the plumbline to which we hold those passages.

*One clarification: Jesus did disregard some purification laws that were in the Torah. However, due to his own purity, when he touched someone who was not pure, instead of becoming impure himself, he made them pure.

Chapter 5:

JESUS AFFIRMING WOMEN

Jesus Used Women to Represent God

One day, Jesus told the Pharisees three parables recorded in Luke 15 (Lost Sheep, Lost Coin, Lost Son). In each parable, one of the characters represented God. In the second one, God was represented by a woman (searching for a lost coin). Today, we miss the significance, but that would have really steamed the Pharisees. They would not have missed that a woman represented God in a story where they were being chided.

It wasn't necessary for Jesus to use a parable with a woman representing God. He had to know that doing this might even distract the Pharisees from the main point. It seems like he went out of his way to do it. Again, God didn't have a problem with revealing his nature using a woman. We learn of God's focused care, diligently seeking out each valuable individual and throwing a party when they repent and come. Apparently, a man just wouldn't do for this illustration.

In another metaphor (Luke 13:20-21), Jesus used a woman putting yeast into bread dough to depict God's activity in the Kingdom. Another time, Jesus compared himself to a mother hen (Matthew 23:37). I own chickens and allow them to hatch their own brood. The dedication of a "broody" hen makes me fear she will lose her life for refusal to get off the nest to eat and drink. Apparently, a male just wouldn't do for this illustration.

Bible-wide Maternal References to God

God is a spirit (John 4:24) and has no body, so does not actually have gender. So why do we think of God as masculine?

First, God sometimes chooses to be known by male metaphors. "Father" might be the first one we think of, but that is in the minority in the OT, 15-20 times. Most "father" references are in the NT, mainly because Jesus referred to God often as Father. Some other typically male roles are "king," "warrior," and a few mentions of "husband." I imagine God wants one of our primary impressions to be of a strong protector and provider, like the good father or husband many people didn't get to experience. Other strong or protective metaphors are "rock" and "shield." These also communicate stability and safety. This makes me think of Maslow's Hierarchy of Needs. The field of psychology discovered what God already knew, that the basic needs of humans are first physiological (water, food, shelter) and safety. Then comes love and belonging. God speaks frequently about being the source of provision for our basic-level needs.

The Bible says God's very essence is love; a characteristic more often connected with the feminine. God is sometimes portrayed with maternal qualities and imagery: mother in childbirth (Isaiah 42:14), nursing mother (Isaiah 49:15; Hosea 11:3–4), comforting mother (Isaiah 66:13), midwife (Psalm 22:9; Job 38:8–9; Isaiah 66:9), female master (Psalm 123:2), housewife (Luke 13:20–21; Luke 15:8–10), mother hen (Matthew 23:37; Luke 13:34), and woman giving birth to creation (Psalm 90:2 CSB).

Then there are additional nongender-typed human metaphors that have to do with occupations such as potter, builder, weaver, baker, crafts/artisan, refiner/launderer, judge, farmer, shepherd, and creator. There are nonhuman metaphors such as rock, shield, tower/stronghold, light, vine, and bird. These metaphors are meant to help us with a rich experience of God relationally and metaphorically. Jesus taught his disciples to pray "Our Father," so we often restrict ourselves to that one metaphor. We would do well to broaden our perspective and explore all of these metaphors in our devotional time.

A second reason we often think of God in the masculine is that the Bible is full of masculine pronouns. As Marg Mowczko writes on her website:

> *The reason God is referred to as "he" is largely due to the limitations of language. There are no divine pronouns or appropriate non-gendered third-person singular pronouns in the biblical languages that we can use when talking and writing about God. So, we are limited to the grammatical genders of masculine and feminine in Hebrew, and masculine, feminine and neuter in the Greek.*[16]

I think the majority of the rest of the world understands grammatical gender far better than Americans who don't speak a language with grammatical gender. Seven out of the ten most spoken languages in the world have grammatical gender as do Hebrew and Greek. Grammatical gender is a system in which nouns are categorized as masculine, feminine, or neuter, which affects the form of related

16 Marg Mowczko, "Is God Male or Masculine?" Exploring the biblical theology of Christian egalitarianism, June 22, 2011, https://margmowczko.com/is-god-male-or-masculine/.

words like adjectives, pronouns, and verbs. It's a linguistic feature, not necessarily tied to biological sex, and varies widely across languages. English does not have grammatical gender so when translating from Hebrew or Greek, gender will appear in the English and can mislead people who only know English and are not aware that grammatical gender has nothing to do with biology.

The Hebrew word for Holy Spirit, *Ruach*, is feminine, which again, is simply grammatical, like the word "table" in Spanish (*mesa*) is feminine, but a table has no gender. Articles and adjectives would be feminine to agree with it. In Syriac, a dialect of Aramaic which Jesus spoke, the word for spirit (*Rucha*) is also feminine and early Christian writers in that tradition used feminine articles, pronouns, and even maternal imagery for the Holy Spirit. Again, from Marg Mowczko:

> *The Greek word for "Spirit" (*pneuma*), however, is grammatically neuter, and so neuter pronouns (corresponding to "it") are often used in reference to the Holy Spirit in the Greek text of the New Testament. Nevertheless, these Greek neuter pronouns are usually translated into English as masculine pronouns simply so that the Holy Spirit does not seem impersonal.*[17]

It bothers me when people refer to the Holy Spirit as "it." In fact, in my own speech, I have dropped "the" in front of "Holy Spirit" as I feel that is impersonal. (We don't say "the Jesus.") I include "the" when writing because people would think there is a typo. I point the reader to Mowczko's article for many other interesting aspects of this discussion. I also encourage the reader to read all the footnotes of Mowczko's articles because they are as interesting as the articles themselves.

A discussion on how evangelicals deal with gender isn't complete without discussing this view from John Piper:

---

17 Ibid.

> *God has made Christianity to have a masculine feel. ... He has ordained for the church a masculine ministry.*[18]

It downplays women to say "God has ordained for the church a masculine ministry." Both men and women reflect the image of God and play important roles as the "Body" and "Bride" of Christ.
Misleading Tactic #17

The Bible compares the church to a wife, to the "bride" of Christ, so how does that give the church a masculine feel and masculine ministry?

I've heard it said that because God calls himself "Father," he must only be represented by males. The book, *The Shack,* by William Paul Young, was highly criticized because "no story should have a woman who represents God" (the character of the Holy Spirit was female). Those who say this should tell that rule to Moses, Paul, God, and Jesus since they all broke it. (This is not an endorsement of every theological idea in The Shack.)

Jesus Was the Son of Humanity

The word "Man" in the phrase "Son of Man" is the Greek word *anthrōpos*. This word (from which we get anthropology) means "humanity" or "person." "Son of Man" is used in most Bible translations because this is the way the title has traditionally been translated. Back when this was first translated in the KJV, "man" meant "mankind" in the minds of translators and readers. Now, this phrase should be translated "Son of Humanity" for the reader's best understanding, that Jesus isn't just the son of the man but of humanity (men

18 Alex Murashko, John Piper: God Gave Christianity a 'Masculine Feel', The Christian Post, February 01, 2012, https://www.christianpost.com/news/john-piper-god-gave-christianity-a-masculine-feel.html.

> *A more accurate translation of Huios tou anthròpou is "Son of Humanity," rather than "Son of Man."*

and women). I don't think this rises to the level of "misleading," but it helps make the point that *tradition has much to do with translation choices.* It is impossible to know the extent to which gendered translation tradition affects our subconscious bias, but no doubt some of that happens.

Jesus Submitted to a Woman

Even as a 30-year-old adult, Jesus submitted to his mother when he performed his first public miracle. She asked him to do something about the wine running out at a wedding and he refused, saying it wasn't his time. She ignored that statement and told the young men to do whatever he told them to do. (Some men would consider that pushy and manipulative!) So, Jesus yielded and did his first public miracle at her request. (This is just one of many examples in the Bible where God changes his mind or his plan at the request of mere humans, and in this case, a female human.) Did Mary know better than he did? Was her posture a commanding one? No and no. But he honored her by submitting to her wishes. Obviously, his male disciples were observing, and John included the exchange in his Gospel. (Did anyone chide Jesus about "who wears the pants" in the family?)

Jesus submitted his very existence as a dependent baby and young child to a young woman, probably in her teens. Who knows how long he submitted as a young man? Even if he took over provision of the home after the death of Joseph, he probably submitted in cooperative ways in the household in support of his mother, especially in caring for the other children. After considering all the information in this book, I am certain there was no particular age at which he declared that he was too old to submit. I am certain that unless his mother asked him to sin, he did as she wished until the day he left the home. (He stayed longer than most, due to her need for his support. In Mark 6:3, the people of his town referred to Jesus as the son of Mary, indicating that Joseph had been gone for so long they may not have known him.) Even after beginning his ministry in his thirties, we see him submit to his mother with the timing of his first miracle. The idea that men should never submit to women is not consistent with the example of Jesus.

My sister had boys removed from her Sunday school class at age twelve because they had supposedly "come of age" and should not be taught by a woman. They were put under the teaching of a man who turned out to be morally corrupt. It was as if the church desperately searched for any man to teach the boys, with the highest criteria being "male." Her heart still aches for those boys.

Jesus Trusted His Body and Blood to a Woman

Amy Peeler, author of *Women and the Gender of God*, says this in chapter two of her book,

> *God's choice to allow the body of a woman, even the most intimate parts of herself, to come into direct contact with the body and blood of the Son stands against any who would deny women, by virtue of the fact that they are women, access to the holy.*[19]

She makes the point that it is oppositional to Scriptural narrative that men restrict women from administering communion as if a woman does not have the status to come into contact with the elements. They forget Jesus allowed his body and blood to have intimate contact with a woman who brought him into the world and cared for him as a child (and who no doubt had incidents such as skinned knees).

---

19 Amy Peeler, *Women and the Gender of God* (Grand Rapids MI: Wm B. Eerdmans Publishing Co., 2022), 62.

Jesus Ordained Women to Evangelize

Jesus chose the Samaritan woman for something today's conservative evangelicals would never consider. Do we think that Jesus didn't know this woman would get so excited that she would run into the city and tell everyone? His allowing her to do that was basically ordaining her to do so. Up to that point, he had specifically told his disciples and people he healed to keep quiet about who he was. She was the first person he did not command, "Don't tell anyone." She was the second crowd evangelist (after John the Baptist; John 1:29) to all the townspeople including men. If today's evangelicals could go back in time, would they instruct Jesus that this is not permissible, and he should find a man to do this task?

Jesus chose to appear to women first when he was resurrected. What an honor! He told Mary to go tell the other disciples, making her the first post-resurrection gospel evangelist. Jesus would ordain/order a woman to go tell the gospel to men, but some of today's religious leaders will not ordain women.

In 2025, the Southern Baptist Convention voted at their annual meeting (for the third consecutive year) on a constitutional amendment to prohibit any woman from having the title of "pastor" even if to just lead women and/or children. The measure again narrowly failed to pass, requiring a "super majority" of 66.6% two years in a row. It did not fail due to lack of conviction but for pragmatic reasons. Some people in favor of the principle do not think it needs to be enshrined into organizational documents for these reasons:

1. *The Baptist Faith and Message* document already states that women cannot be pastors. (The assumption was "lead" or "senior" pastor, and some wanted it clarified.)

2. They fear it would cause a burden on committees to suddenly have to investigate and kick out hundreds of churches. (I feel like it would become a modern-day Inquisition.)

3. They have already lost a few hundred churches over this issue and could quickly lose more if they keep pressing it.

4. Black churches are especially against it, so pressing it further damages race relations.

The SBC has had single women missionaries go to foreign countries for many years while it conveniently ignores the fact that those women preach and lead in a way that would not be allowed in the USA. The SBC even takes up a Lottie Moon missions offering every Christmas but doesn't acknowledge that Moon was used by God mightily when preaching to mixed-gender crowds. They don't acknowledge that Lottie left the SBC because of growing restrictions on women. (The final straw was when she was informed that women weren't allowed to vote regarding the missions committee which she did much to develop.) She resigned and went to a different area of China (so she couldn't be accused of building on the work supported by the SBC) where God once again used her mightily. I doubt she would be in favor of the SBC now acting like she was all theirs while they continue to limit women even more.

Jesus Enabled Women to Be Prophets

The Gospel of Luke says that as soon as the angel left Mary, she got ready and hurried to see Elizabeth roughly 70-80 miles away. There is no indication that she sent word to Zechariah and Elizabeth that she was coming and that she was pregnant. When Mary greeted Elizabeth, and John leaped in Elizabeth's womb, Elizabeth burst out with a greeting regarding "the child you will bear" and "the mother of my Lord." She had specific divine revelation. The record preserved how both women were filled with the Holy Spirit in a time when the Holy Spirit did not fill every believer. They both prophesied and spoke words that became holy Scripture.

Later, when Jesus was taken to the Temple to be circumcised, the "prophetess," Anna, recognized Jesus as the Messiah and told everyone around that the Messiah had come.

These examples of female prophets and evangelists are only the examples where the women were in contact with Jesus. See the chapter on female prophets in Part Three for more examples and the larger meaning.

Jesus Yielded a Debate to a Woman

Thanks to Jessica LM Jenkins of Women of the Bible in Context Podcast, Episode 21, for insights regarding the Syrophoenician woman. Matthew 15 and Mark 7 relate how Jesus taught the disciples and Pharisees a lesson about purification being what is in the heart and what comes out of the mouth rather than rule keeping. Then he and the disciples went deeper in Gentile territory and encountered a woman who begged him to heal her daughter. She proclaimed him as Messiah when the first words out of her mouth were "Lord, Son of David." This is the first recorded human proclamation of Messiah after John and Peter. Jesus ignored her at first, and often people interpret this as putting the woman's faith to the test. But Jesus knew her heart and faith and recognized she would help him make a point to the disciples. His delay and her insistence drew a larger crowd for what followed.

In this honor/shame culture, people often debated Jesus publicly in the challenge/riposte manner, and he always won. Jesus could have just healed the woman's daughter, but he challenged her in a way the Jews (including the disciples) would have done (with their purification standards), by saying, "It is not right to take the children's bread and toss it to the dogs." She courageously answered, possibly with a direct contradiction, "Yes, it is, Lord. Even the dogs eat the crumbs that fall from their master's table." He granted her the debate "win" and healed her daughter. She left with not only healing, but the honor of having won a challenge and been commended. (Was her answer/theology less valid because she was female?)

I have received teaching that I should protect the man's honor more than my own, such as, "Plant an idea and let him think it was his" and "Do not correct him and show him up because that is disrespectful." I have been in meetings where a woman's suggestion was ignored and then 20 minutes later a man presents the same idea as his own, and the women don't dare say anything. Also, the men repeatedly interrupted women but wouldn't stand for reverse behavior. Such instances contradict the example set by Jesus. He never honored a man by conceding a debate to him!

Besides having her daughter healed, her honor was elevated in the community, taking away the shame of her daughter's former demon possession. Jesus did not just grant physical healing to people. Time and again he gave words that restored relationships, dignity, and honor.

Jesus's Teaching on Divorce Gave Women Equality

In Mark chapter 10, when the Pharisees tried to trap Jesus in a discussion on divorce, he raised the standard by explaining God's high view of marriage in Genesis, including that a man leaves his parents to become united to his wife. He's not taking her in as property or a maid, but as a one-flesh partner. Then in further teaching with the disciples, Jesus says, "Whoever divorces his wife and marries another commits adultery against her." Mark Strauss gives this insight on what Jesus said:

> *This "against her" would have shocked the disciples because in Judaism, adultery was always assumed to be against a husband because a woman had no rights. This "against her" was so countercultural that some translators have attempted to strain the text*

> *for it to read "with her" meaning adultery with the new wife. Paul continues this countercultural teaching by stating a wife has authority over a husband's sexual behavior the same as he has over hers.*[20]

Jesus Chose Women to Be Key Witnesses to the Resurrection

This is significant because women were not viewed as reliable witnesses in Judaism.[21] (This could also be an example of Jesus balking at illegitimate "law.") The importance of the resurrection to Christianity cannot be overestimated. Yet, Jesus decided to have women be the key witnesses. The women discovered the empty tomb, spoke with an angel, and went to report it. The men didn't believe them. Jesus could have appeared to Peter and John when they came to check out the empty tomb, but he chose Mary Magdalene. (This is strong evidence for the historicity of the resurrection account because if someone had fabricated it, they wouldn't have chosen women as key witnesses!) I believe Jesus chose women as his key witnesses to 1) demonstrate he valued them as proclaimers, and 2) requite their devotion as the disciples who ministered to him during his death and burial.

For the Skeptic

Someone might wonder, "If Jesus really wanted to honor women as equal to men, why were there no women among the twelve disciples?" (Notice in Acts 6 they were referred to as "The Twelve" (capitaliza-

---

20 Mark L. Strauss, *Zondervan Exegetical Commentary on the New Testament: Mark* (Grand Rapids MI: Zondervan, 2014), 426.

21 Josephus, Ant. 4.219: "But let not the testimony of women be admitted, on account of the levity and boldness of their sex." Cf. Mishnah Rosh Hashanah1:8; Mishnah Shevuot 4:1; Sipre on Deuteronomy 19:15.

tion not in the Greek). Good question. Let's add more questions such as, "Why were all the disciples Jews?" After all, Jesus came to save the world—all ethnicities. Gentiles tried to join (example Mark 5:18-19) but Jesus refused. "Why were there just twelve special disciples, and why were there no slaves represented by the twelve?" Gentiles, slaves, and women among The Twelve (or more) would have been nicely inclusive!

A solid theory is that God was faithfully fulfilling his promise to the twelve tribes of Israel. The establishment of Jesus as the promised Messiah was hugely significant, so this symbol was significant. God symbolized his faithfulness to the twelve tribes many times (for example, the twelve stones taken out of the Jordan River). Since we who are believers already accept that he was Messiah, we overlook how people back then still needed to be persuaded and how symbolism was important to them.

Furthermore, Jesus was working within the patriarchal, Roman, and Jewish culture. He didn't go to all the world while on earth, but he predicted that his disciples (including women) would do greater things. When he left, he gave all his followers (including women) a command to go to all the world. He included women in receiving the Holy Spirit and all the Spirit's gifts. He had Paul write that there was no longer Jew or Gentile, slave or free, male or female. Gentiles and slaves became church leaders, but are we to believe that women didn't become church leaders? That would be incredulous (except to those of us who have had it pounded into us that women cannot be leaders).

> *It is illogical to believe that Gentiles and slaves became church leaders but not women.*
> Misleading Tactic #1

With our modern western experience, we miss all the radicalism of Jesus on behalf of women who were oppressed by both the culture and the spiritual leaders of the day. Failing to understand the heart of

Jesus on this issue is a great loss because, if we can grasp how he was willing to radically intervene on this issue, then we can grasp that his heart is still for us to practice that same radical intervention now for anyone who is being marginalized by the spiritual leaders of the day. Jesus's followers should be concerned about whether we are ignoring his heart on this matter. Jesus said to the Pharisees in Matthew 15:6:

> *"You nullify the word of God for the sake of your tradition."*

Jesus truly went to the most distressed and oppressed people in his time and in his physical proximity and he empowered them to do things they were not doing before meeting him. Besides women in general, there were widows, children, and diseased whom Jesus empowered and granted respect. If Christian men want to be Christ-like, they will show honor to physically "weaker vessels" and do whatever they can to empower women and anyone else who finds themselves held back. Jesus could have taken the position that letting women "stay in their place" or even "go lower" gave them more opportunity to be humble like him. But instead, at every turn, he empowered them. He still gives every person plenty of opportunity to learn humility, but he obviously also cares about justice, basic human dignity, and respect.

Finally, Jesus said, "I will build my church…." He is the builder and the cornerstone which others build upon. The example he set regarding women should influence how we interpret what was written later by others.

Chapter 6:

JESUS'S FEMALE DISCIPLES

"Many" Female Disciples

Luke 8:1-3 names three women among the women who travelled with Jesus and The Twelve and mentions "many other" women who supported them out of their own financial means. Mark 15:40-41 names three additional women who followed him in Galilee and ministered to him, and references "many other women who had come up with him to Jerusalem." The Greek word in Mark for "follow" *akoloutheō* (G190) is the language of discipleship, something that is shocking in its first-century Jewish context, confirming that, unlike other rabbis, Jesus elevated women to the position of disciple. [22]

When the Gospels refer to Jesus's disciples in general, they are most likely referring to both men and women. However, we have a gender bias in favor of men when we hear the word "disciples" because we put so much focus on The Twelve. For example, people assume that the

22 Strauss, Zondervan *Exegetical Commentary on the New Testament: Mark*, 706.

> *Akoloutheò is the language of discipleship, confirming that, unlike other rabbis, Jesus elevated women to the position of disciple. Why is this not widely known?*
> Misleading Tactic #17

two disciples on the road to Emmaus were two men. They could have been a married couple. In Luke chapter 2, when Jesus sent out 72 disciples two by two, it would have made sense to have couples among them so they could speak to mixed gender groups. If you never imagined the two or the seventy-two having women among them, ask yourself, "Why?" During my youth, all the Sunday school pictures of "disciples" were of 12 men. Every reference in the Gospels to "his disciples" was assumed to be The Twelve. If I had this perception, surely others do.

Mary Magdalene

Mary Magdalene is the most prominent female disciple, almost always named first when there is a list, and Jesus appeared to her first after the resurrection. She is mentioned as being at the cross with Mary the mother of Jesus, Mary the mother of Joseph, Mary the wife of Clopas, Salome the mother of James and John, and the only male disciple there, John. Since John was present, other male disciples could have chosen to be present, but it seems the women were more devoted. The women who were present at the cross, burial, and resurrection of Jesus were critical witnesses to his death, burial, and resurrection. They watched the preparation of Jesus's body by Joseph of Arimathea and Nicodemus and watched them lay the body in the tomb. This was not only difficult emotionally, but probably felt dangerous, and it had to be a difficult job physically—where were the male disciples?

Mark 16:1 says the women brought their own spices on Sunday morning. They had watched the burial so must have known Nicodemus already provided a lavish amount (equal to 75 pounds, only done for royalty). Apparently, nothing could keep them from purchasing their own and going to honor Jesus's mangled body. No men came because the women wondered who would roll the stone away. This was incredible devotion. If I am piecing the narrative together correctly from the four Gospels, the women obeyed the angel and ran back to tell the men. The men, however, didn't believe them, though Peter and John ran to see the tomb but Jesus did not reveal himself to them. Then Mary Magdalene stayed around until Jesus came to her and she first thought he was a gardener. It was a deeply personal interaction between Jesus and Mary, and only John recorded it.

Mary and Martha

John 11 reports that Jesus loved Martha, Mary, and Lazarus. When Lazarus died, Jesus let Martha scold him and then met her where she was, mentally and emotionally, with Scripture. Then he met Mary where she was emotionally, with his own tears. He knew their personalities and responded to them the way each needed.

Due to learning more about the gender issue from a biblical perspective, I have grown in confidence that Jesus "gets" me and endorses my God-given personality. It needs to be under Spirit control, but it is God-given. I have always had consternation about why God would be so cruel to give me an assertive personality and giftedness in the area of administration if I am not supposed to take initiative and lead. I am now much more at peace that if I feel called to do something bold in the future, I should do it alongside those without gender bias. That is the community God will bless with fruitful ministry because they are focused on the Great Commission and not wasting bandwidth on who is allowed to hold which office, and whether it is appropriate for a woman to speak, take initiative, or lead.

The Samaritan Woman

The handling of the narrative in John 4 is an example of problematic interpretation (not translation) that adds assumptions to Scripture, repeats the assumptions so frequently that people don't question it, and strings assumptions together for more questionable conclusions. After we delve into this example, we will consider the repercussions of this approach.

How many times have you heard it said that the Samaritan woman was sexually immoral? I have heard it from the pulpit and seen it in writing countless times, but the Bible doesn't say she was immoral. It says she had five husbands and the man she was living with was not her husband. The assumption is that she was something of a first-century Liz Taylor who married and divorced at whim, or she slept around and didn't even bother to marry her current lover. This doesn't align with first-century culture.

First, women couldn't divorce without the husband granting her petition, or without a male relative sticking out his neck to represent her, so unless the situation was dire and legitimate, it just didn't happen. The vast majority of divorces occurred when the husband decided the woman was unworthy of him, perhaps due to some minor offense or because he wanted someone else. Not producing babies, especially sons, was an offense and considered the woman's fault. If a woman was found displeasing to a husband who divorced her, it's unlikely that another man would marry her, because he would essentially be stating that he was not as good as the man who discarded her. Divorce in modern times can be financially and socially devastating for women, but it could be more so in that era. It is possible this woman had been divorced five times, but highly unlikely due to her being immoral.

Second, Jesus didn't say, "You've been divorced five times"; he said, "You've had five husbands." It is more likely that she was widowed repeatedly than divorced. In that era, fathers often married off their young daughters to much older men. Death of a husband from old age or disease could happen while a woman was still very young. War, violence, or accidents during hard manual labor were also common.

Third, young people often didn't choose their marriage partner. Sometimes, if the father felt a better opportunity came along, he paid off her husband, then married her to someone else.

Fourth, it could be more difficult for women to own property or do business on their own, so each time she was widowed or divorced, it would have been imperative to remarry as soon as possible, even if he was less than desirable. If she couldn't get a husband and had no male relative alive or willing to take care of her, she might need to resort to living with a male "sponsor" though unmarried to him. Some possibilities of a sponsor could be a person with the means to employ her as a house servant or a man that required sexual services for living in his home but wouldn't dignify her with marriage. The passage doesn't explain the circumstances, but there are many possibilities, and given the culture, it's unlikely they were due to her being immoral.

Therefore, Jesus was likely acknowledging her difficult life and that her current man would not dignify her with marriage or that it was a sponsorship. People have assumed the tone of Jesus's voice to be a reprimand when we can no better assume his tone than we can assume the tone of a text message from someone today without the aid of emojis. I've heard many preachers read Jesus's words about having five husbands with the "gotcha" tone. Try reading the dialogue out loud with this new perspective in mind and when Jesus says, "You are right when you say…" slow way down, and when you get to the words "five husbands" say it with heartfelt compassion, recognizing that each of those was a gut-wrenching disaster. Watch her face in your mind as she feels truly seen and understood by a man for the first time. This is the Jesus we should know.

When Bible scholars assume the worst about a woman in the Bible and write it in a commentary, why does everyone take it as gospel truth? They tell us it's because this woman was drawing water at noon. Is that a good reason? Her household could have run out of water due to extra need that day. They could have had an accident with their water, or perhaps something came up that morning to delay her usual trip. It's a HUGE speculation that she came at noon because she was immoral and ostracized by other women. That is nowhere in the passage. Nor is there evidence from history that moral women drew water at one time of day and immoral women at another time of day. It's possible, but it's speculation. No doubt there were people of all kinds going to the well all day long with the preferred times in the morning and evening when it was cooler.

I believe God knew this woman was a sincere seeker so he orchestrated her water circumstances so Jesus would be able to speak with her. Could it be that people viewed the five marriages from a modern-day perspective which caused a bias that, in turn, led to the assumption that drawing water at noon was because of rejection? This is an example of how one erroneous assumption can affect another assumption, leading to an erroneous conclusion.

Another reason the unfavorable narrative does not make sense is that the townspeople willingly listened to her and believed her when she told them about Jesus. It seems she had some respect because they dropped what they were doing and ran out to see this stranger whom they hadn't heard about from anyone else. That is a bigger clue about her reputation than speculation about drawing water at noon, because it actually includes interaction with people.

Because of the aforementioned assumptions, when she said, "He told me all I ever did" we assume she means something like, "He told me all my secret sins." We need to remember that translation to English can lose some nuance, so it could have more like, "He told me all about my life (everything I've done)."

Marg Mowczko tells how she noticed the same Greek phrase "all I've done" used by the man from Gerasene so she did a study of the phrase (*hosa* and *poieo*) used elsewhere. The closest parallel to the use of those Greek words in the NT is the testimony of the twelve in Mark 6:30 and the man from Gerasene in Luke 8:39. The phrase was used in a positive way in those two passages, but in the case of the Samaritan woman, we are supposed to assume something negative.[23]

For the reasons explained, multiple marriages were common in that day, but five was still a lot. Therefore, it couldn't have just been a lucky guess when Jesus named five, and then her current living situation. This clued the woman in that he was a prophet. It would be like a woman having a first-time encounter with a stranger from another country and saying, "I have no children" and the stranger says, "That's true, you've had five miscarriages and the child you have living with you is a foster child." The woman would be saying, "Wow, how could you have known my life story like that? You must have supernatural powers!"

It should also be noted that Jesus never said to the Samaritan woman, "Go and sin no more" like he told the woman caught in adultery and other people whom he healed.

I always wondered why this woman didn't run away in shame when Jesus named her worst sins, but instead, she calmly pursued a theological question. Now that I have a different perspective on the conversation, I believe there's a good explanation for her calmness. Because she wasn't being confronted, but rather receiving empathy, she was touched by his compassion. She was able to be amazed, say, "I can see you are a prophet," and then think about what she would like to discuss with a prophet since she has this opportunity.

I've heard it said by spiritual judges, "She was just trying to deflect from her guilt and change the subject by asking a question about

---

23 Marg Mowczko, "A note on 'everything I ever did' (John 4:29)," Exploring the biblical theology of Christian egalitarianism, September 7, 2022, https://margmowczko.com/everything-i-ever-did-john-4/.

where to worship." It is quite amazing how they can see into her heart's motivation from 2,000 years and a different culture away!

She could have asked him any question and focused on her own pain, such as, "If God is good, why have I suffered such a hard life?" But instead, she focused on how to worship God. Perhaps this is why God orchestrated the circumstances which brought her to the well at noon, because of the sincerity of her heart for relationship with God. She feared that the only way to worship God acceptably was out of her reach.

This reminds me of how there was only one person (a woman, Rahab) in the huge city of Jericho who wanted to express faith in the one true God, so God sent some incapable spies to meet her and become indebted to her, so that she would be spared in the assault on the city. (They were incapable because they blew their cover as soon as they entered the city, had to be hidden by a merciful woman and make a narrow escape.) The Bible doesn't report any other accomplishment in that quick mission except to meet up with a woman God wanted to save. That is how far God was willing to go to rescue one woman and then honor her with Messianic lineage and in the "Hall of Faith" (Hebrews 11). The Samaritan woman demonstrated the same kind of faith with her bold declaration.

Jesus honored this woman with one of the most theologically deep conversations ever recorded between Jesus and an individual. His answer was that true worshippers could worship anywhere in the spirit. He was telling her that God was with her wherever she worshipped—truly an exciting comfort! I am certain she taught this to men and women for the rest of her life.

Jesus knew what she would do with the truth he had just given to her. It appears she was the second believer to be freed to proclaim Jesus as Messiah (after John the baptizer). That is huge!

What Is the Point?

I gave copious space to the narrative about the Samaritan woman. Following are five reasons why I think this (mis)interpretive example is crucial:

1. **Contextualization Failures** – We will continue to see how commentators and preachers fail to contextualize both the OT times and especially the first and second-century lives of women in many passages. Thus, the average person in the congregation also fails to understand context. Without accurate guidance, we have no idea of the challenges of correctly understanding something that was written 2,000 years ago, in another language, on another continent, in a culture wildly different than ours, especially as it relates to women. It is easy to impose our western, twenty-first-century perspective onto the Bible without realizing it. Transferring the ability of today's women to divorce onto a first-century woman is a huge cultural transference—how many other times do we commit a gross transference?

2. **Research and Curiosity Failures** – Over the last several decades, new discoveries of first- and second-century documents have not only brought more cultural light, but more understanding of how specific Greek and Aramaic words were used, helping with both translation and interpretation. Yet, we are still using commentaries by people who didn't have access to these discoveries, allowing misunderstandings to continue and keep us stuck in our perspectives.

This negative view of the Samaritan woman may have originally come all the way back from John Calvin if not further back. In his commentary on John 4,[24] he calls her a prostitute right away, casts

24 "Calvin's Commentaries," Bible Hub, accessed September 12, 2025, https://biblehub.com/commentaries/calvin/john/4.htm

everything she says as mockery, and says she was probably a forward and disobedient wife who constrained her husbands to divorce her. He did attribute the "change the subject" idea on others. How many other interpretations are simply old tradition from venerated teachers?

This passage shows how far afield we can get when we neglect to question what we are told and search things out. It is inconsistent to claim that we only believe what the Bible actually says but then impose unfounded interpretation onto it. (Interestingly, the church father Origen, AD 185-253, called the Samaritan woman a preacher.)

3. **Confirmation Bias Failures** – We have a bad habit of assuming things that aren't in the Bible, adding several weak assumptions together to form a "rock-solid" conclusion, then repeating it until everyone has the same perspective. Not only can this happen in one short passage, but it also occurs with an assumption regarding a topic in a certain book of the Bible, another assumption happening in a different book, then a third somewhere else, with all of them affecting each other. For example, we noted that Reformation theologians decided that "desire" in Genesis 3:16 was negative. That weak assumption would be added to the assumptions in this John 4 passage and others. We saw the following three weak assumptions: why the woman went to the well at noon, why the woman had many men in her life, and what the woman meant when she said, "all I ever did." We will see more of this pattern of gathering weak arguments and putting them together for a "strong" conclusion that is actually confirmation bias.

4. **Negative Assumptions Failure** – It seems typical that negative interpretations will be chosen for female Bible characters. There are not many sermons extolling the virtues or wonderful lessons learned from women in the Bible. (Perhaps they're all in women's books, not fit for men to hear.)

Let us start with Bathsheba. All my life, I heard how she was immodest and that she was complicit in "having an affair" with King David. It wasn't until a few years ago that I heard voices pointing out the power differential in the situation and I began to really think about it: She didn't know why she was being summoned to the palace—perhaps there was news of her husband. Had he been killed and the king wanted to tell her himself since her husband was one of his "mighty men"? She probably became alarmed, rushed over, and was unprepared for the shock of the king's sexual advances. In those days, who said no to a king, or even had the courage to displease him with hesitancy? Historically, there has not been a compassionate telling of what Bathsheba would have gone through: shock, confusion, guilt when she discovered her pregnancy, and grief over the deaths of her husband and baby. She did not ask for all that trauma, and her reward was "getting to be queen" to a very busy man with a harem, other wives, and their sons who resented her? Lovely.

Where is the teaching of compassion and praise for Tamar who had "greater righteousness than Judah" when she took matters into her own hands to get pregnant by him because she was denied justice? She was honored by God at the end of the book of Ruth and in Matthew chapter 1.

What about Queen Vashti who was deposed for disrespecting her husband? The popular Christian marriage book, *Love and Respect* by Emerson Eggerichs, quotes the pagan counselors of the king as if they are giving godly counsel when they say the king must make an example of her or else all the wives in the kingdom will disrespect their husbands. However, the king had commanded her to parade around in front of a bunch of drunken men so they could objectify her. It is a problem that I have never heard Vashti used as an example of when not to obey one's husband.

There are assumptions that Euodia and Syntyche (Philippians 4:2-3) were silly women with a petty argument. The Greek phrase rendered "to be of the same mind" just means to think the same thing. Paul has been talking about what kind of mindset to have "in the Lord" during the whole letter. ("let this mind be in you" etc.). It is unjustifiable to assume a silly disagreement and not a serious one that Paul has addressed in the letter.[25] In addition, Paul highly praises the women as having labored side-by-side with him and Clement. (Sounds like partnering to me!) He asks someone to assist the women (in their ministry?). Is a negative interpretation assumed because someone fears that these women were in fact leaders and this interpretation helps to dismiss them?

God showed honor to Hagar by sending divine messengers to her twice and reassuring her with promises. How many people in the Bible had two divine messengers? When do we hear a sermon about Hagar in a positive light or compassionate light (mistreated by God's people) rather than just the Galatians 4 context of the illegitimate woman representing the law?

There is a completely unfounded myth that Mary the Magdalene (from Magdala) was a prostitute. The myth might have arisen from conflating various women by the name Mary, but why was there not careful study and distinction made such as was made for the men with the name "James"?

Where has the compassion for the Samaritan woman been? Obviously, all these women are long dead and don't need our respect and compassion, but the woman sitting in the church congregation, the Bible study, or across the table at the coffee shop needs to see respect and compassion through these Bible passages. They need to know we get it when they have been in impossibly desperate situations or unable to resist pressure from a man, and not hear things like, "If that really happened, why didn't you report it 20 years ago?"

25 Mowczko, "What were Euodia and Syntyche thinking?!" July 11, 2018, https://margmowczko.com/euodia-syntyche-philippians-quarrelling/.

They need help sorting out truth so they know where responsibility belongs. They need to know how much God values them, has seen everything, truly understands, and will help them walk in freedom instead of shame.

5. **Application Failure** – One man I spoke with strongly objected to this different interpretation of the Samaritan woman and said, "So what? She was still a sinner, like we are all sinners. Why does her being less of a sinner matter?" My answer is that it affects our takeaway or application from the passage.

The primary takeaway we get from the historically entrenched view (that the woman was immoral) is this: "Jesus cares about all sinners and takes time to minister to them regardless of ethnicity, popularity, or gender." We have examples of that elsewhere in the Gospels so that takeaway, although true, isn't unique.

The negative assumptions with this passage interfere with the following takeaway: "Jesus knows who is seeking him with a sincere heart. He will go out of his way for that person, even (or especially?) a person who is disadvantaged (such as a woman with a hard life), conveying deep truths to her and commissioning her to be his evangelist or minister." This application makes me look around at a gathering and pick out the least likely person and imagine them as an effective evangelist or minister.

People today who do not want to recognize that women can have revelation from God, and that women can and should be authorized to teach God's Word to men and women—would not like the second takeaway nearly as much. Because Satan has such enmity

> *To make negative and uncompassionate assumptions about female Bible characters interferes with good interpretation and application.*
> Misleading Tactic #8

with woman, it is no wonder that he distracts from that impactful application.

Part Two Closing Thoughts

I'm intrigued by the timing of Jesus's arrival on earth. Yes, it is significant that his arrival coincided with the dawn of the Pax Romana which facilitated the spread of the gospel throughout the world. But what if another factor goes back to the Garden of Eden when God predicted enmity between Satan and the woman?

When Jesus arrived, Jewish women in Pharisaic and Rabbinic circles (not the broader Jewish world) were more oppressed in the first century than in previous Israelite history. Quite a contrast between the women of the OT (such as the women of Psalm 68 who mightily proclaimed the Word of God). Satan was at the height of his attack on women, and this is when her "offspring" Jesus chose to come intervene, quoting Isaiah 61:1-2 (account of the quote is in Luke 4:16-20):

> *The Spirit of the Lord is on me, because he has annointed me to proclaim good news to the poor. He has sent me to proclaim freedom for the prisoner and recovery of sight for the blind, to set the oppressed free, to proclaim the year of the Lord's favor.*

He openly defied the religious powers who were committing spiritual abuse. However, he did little about the secular world and its power structure except a quiet subversion by redirecting his believers. I believe he wanted his people to lead the way in all matters of justice, mercy, and humility (Micah 6:8).

PART THREE
WOMEN IN THE CHURCH

The Religion of Slaves and Women

This article by historian Michael Kruger, "How Early Christianity Was Mocked for Welcoming Women," cites five examples of early secular literature denigrating Christianity for being the religion of women and slaves: https://michaeljkruger.com/how-early-christianity-was-mocked-for-welcoming-women. The sheer volume of converts meeting in homes, courtyards, and catacombs (no known church buildings until circa AD 250 and then still modest) required many leaders or disciplers. Celsus was a second-century Greek philosopher and polemicist who authored the earliest known comprehensive critique of Christianity. He accuses Christians of hiding out in their private houses.

When Paul went into a city he started teaching in the synagogue until he no longer felt welcome, then possibly a public hall or city forum, and before long, house churches were formed. Acts 19 says all of Asia heard the gospel in two years. I believe women were significantly instrumental in that quick spread through their common laborer network. Origen of Alexandria (AD c. 185–c. 253), the "father of Christian theology," responded to Celsus's criticism:

> *"Celsus ridicules the fact that Christians make converts in kitchens and shops, among wool-workers and cobblers and laundresses. But we say that the word of God is not dishonored by being preached in humble places, nor is it less divine because it reaches the lowly."*[26]

It was unusual that slaves and women were highly represented and in leadership in spite of their social status. For example, we learn in Philemon that Onesimus was a slave, and then later in Colossians 4:9 he is mentioned as on mission from Paul. In my opinion, to think slaves were recognized as leaders but women were not is highly unrealistic. As we've seen, although women were lower in social status than men, there were free, wealthy, and powerful women. Male slaves were considered lower status than free-born women.

The passages most frequently used to limit women in the church are 1 Timothy 3:1-13 and Titus 1:5-9 (qualifications of a bishop/overseer), 1 Timothy 2:11-15 (Paul does not permit a woman to teach), and 1 Corinthians 14:34-35 (women should be silent in church).

In chapter 7, we will look at church "offices" and then at the offices of deacon, pastor, elder, and bishop/overseer. We will see where and how the Bible uses these titles, Paul's favorite titles and compare everything we learned to the offices in today's modern church. In chapter 8, we will look at the qualifications for holding these titles in 1 Timothy 3. Chapter 9 covers some first-century context before we dive into the

---

26 Origen, Against Celsus 3.55 Origen. Translated excerpts available at Early Church Texts, Accessed 09/23/2025, https://www.earlychurchtexts.com/main/origen/celsus_objections.shtml

supposed prohibitive passages of 1 Timothy 2 and 1 Corinthians 14 in chapter 10.

Chapter 11 covers passages and people which demonstrate Paul permitted women to teach and lead. Then we examine women and prophecy in chapter 12 and how Paul elevated prophecy more than teaching.

Chapter 13 gives some of the extra-biblical evidence for female leaders. Chapter 14 explains some of the fallacies that prevent USA Protestant denominations from ordaining women and some of the recent influences on the issue.

The church is suffering from an abuse-of-power crisis. Chapter 15 analyzes the crises including how patriarchy plays a role, what changes are in the air, and what can be done to remedy the situation.

Chapter 7:

GIFTINGS AND OFFICES

Ministry Giftings

The Bible teaches that *every* follower of Jesus has been gifted by the Holy Spirit who gives ministry gifts and abilities without apparent regard for gender. Notice I used the phrase "ministry gifts." All my life I've heard them called "spiritual gifts." Then I saw Mowczko and others point out, "What are spiritual gifts for, if not to minister to others?" It dawned on me that the church came up with this term, "spiritual gifts," used it as theological shorthand, and it took on a life of its own that became a bit mystical, in my opinion. All lists of ministries in the NT, without exception, give no hint that some ministries within the body of Christ are only for women and others are only for men. Isn't that strange? If it were true that some ministries should only be performed by men, surely that would be mentioned in at least one of the following lists of ministries.

Romans 12:6–8; 1 Corinthians 12:7–11, 27–28; Ephesians 4:11–12; Hebrews 2:4; 1 Peter 4:9–11; Acts 2:17–18 list specific gifts. We could also include many passages such as Colossians 3:16 and 1 Corinthians

14:26 that list ways of ministering to the rest of the body of Christ. None have restrictions on women.

The NT puts far more emphasis on giftings and ministries than on human offices and authority. And yet, today's church flips that, putting far more emphasis on offices and authority, along with an unbalanced emphasis on "leadership," which is not a biblical term. (See the glut of Christian leadership books over the last few decades.) There has been a rash of celebrity pastors and megachurches that require corporate-style management to operate due to size. Thankfully, there is some recognition that men who gravitate to these roles tend to abuse power and there needs to be more accountability.

Besides local church hierarchy structures, there are denominational corporate structures which prioritize the protection of the institution over protection of individuals. It would be comical for Jesus to visit any of these big-name leaders and institutions. Would he be honored and awed to be in their presence and facilities? I wonder if he could even get an appointment with such important leaders. Paul set a wonderful example by saying he could claim all kinds of authority and credentials, but he didn't exercise them.

Offices

Complementarians would say there are "offices" in the NT that are for men only. Because there is actually very little said in the NT about offices (the word itself or any equivalent is not in the Greek), this position skates on thin ice. Because the Bible does not spell out organizational structure, offices and structure are one of the significant differences between denominations. Often, the issue is referred to with the term "church government." Notice that term is about "governing" which is the system by which a church operates (episcopal, presbyterian, congregational, etc.). Another term used is "church polity" which is more about the principles and policies that guide church governance (theological and procedural framework).

No word for "office" is in the Greek. That's right, it is NOT in the Bible except where the English word is added, found in the ESV, the NASB, and the KJV (not the NIV or NKJV) in 1 Timothy 3:1. "If anyone aspires to 'overseership' (*episkopēs*)..." There is translation liberty taken to add the words "to the office of." The only other occurrence of the word "office" is where the KJV also adds the word "office" in verses 10 and 13 in the same chapter. So, in my opinion, the emphasis on "offices" is overblown; hence, I'm putting it in quotes for the first several mentions to remind the reader this is a made-up construct.

The word "office" appears nowhere in the Greek of 1 Timothy 3 or elsewhere in Scripture—only in three verses in this chapter where translators added the English word. From this, formal "offices" emerged that exclude women.
Misleading Tactic #7

1 Timothy 3:1 (Bolded words are not in the Greek.)

Whoever aspires to be an overseer desires a noble task. (NIV)

If anyone aspires to ***the office of*** *an overseer,* ***he*** *desires a noble task. (ESV) (adds "office")*

If ***a man*** *desires* ***the position of*** *a bishop,* ***he*** *desires a good work. (NKJV) (adds "position")*

If any ***man*** *aspires to* ***the office of*** *overseer, it is a fine work* ***he*** *desires to do. (NASB) (adds "office")*

Jesus said this in Matthew 23:8-12 (Remember, "Rabbi" means "teacher" and their only teacher is Jesus, and then the Holy Spirit):

But you are not to be called 'Rabbi,' for you have one Teacher, and you are all brothers. And do not call anyone on earth 'father,' for you have one Father, and he is in heaven. Nor are you to be called instructors, for you have one Instructor, the Messiah. The greatest

> *among you will be your servant. For those who exalt themselves will be humbled, and those who humble themselves will be exalted.*

Rather than using titles, I think we want to refer to a person's ministry in a way that doesn't suggest title depending on the cultural environment. Attaining titles can be a pitfall for both men and women. Women do often serve without any title and God will reward them. Men should bear that same servant attitude. In just about any endeavor, someone will be taking the most initiative and leading from a God-given passion. That can be recognized, but a humble attitude is most interested in equipping co-laborers so the one leading is as nonessential as possible.

If the NT doesn't spell out organizational structure or "offices," why has the church repeatedly (and elaborately) set it up? Probably because people are so enmeshed in the world's way of doing things with a vertical hierarchy, it has always been difficult to conceive of any other way. Also, our sinful hearts are drawn to having power, to admiring others who have power, and to setting others up to take the burden of responsibility which we don't want. The Israelites desiring a king against God's will is a great example.

We will look at why women should be included in today's "offices," if there is such a thing. I will list common "office" terms, their Greek word origins, and their NT usage but I will not give definitions because definitions vary by denomination. There is much church tradition that influences these titles. It should go without saying, but tradition is not equal to Scripture.

Deacon – The Greek word is *diakonos* (G1249), which means "one who serves." It appears 29 times for a person. It is translated as "deacon" only 2-3 times by the four versions I'm comparing in this book, "minister" anywhere from 4-7 times, and as "servant" anywhere from 8-19 times. This accounting is just to remind you that translators make choices and it's good to use an interlinear Bible before getting excited about an English word you are reading. See each of the 29 uses here: https://biblehub.com/greek/strongs_1249.htm.

It is significant that only twice in all the epistles is an individual identified in a specifically named church as holding any of the "offices" in discussion here. That "office" is deacon. One person is a woman, Phoebe, named in Romans 16:1, associated with "the church in Cenchreae," and the other person is Epaphras with the Colossian church, commended by Paul in Colossians 1:7. The other individuals called *diakonos* are Paul, Tychicus, and Timothy, but they're not clearly associated with a specific church when *diakonos* is used. (I will explain the misleading translation tactic concerning Phoebe in Chapter 11.)

A significant mention of *diakonos* (related to the topic of women) is in 1 Timothy 3 along with *episkopos*, so it is addressed below under the "office" of overseer.

Many people believe the seven men in Acts 6 were the first deacons. However, the Greek word (*diakonos*) is not in the book of Acts at all. "The Twelve" disciples called a meeting of all the multitude or congregation of disciples. The Twelve instruct the crowd to choose from among themselves seven men (*anēr*, the actual word for adult male person) for the task (*chreia* - need or duty). They laid hands on them and dedicated them for the task. They were not granted a title; it was just said they would serve. Interestingly, Mowczko has an article[27] which aggregates three

> *The word "diakonos" (deacon) is not anywhere in the book of Acts. To claim all deacons in the future must be men based on the narrative of Acts 6 is an interpretive overreach.*
> Misleading Tactic #19

27 Marg Mowczko, "3 views on the ministry of the Seven in Acts 6," Exploring the biblical theology of Christian egalitarianism, February 4, 2014, https://margmowczko.com/the-ministry-of-the-seven-men-in-acts-6/.

views of the ministry of these seven men, and why serving food is the least likely. It's a great short study on the use of *diakonos* in the NT. (Don't skip the footnotes!)

I think the best explanation for why those chosen were all men is just that the cultural environment positioned them as the best candidates. If this were a Roman city, there would have been plenty of women skilled in managing the finances of an organization, but this is Jerusalem. Also, Greek-speaking men were chosen, probably because it was Greek-speaking widows who needed better service. The job description had some specific criteria. It is an interpretive overreach to decide these were the first deacons and they were men, so for all of time, all deacons should be men. (Chapter 9 includes a quote from Clement of Alexandria about the women in ministerial roles accompanying the apostles.)

If hands were laid with a prayer of dedication for this particular task, how much more should we do the same for every little task we agree to do in service for each other? Perhaps rather than glamorizing this occurrence as a great commissioning and trying to re-enact that in our church gatherings, we should be making more of seemingly insignificant occurrences of service and intentionally blessing them.

Because of the events in Acts 6 (where people were selected to serve) and the qualifications in 1 Timothy 3, "deacon" is a reasonable "type of service" for a person who volunteers for service/ministry. However, I think the esteem associated with the "deacon" title has become overblown. In my opinion, we should revert to the word "servant" since it is less pretentious than "deacon" and it reminds people what the role is—service. And we could drop a lot of the formalities and include as many people as possible. This is easier to do with a smaller group than with a large church which necessarily needs to run more like a business.

In summary, "deacon" represents a person performing service tasks for which they are equipped. Servants shouldn't be put on a pedestal and all people should be welcomed to service based on character, spirituality, and ability.

Pastor –Ephesians 4:11 is the only time the word "pastor" is used as a noun in the New Testament and applied to ministers other than Jesus.

> *So, Christ himself gave the apostles, the prophets, the evangelists, the pastors and teachers, to equip his people for works of service, so that the body of Christ may be built up until we all reach unity in the faith and in the knowledge of the Son of God and become mature, attaining to the whole measure of the fullness of Christ. (Ephesians 4:11-13)*

The answer to the question, "Show me where a woman is called or permitted to be a pastor in the NT" is "Show me where a man is called or permitted to be a pastor in the NT." I'm going to lean on Mowczko for a short description of "pastor":

> *The Greek word for "pastor" (which is the same Greek word for "shepherd") occurs as both a verb (*poimainō*) and a noun (*poimēn*) in the New Testament. But unlike the words minister/servant (*diakonos*), elder, apostle, prophet, or teacher, "pastor" is not used in the New Testament as a title or description for any named individual, man or woman, except for Jesus Christ. Paul was not referring to a specific person, and no gender is specified in the Greek of this verse. Again, gender isn't mentioned in any New Testament verses that list ministry gifts.*[28]

In ancient Israel, women were also shepherds, especially in their youth, taking care of flocks close to home and then the men herded

28 Mowczko, "There are Women Pastors in the New Testament," May 9, 2021, https://margmowczko.com/women-pastors-new-testament/. (Again, the whole article is must-read.)

them farther away. So, there wasn't even a male connotation to the word "shepherd" in the first century.

First Peter 5:1-4 describes shepherding as a function of an elder. Therefore, some denominations recognize that pastoring/shepherding is not a separate office, but a description of a gift or activity. It does not indicate that shepherding can only be done by an elder; rather, it commands that elders already be shepherds.

> *To the elders among you, I appeal as a fellow elder and a witness of Christ's sufferings who also will share in the glory to be revealed: Be shepherds of God's flock that is under your care, watching over them—not because you must, but because you are willing, as God wants you to be; not pursuing dishonest gain, but eager to serve; not lording it over those entrusted to you, but being examples to the flock. And when the Chief Shepherd appears, you will receive the crown of glory that will never fade away.*

Jesus chose to associate with shepherds by being the first to refer to himself as an honorable shepherd who cared for the sheep more than the hired shepherd. The fact that in Ephesians 4:11-12, "shepherd" is on par with apostles, prophets, evangelists and teachers, to me, either elevates shepherd or diminishes the other "titles."

Notice that the purpose of all of the gifts is to "equip his [Christ's] people for works of service" so that:

- the body of Christ may be built up
- we all reach unity in the faith and in the knowledge of the Son of God
- we become mature, attaining to the whole measure of the fullness of Christ

Gifts are to be used to equip others so they can turn around and equip others. They are not for making ourselves indispensable. As soon as someone performing an equipping service thinks more highly of themselves than someone else, it derails the purpose, because they don't see others as able to turn around and do the same thing, and others won't see themselves as capable. Only Jesus is indispensable.

Jesus did not use a title for himself or allow his disciples to use any title except the following:

- "Rabbi" which simply means "teacher."
- "The Son of Man" which I discussed earlier. It is a lowly title of humanity, not authority.

Finally, the word *poimēn* in this passage is grammatically linked with the word "teacher," indicating that teaching is one of the functions of pastors. (In English, the word "and" is used to signify the end of a list, but in Greek, it has additional uses, such as linking similar things together.)[29]

Teaching is essential to shepherding. Do women have the spiritual gift of teaching? I believe any woman who is intentionally teaching others is pastoring/shepherding them, regardless of whether any person has formally recognized it or bestowed the "title" –the Holy Spirit recognizes it. When someone says a woman shouldn't be a pastor, they mean a woman shouldn't have recognized "ordination" or "authority," but those ideas are not accompanied with "pastor" in the Bible. I watched a "tradwife" on Instagram exuberantly teach that women should not pastor. I looked at her other teaching posts and her large and engaged following and had to laugh at the incongruency—she was both preaching and pastoring. Unfortunately, a digital platform is not as personally edifying as in-person interaction. I believe she should drop the digital and do it in person.

In summary, "pastor" seems to be a gift, not a position or office. We all know people who have this gift of being able to care for others like

29 Ibid.

a shepherd. There is no reason to quench the Holy Spirit by failing to recognize the pastoral gifting when God gives it to women.

Elder – The Greek word is *presbyteros* (G4245), which means an older person (but not elderly—that's another word). It was used a total of 67 times in the Greek NT, for esteemed older people, such as for the members of the Sanhedrin, and around 15 times for church leaders. It can imply maturity and experience. Titus 1:5 is a sample of usage for church leaders:

> *The reason I left you in Crete was that you might put in order what was left unfinished and appoint elders in every town, as I directed you.*

The Greek word for "elders" in Titus 1:5 is a plural form of *presbyteros* and is *grammatically* masculine, signifying that the group includes men. It doesn't mean that women are necessarily excluded. Titus is to appoint *people* to be elders. Once again, Paul could have specified males (*andres*), but didn't.

The Greek verb translated "appoint" is *kathistēmi* (G2525), used 20 times throughout the NT in clear context of setting someone to be in charge. Note that Paul told Timothy to appoint elders in every town, not every church. This tells me that hierarchy is not needed in every individual group. Note also that a town gets a plurality of elders, not a single person. I believe these people should be appointed based on track record of being wise peacemakers, not because they are productive and have great leadership skills. People are already following them because they want to be like them in spirit.

In 1 Corinthians 6:5 Paul scolds the Corinthians for taking disputes with fellow believers to secular courts, asking if there is no one wise enough among them to help them. I believe elders should be people of peace, of the age and experience to see the big picture, bring justice to those who need it, and pronounce someone to be too stubborn in sin or too contentious to stay in fellowship (1 Corinthians 5:11; Titus

3:10). These people, if they are concerned about a whole city and not one church, should also be able to see where the Holy Spirit is moving and encourage people to work with God in a collaborative way rather than only doing things under the banner of their local church or gathering. This would encourage unity and be a far better testimony to the world. Perhaps each cooperating church could send an elder to the board and try to choose different people every so often. When a church has a dispute, having elder arbitrators from outside who are not enmeshed in the personality politics could be a help.

Are Elders Responsible to "Rule"?

There is the idea from 1 Timothy 5:17 that elders have a ruling responsibility. Modern impressions regarding the word "rule" are much stronger than what was meant.

The NIV and NASB translation teams recognized that the word *proistēmi* (G4292), translated as "rule" was too strong and translated it as follows (respectively):

> *The elders who direct the affairs of the church well are worthy of double honor, especially those whose work is preaching and teaching.*

> *The elders who lead well are to be considered worthy of double honor, especially those who work hard at preaching and teaching.*

I am not surprised that the NKJV and the ESV prefer the word "rule" as follows (respectively):

> *Let the elders who rule well be counted worthy of double honor, especially those who labor in the word and doctrine.*

> *Let the elders who rule well be considered worthy of double honor, especially those who labor in preaching and teaching.*

We will see this word, *proistēmi*, again.

The same thing happens in Hebrews 13 where three times the NKJV renders the word *hēgeomai* (G2233) (unrelated to *proistēmi*) as "rule over" and the other versions render it having to do with "leading." Again, generations were brought up on the KJV and conditioned that "ruling" is biblical.

The following is a commentary on the word "rule" in this passage in 1 Timothy 5:17, opining that it was likely a bench of elders, not just one or two.

> *That rule well - Presiding well, or well managing the spiritual interests of the church. The word rendered "rule" - προεστῶτες proestō [perfect participle of proistēmi]- is from a verb meaning to be over; to preside over; to have the care of. The word is used with reference to bishops, Titus 1:5, Titus 1:7; to an apostle, 1 Peter 5:1; and is such a word as would apply to any officers to whom the management and government of the church was entrusted.*
>
> *... It is probable that not precisely the same organization was pursued in every place where a church was established; and where there was a Jewish synagogue, the Christian church would be formed substantially after that model, and in such a church there would be a bench of presiding elders; see, on this subject, Whately's "Kingdom of Christ delineated," pp. 80-84. The language here seems to have been taken from such an organization.*[30]

> *Translation teams that believe in hierarchy would have us believe that the Greek word for elder activity, "proistèmi" is properly understood as "rule."*
> Misleading Tactic #2

30 Verse-by-Verse Bible Commentary: 1 Timothy 5:17, StudyLight.org, Accessed September 12, 2025, https://www.studylight.org/commentary/1-timothy/5-17.html.

A group of people coming to a consensus is a much different picture than a dictator. I hope the reader is coming to see that translator choices can greatly affect the reader's impression, especially if passage after passage leans in a particular direction due to those translator choices.

In summary, "elder" seems to be a position primarily based on experience and character, attributes held by both men and women. There is nothing to indicate men only. They have a sense of being in charge, appointed for a whole town--not every church gathering, and there is a plurality.

Overseer/Bishop – The Greek word for "overseer" is *episkopos* (G1985), which comes from *epi* (over) and *skopos* (a watcher). It is used five times in the Greek NT, once for Jesus and four times for ministers, sometimes translated as "bishop" and other times as "overseer" (depending on the Bible version). In today's vernacular we would say "supervisor," which is to oversee. The word "bishop" developed from the Greek *episkopos* which was adopted into Late Latin as *episcopus*. It then morphed into Old English *bisceop*, which evolved into bishop.

Some commentators say this word seems to be used interchangeably (by epistolic authors) with *presbyteros*. In other words, there seems to be no distinctive difference between elder and overseer, and they are used the same way, like synonyms. Again, I think an elder/overseer can have better perspective on life after more years of "been there, done that mistake" if indeed they can demonstrate ability to self-reflect and repent.

In summary, "overseer" seems to be very similar to elder without the qualification of age (and again no gender).

Paul's Favorite Titles

We read in 1 Timothy 1 and Titus 1 that Paul left Timothy and Titus behind to wrap things up and appoint elders (in Ephesus and Crete, respectively). Clearly, Titus and Timothy were leaders. It seems they would be worthy of a special title since they were appointing elders. However, Paul just calls them "coworker" and "servant," the same Greek words we see repeatedly, including for women. Edward Earle Ellis researched the designations Paul uses for fellow workers.

> *The designations most often given to Paul's fellow workers are in descending order of frequency as follows: coworker* (synergos)*, brother* (adelphos) *[or sister* (adelphē) *as in the cases of Phoebe and Apphia]†, minister* (diakonos) *and apostle* (apostolos)*.*[31]
> *†Mowczko*

Here is a final point for those who would say, "Even if Paul called Phoebe a deacon, it isn't as important a title as elder, showing that women had lesser position." Some churches today, due to recognizing that Paul called Phoebe a deacon, permit women to be deacons, but not elders. The problem with that line of thinking is that Paul called himself a diakonos in the same letter (Romans), so it is illogical to claim he was diminishing her role. If anything, he was elevating it by calling himself the same.

> *The "titles" Paul used were service-oriented descriptions. Today's church has turned them into power titles and then denied them to those less powerful in an ironic reversal of Paul's intentions.*
> Misleading Tactic #19

These facts about Paul's designations influenced me to form the opinion that titles are way overused today and they bestow overblown importance, further emphasizing how the exclusion of women from them is unjustified and counter-productive to helping churches thrive.

I pointed out that in 1 Timothy 3:1, English translations added the

31 Edward Earle Ellis, Dictionary of Paul and His Letters, Gerald Hawthorne and Ralph Martin, eds. (Downers Grove, IL: InterVarsity Press, 1993), 183.

word "office." Then with "elders" I conceded that elders are appointed and put in charge over a town with multiple gatherings. Also noted is that the NT seems to use "elder" and "overseer" interchangeably. There is no additional hierarchical level of bishop prescribed, even though the early church set it up within a hundred years. The shift toward "monarchical episcopacy" (one bishop per city) is evident by the mid-to-late second century, especially in urban centers like Rome, Alexandria, and Antioch. The title "pope" (meaning *papa/father*) was originally used more broadly for bishops (directly disobeying Jesus's command to call no one "father"), but by the sixth century it became closely associated with the bishop of Rome.

The early church might have given too much authority to elders, and then I believe it was certainly a mistake to set one person over each city. Sadly, the church already adopted a hierarchical system in the second century. God's first chosen people, the Israelites, demanded a human king and God's people today still set up human kings instead of cooperating with the indwelling Spirit of God in ourselves and fellow believers.

Offices in the Modern Church

The reader may have noticed that the Greek words *presbyteros* and *episkopos* have English cognates in the modern denominational names Presbyterian and Episcopal. These names have become almost synonymous with the type of church governance practiced by these denominations, demonstrating today's emphasis on chain-of-command authority up to the national and international level. This is also true of Anglican, Methodist, Eastern Orthodox, Roman Catholic, and Coptic Orthodox churches with "Bishops" being at the highest level (other than the Roman Catholic Cardinal and Pope and the Alexandrian Coptic Pope).

Baptist history is free from denominational hierarchy, so there are many loose fellowships and denominational memberships where local churches have a high level of autonomy, owning their own properties and making all internal decisions. However, lately, there have been votes (by representatives of the churches) to forcibly disfellowship churches which don't abide by denominational standards (such as no female pastors for any ministry). The denominational officers (i.e. president and executive committee) claim no responsibility for the autonomous churches, yet are called on to provide leadership, resources, cooperative programs (which financially support missionaries and seminaries), and to absorb litigation when things go wrong. It's an unwieldy structure but provides a common voice with significant influence and streamlined financial support for missionaries and seminaries. Even though Baptists have a long history that is free of denominational hierarchy, the local churches were certainly not free of little dictators, a strong emphasis on authority, and hierarchical homes.

Several other denominations such as Pentecostals and Assemblies of God have a similar structure where local churches voluntarily affiliate with national leaders primarily for credentialing and missions. Then there are denominations with moderate accountability to district leaders (i.e. Nazarenes, Wesleyans).

Jesus wants unity in the church. All of these denominations cause the world to wonder what is wrong with Christianity that no one can get along so we have all these denominations. There are estimated to be 45,000 Christian denominations worldwide, with 41,000 being Protestant. A lot of the division has to do with differences on church polity and governance. A lot more has to do with doctrinal differences, but it would be interesting to know what percentage of those are salvific, and which are secondary or tertiary issues. Perhaps we need a lot less quarreling and more prayer (1 Timothy 2:8). If the American church was under persecution, which of these differences would keep us from fellowship with other believers?

Chapter 8:

QUALIFICATIONS - 1 TIMOTHY 3, TITUS 1

Do the qualifications for overseer (aka bishop), elder, or deacon include being a man? Some say yes, and their primary proof text passages are 1 Timothy 3:1-13 and Titus 1:5-9. These are often referred to as "the qualification passages."

The following explains why 1 Timothy 3 does not exclude women, verse by verse. The Bible words under discussion are bold so it's easier to follow along with what is being explained in each paragraph. Everything in this section also applies to Titus 1:5-9.

"Anyone" is Gender Accurate

1 Timothy 3:1

Whoever [ESV uses "if anyone"] aspires to be an overseer [NKJV uses bishop] desires a noble task. (NIV)

...if any man aspires to the office of overseer, it is a fine work he desires to do. (NASB)

If a man desires the position of a bishop, he desires a good work. (NKJV)

The Greek word *tis* (G5100) is an indefinite pronoun and is correctly translated "whoever" in the NIV and "anyone" in the ESV. It is "common gender." It is also used in 2 Corinthians 5:17

Therefore, if anyone [tis] is in Christ...

Paul could have easily used a word to clearly indicate a male, such as "If a man (*anēr*) aspires..." or Paul could have listed "is a man" in the list of qualifications, but he did neither.

The NKJV translators **chose** to render it "if **a man** desires" and the NASB translators **chose** to render it "if **any man** desires." **These are misleading translations.** Some people might think it's a holdover from back when "man" was understood to be "mankind." However, there have been enough recent editions to update the language. Even the ESV, which has egregious translations elsewhere, has this correct.

The average person doesn't know there is no Greek word that means "man" in 1 Timothy 3:1. They believe they see the "plain reading of God's Word." People might assume that the NIV is wrong, especially if they read an author who mocks the NIV as "the feminist's Bible." The NIV (2011 edition) was heavily criticized when first published, but most of those critiques have not held up over time as people learn the difference between forcing something to be gender neutral and accurately reflecting something

> *Translating "a man" instead of "anyone" or "whoever" is misleading. The Greek has "tis" which is an indefinite pronoun and means "anyone."*
> Misleading Tactic #7

that is gender neutral. Forcing male generics is just as wrong as forcing neutrality. We simply need accuracy.

Husband of One Wife

Now for the big "husband of one wife" argument in 1 Timothy 3:2:

Now the overseer is to be above reproach, faithful to his wife, temperate, self-controlled, respectable, hospitable, able to teach.

The NIV above reads "faithful to his wife" and the ESV reads "the husband of one wife" with a footnote that reads "Or, *a man of one woman*, also verse 12." I believe "a man of one woman" is the best translation and it means what it sounds like—married one time to one woman. There are other ideas which can be refuted. I have heard this used many times as the primary reason for male-only leadership, "Only a man can be a husband!" There are three problems with this thinking:

1. The list of qualifications could have easily included being a man, but it does not in the Greek. Acting like it is there when it is not, is essentially adding to Scripture. It would not be surprising if Paul assumed that most of those chosen or recognized as church leaders would be men, considering the cultural norms, but he did *not instruct* it to be so. In a patriarchal society, it is just a fact; men had more opportunity to be out of the house and more opportunity to gain skills and broaden relationships. We need to distinguish between observation of *what is true culturally* versus what could be God's more perfect will.

2. Colossians 2:11-15 talks about the privileges we have in Christ because our hearts have been circumcised and not just our bodies. If we were to use the same logic that is used by complementarians with 1 Timothy 3, then the privileges in Colossians 2 could not apply to women because only men were circumcised. Does anyone want to claim Colossians 2 only applies to men?

Nijay Gupta has a great illustration for this. He suggested that one might enter a golf course where a sign read "The facial hair of golfers must be neatly groomed." It is true that more men golf than women, so the sign is directed at them. But does the sign exclude women from playing?[32] The better understanding is that this phrase regarding "a man of one woman" and the circumcision of male bodies are both representative illustrations.

> *It is frequently said that elders can only be men because only men can be husbands. There are three reasons to view this phrase as illustrative for either gender.*
> Misleading Tactic #19

3. The phrase "man of one woman" is also used in the qualifications for deacons and Paul calls Phoebe a deacon. I believe this fact conclusively shows the phrase is not excluding women, but is illustrative as a general moral standard. I believe all the character qualifications are illustrative—women should be held to all the same standards as men—temperate, self-controlled, etc. This is why Paul says, "In the same way, women…" and men held to the same standards as listed for women. (Who would want a male elder who is a malicious talker, intemperate, and untrustworthy?) Although this phrase "man of one woman" suggests that Paul had men in mind, it is going too far to use it to preclude women, especially as the only reason to do so.

Verse 7 says "must also have a good reputation with outsiders, so [as] not [to] fall into disgrace and into the devil's trap." How church leaders are viewed by the world is important to Paul, so he seems to be setting this standard of one marriage for the sake of testimony. If

32 Nijay K. Gupta, *Tell Her Story: How Women Led, Taught, and Ministered in the Early Church* (Grand Rapids, MI: Brazos Press, 2023), 91. See more about Dr. Gupta https://www.seminary.edu/faculty/nijay-gupta/.

a man or woman in Roman culture was punished, marginalized, and considered not respectable due to adultery, and conversely elevated for only being married once, Paul would understandably want the same high standard for leaders in the church.

No doubt, there are some readers who are upset with the interpretation that Paul says people were only to be married once, even in case of spousal death. I believe that instruction was highly dependent on that culture and the early church proceeded to abuse it and take it to an extreme. They also had some strange ideas about celibacy (even within marriage) which I won't get into. There were legalists then just as there are legalists now. In short, I believe this issue should be considered on a case-by-case basis by wise elders. Having a divorce in one's past is not the same thing as currently struggling with the character issues listed.

This phrase (man of one woman) has also been interpreted to mean "a man must have a wife" so unmarried men are excluded from offices, even though Paul himself had no wife (nor did Jesus). These people would disqualify Paul—and Jesus! If a man must have a wife, then he also must have children so he can keep them in line! There is quite the range of harsh interpretations in this passage, causing harm to men as well as women. I don't believe God is watching and saying, "If you want to please me, you must take the strictest interpretation possible to guarantee you didn't cross a line." That would be like what the Pharisees did with fence laws, heaping a burden on people (Matthew 23:4). If we are going to take the phrase "man of one woman" and interpret it that

> *To be consistent, if "man of one woman" excludes women, then unmarried and fatherless men must be excluded since "qualifications" are made related to those responsibilities. That would exclude Paul and Jesus.*
> Misleading Tactic #1

women are excluded as leaders, then to be consistent with a narrow interpretation of everything mentioned, we would need to exclude unmarried men and married men without children, no matter what the circumstances.

Masculine Pronouns

Now for the many masculine pronouns in 1 Timothy 3:4-7:

> *He must manage his own family well and see that his children obey him, and he must do so in a manner worthy of full respect. (If anyone does not know how to manage his own family, how can he take care of God's church?) He must not be a recent convert, or he may become conceited and fall under the same judgment as the devil. He must also have a good reputation with outsiders, so that he will not fall into disgrace and into the devil's trap.*

The masculine pronouns in this passage were added by English translators. The way many languages work is the verb carries the person and number, so a pronoun isn't needed unless the author wants to name a specific person or group. The many Greek verbs in this passage are third person singular, not gendered. Because English uses pronouns separate from the verbs, translators needed to add pronouns. They did not have to choose male pronouns. "One who manages home and children well" would have been accurate. If Paul had intended males only, he could have used the Greek male pronoun *autos* (G846).

KJV translators decided to add male pronouns (understandably, because of the male default back then) and the tradition stuck. The NIV, ESV, and NASB all have them. Removing these pronouns would go a long way in clearing up misunderstanding. **When an edition is published with the claim that it now has "gender accuracy" this becomes a seriously misleading problem.** All three (NIV, ESV, and NASB) claim gender accuracy while using various terms and philosophies. There is acknowledgment that modern readers may misinterpret masculine terms as exclusive (putting the responsibility on the reader to know what is going on). I studied this issue in Hermeneutics and again for this book. I understand their various gender terms and translating philosophies and feel they are setting a high bar that has to be met in order to prevent a default to masculine (an epistemic double standard.) I believe they should stay faithful to the Greek and not add male pronouns and gendered words such as "any man."

Just to be clear, even though I concede that Paul had men in mind with the "man of one woman" phrase, I don't believe it specifically excludes women, and others might agree if they weren't given the wrong impression by also seeing "a man" in verse 1 and all the masculine pronouns in verses one through seven.

> *Masculine pronouns were added even though the passage is gender neutral. Also, the list of qualifications could have easily included "is a man" or disqualifiers "is a woman" but they do not.*
> Misleading Tactic #7

As mentioned at the beginning of the chapter, all of this is applicable to Titus 1:5-9. Some people assume males in that passage because they feel the vices listed in verse 7 (i.e. violent or hot-tempered) are more likely to apply to men. However, the truth is that males are not specified in that passage either (specifically or inferred by pronouns), and these temptations can apply to women. If we claim to be meticulous about adherence to the infallibility of the Word in the original language, we should not add words when they are unnecessary for understanding. We could still understand the passage above if it said, "One who manages home and children well," etc.

Here is another example of male pronouns being added inconsistently, this time in Romans 12:6-8, a passage on gifts. It has five male pronouns in the NKJV English.

> *Having then gifts differing according to the grace that is given to us, let us use them: if prophecy, let us prophesy in proportion to our faith; or ministry, let us use it in our ministering; he who teaches, in teaching; he who exhorts, in exhortation; he who gives, with liberality; he who leads, with diligence; he who shows mercy, with cheerfulness.*

It has the gender inclusive "us/our" six times. But then when the list gets to "teaching," now male pronouns are added in front of each ministry gift. The reason is because the Greek changes from plural to singular and Greek does not have a singular, non-gendered pronoun, so it defaulted to masculine articles (which can function as pronouns). We know that women were also among those who gave generously and showed mercy, so these were simply masculine defaults.

Below are the same verses in the NIV. Instead of moving from the plural "us" to the singular "he," they moved from "We" to the singular "each of us" and then to "you," which in English, can be singular. Because they understood that the Greek articles were simply masculine by default, they found a way to switch to singular without using masculine pronouns. This is more accurate.

> *The ESV makes the pronouns in front of giftings all gender neutral, but if it is a gift they deem for males only, they add a male possessive pronoun.*
> Misleading Tactic #7

> *We have different gifts, according to the grace given to each of us. If your gift is prophesying, then prophesy in accordance with your faith; if it is serving, then serve; if it is teaching, then teach; if it is to*

encourage, then give encouragement; if it is giving, then give generously; if it is to lead, do it diligently; if it is to show mercy, do it cheerfully.

Now let's look at how the ESV handles it:

Having gifts that differ according to the grace given to us, let us use them: if prophecy, in proportion to our faith; if service, in our serving; the one who teaches, in his teaching; the one who exhorts, in his exhortation; the one who contributes, in generosity; the one who leads,[a] with zeal; the one who does acts of mercy, with cheerfulness.

When it is time to switch to singular because the Greek switched to singular, the ESV appropriately used "one" because, in English, that is how we refer to a singular person in a non-gendered way. Oh, but wait, for the two gifts which they ideologically believe belongs to males and not females (teaching and exhorting), they add male possessive pronouns (his). Then they continue without any male pronouns.

But one might wonder why they didn't add a male pronoun with "leads" since they believe only men should lead. They added a footnote to "leads" which says "Or *gives aid.*" Perhaps their inconsistency would be a little too obvious if they kept switching back and forth with "his" for male-only "roles" so diminishing the gift of leading to giving aid helps to smooth that gift over to what they consider a non-gendered role. I don't think it makes sense to render it "gives aid" when "generous contribution" is right before it and "acts of mercy" right after, so the idea of "giving aid' is already well covered, whereas "lead" or "manage" adds a little more to the picture. I've been part of many ministry endeavors where someone needs to be the primary point person and manage the project or it's just chaos. Some are obviously more gifted at it than others. There would be a big hole in this list without it.

> *When the ESV encounters "proistèmi" where women are included in the passage, they prefer "give aid" or "good works." When they believe only men are included, they prefer some form of "rule" or "manage."*
> Misleading Tactic #15

Furthermore, the Greek word here in 12:8 (that other versions translate to some form of "lead," "manage" or "rule" here) is *proistēmi*. The ESV itself translates *proistēmi* to lead, manage, or rule in five other places. Unless, women are included. The two other places where the ESV renders *proistēmi* as "good works" is in Titus 3:8 and 14 a passage where women are included, similar to Romans 12:8. The meaning of *proistēmi* encompasses leading, managing, caring for, and providing for. But there is no good reason to selectively apply those meanings which imply leadership to men and those which imply service to women.

(I have to wonder if this footnote for 12:8 is a precursor to putting "gives aid" in the text, like they put the word "contrary" in Genesis 3:16 into a footnote first and then put it in the text in a later version—see Chapter 2.)

If Paul had intended males only with those two particular gifts, he could have used the Greek male pronoun *autos* or given separate lists for men and women. No gifts in Romans 12 were gendered--not teaching, not exhorting (preaching?), and not leading. They were for men and women.

Notice that all four versions: (NKJV, NIV, ESV and NASB) have gradually switched over to what they believe to be gender accurate and leave out the male pronouns in this passage (except the ESV puts "his" in front of just "teaching" and "exhortation"). Why did they have no problem recognizing here in Romans 12:6-8 (and in other passages) that masculine pronouns are not required. But in 1 Timothy

3 and Titus 1, the so-called "Qualifications for Elders" passages, they decided to add masculine pronouns. They would explain their reason to be, "context." If they believe, ideologically, that the context is about males, they will translate it as such, even if it means the translation is inconsistent (and therefore misleading). It has more to do with their belief than the text. Because the ESV committee is complementarian, then of course, "teaching" and "exhortation" in Romans 12:6-8 are male-only activities and (*proistēmi* G4291) is less likely to mean "lead" (or manage) here even though they are confident it means "lead" (or manage) elsewhere. For example, in 1 Timothy 3:4-7, the word translated "manage" one's family and household is *proistēmi*. Since they added male pronouns, they have no problem using the word "manage" rather than something along the idea of providing aid and financial resources.

> *The major versions compared in this book chose to recognize some male-default passages as needing to be translated more accurately as gender neutral, but not other passages which are more impactful to the issue of women being recognized as leaders.*
> Misleading Tactic #13

Again, the reader needs to understand that translators make many interpretive choices and those choices are affected by their ideology.

Finally, related to masculine pronouns, the so-called "Qualification Passages" of 1 Timothey 3 and Titus 1 do not have a job description. They are a character description. The only job description activity is to be "able" or "skilled" in teaching. I believe this is why the complementarians/hierarchalists are so intent on adding a male pronoun to the gift of "teaching" in Romans 12:7 but not to all the gifts in verses six and eight which have the same articles. There is no other explanation for why they added male pronouns.

In the Same Way

Back to our verse-by-verse look at 1 Timothy 3:1-13, and we are up to verses 8-11 (emphasis added):

> ***In the same way****, deacons are to be worthy of respect, sincere, not indulging in much wine, and not pursuing dishonest gain. They must keep hold of the deep truths of the faith with a clear conscience. They must first be tested; and then if there is nothing against them, let them serve as deacons.*
>
> ***In the same way****, the women are to be worthy of respect, not malicious talkers but temperate and trustworthy in everything.*

If "In the same way, deacons…" refers to their conduct being above reproach like the overseers, then "in the same way, women…" means their conduct is also to the same high standard as the elders and deacons.

The ESV renders this verse,

> *Their wives likewise must be dignified, not slanderers, but sober-minded, faithful in all things.*

> *The addition of the word "their" by ESV translators to support the reading of "wives" instead of "women" is dishonest. There is no possessive pronoun and not even an article that could function as a pronoun.*
> Misleading Tactic #7

Then it has a footnote "Or *Wives likewise*, or *Women likewise*." Therefore, the ESV is acknowledging that "their" is not in the text and "wives" is not a certain translation (but who reads footnotes?). The NIV quoted above has this footnote: "possibly deacons' wives or women who are deacons." The translation team is acknowledging that they are also not certain which way it should be, but at least 70% of the team chose "women" rather than "wives" for the primary text.

Note that the ESV starts the verse with "their" wives. There is no possessive pronoun and no article (which can function as a pronoun). In short, there is nothing in the Greek that indicates the women in verse 11 belong to the male deacons. I believe that adding "their" is dishonest. The Greek word *gynē* (from which we get the word "gynecology") means woman or wife. Which one the author meant must be determined from context. Adding "their" gives the appearance of context for "wives."

If the context is not clear, translators will make a choice based on their ideology. How many people know this happens? Most people think they are looking at solid, "plain reading of the Word of God." Recognized translators for the most-used versions have all been male for thousands of years. Then there are the famous teachers who write their own study Bibles. What motivation would any of them have to be inclusive instead of holding onto traditional power? And even with those who wish to be more even-handed, who among them wants to implode their career by having other evangelicals label them "liberal" and put all their other work under suspicion?

Over the past two decades, accomplished female scholars have increasingly been invited to join all the major Bible translation teams except the ESV (teams usually have over 100 people). With their higher level of awareness regarding women's issues, they are pointing out the damage that has been done by some translation choices, but it takes time for a decision-making committee to come to a (for example) 70% vote on changes. Making changes may cause it to appear as though they, or their revered prede-

> *Assuming "wives" instead of women obfuscates the possibility of female elders.*
> Misleading Tactic #4

cessors, were mistaken. Even agreeing on footnotes can be extremely difficult.

Ruling vs. Managing

Continuing with 1 Timothy 3:4-5, we turn from pronouns to give a little more attention to the word *proistēmi* as it relates to the home.

(NKJV) one who rules his own house well, having his children in submission with all reverence.

(NIV, NASB) He must manage his own family well and see that his children obey him, and he must do so in a manner worthy of full respect.

(ESV) He must manage his own household well, with all dignity keeping his children submissive.

Those of us brought up on the KJV hear the word "rule" in Genesis 3:16 and immediately remember 1 Timothy 3:4-5 as an overseer qualification including "ruling" their home well. The NASB, NIV and ESV concluded that the word *proistēmi* (G4291) is better translated as "manage" the home and children.

Furthermore, the NIV and NASB describe the behavior of overseers (who are parents) as *"in a manner worthy of respect."* And then the ESV indicates the parents acts with dignity, so three out of the four versions assign good behavior to the parent in managing the household and children (rather than the children being the ones with dignity, although that is required of them in Titus 1:6). Certainly, in Paul's time, those with positional authority commanded respect due to their position, not because they earned respect. However, we know from the teachings of Jesus regarding exercising authority (more on that in Chapter 15) and other passages which we will look at later from Paul about how leaders are to behave, that God's family is to operate in a relationally wise way compared to the world's way. So, Paul may be implying that parents manage in a way that earns respect, but it's hard to conclude that just from the language in 1 Timothy 3:4-5.

"In a manner worthy of respect" or even "dignified" puts responsibility on the parent to earn respect, in contrast to, "keeping his children submissive." This is an interpretive choice, supporting either authoritative or authoritarian parenting.

Numerous scientific studies have shown that authoritative parents have more impactful influence and healthier outcomes than authoritarian parents. Although Paul cared a lot about witness and appearances to the world, he cared about what was happening to the young person's heart as evidenced by his command in Ephesians 6:4 to not exasperate or provoke children. So, although the Greek wording of this passage is debatable on whether it implies that parents conduct themselves in a way that earns respect or that it merely commands dignity (which is not too far from the same meaning), I believe the broader witness of Scripture affirms the interpretative translation of the NASB and NIV. I believe that if my generation and many generations prior were raised with this translation instead of the ruling, authoritarian parenting of the NKJV, untold harm would have been avoided.

1 Timothy 5:14 instructs women to *oikodespoteō* (G3616) rule, guide, or manage the home. It is similar in meaning to *proistēmi* (G4291) above except that *proistēmi* has a more implicit sense as a provisionary source. I was puzzled over why a much stronger word was used for women. *Oikodepoteō* implies the action is done by a person in a position of authority or position of senior responsibility in a household. If Paul wanted to imply a male authoritarian "master of the house" he could have used *oikodespotēs* (G3617) which is used twelve

times in the Gospels. The KJV had "guide" for the woman's activity in 1 Timothy 5:14, which is a weak word, but now the NKJV, NIV, NASB and ESV all have "manage" (the home) for women which still doesn't really rise to the level of *oikodespoteō*. I think it's appropriate that *proistēmi* is used for church work and *oikodespoteō* or *oikodespotēs* is used when one's own home is referenced, so I conjecture that use of *proistēmi* is used in 1 Timothy 3:4-5 because it is in reference to other people (children) and not the economic aspects of managing a home. Anyway, a teachable spirit in men will view a female partner as a co-manager and be willing to collaborate rather than viewing her as trying to grasp his authority.

Finishing up with verses 12 and 13 of 1 Timothy 3, the same things apply. The reader has to remember that the footnote for verse 2 also applies to verse 12 where "faithful to his wife" means "one-woman man." And once again, masculine pronouns have been added in some versions.

Conclusion on Qualifications - 1 Timothy 3 and Titus 1

The case for male-only leaders in these passages is so weak, that in truth, it is scandalous to build such a major doctrine with this being the lynchpin. (Especially considering the evidence for mutuality seen elsewhere in Scripture.) Hundreds of thousands of men who have done their best to lead their churches well and be faithful to Scripture have been misled to exclude women and now would either have to admit (with great pain) that they were misled (but who could blame them?) or stubbornly dig in. How many would even carefully read and consider these facts since the prospect of being wrong for decades could be devastating?

And then there are the young men who are learning from them. One Sunday, I was working in the sound booth at a "soft complementarian" church and adding songs from the CCLI online database to the morning's slide lineup. I asked the worship leader which version of a song to use, one arrangement being by a well-known church band. He said not to use that one and commented that church is apostate because they approve of women teaching. Apostasy is the total desertion of one's religion, so I protested that the word should be reserved for those who deny the divinity of Christ or similar foundational doctrine. I give this example to demonstrate the extremism that is grounded into young men on this issue, whether intentional or not. As he and I discussed it, the phrase in 1 Timothy 3, "husband of one wife," along with all those male pronouns was his go-to clincher passage.

There was a lot of detail in this chapter, so let me recap with these points:

- In that day, because women had fewer developmental opportunities, it would not be surprising if Paul assumed that leaders would primarily be men, using the phrase "man of one woman" but that doesn't mean he opposed women leaders.

- Paul also said deacons (not just elders) should be "man of one woman" but called Phoebe a deacon, demonstrating the phrase was illustrative and not exclusionary.

- It is significant that being male was not specifically mentioned as a qualification, nor were women specifically forbidden among the disqualifications.

- Translators biased us toward believing Paul strongly intentioned only men by adding "any man" instead of "anyone" in verse one, by adding all the male pronouns, and by adding "their" (wives) so the focus is on wives of leading men instead of on women who are serving in a leading capacity.

- *Proistēmi* is used for management that relates to people. It has a range of meaning for management and provision, unlike much stronger words that would connote authoritarian conduct.

- The larger Scriptural witness is inclusion and servanthood, not exclusion and hierarchy. I believe Paul knew that a spiritual following is earned and not merely positional, encouraging people to follow his example as he followed the example of Christ" (1 Corinthians 11:1). Those who conducted themselves well as servants would have a following *without the need for titles,* and only several titled (elder) people were needed for each city. From all that Paul wrote that does not include formal titles and structure, I don't believe he foresaw or would have endorsed the hierarchical system we have today and the rigid exclusion of women today in some circles.

> *Translating proistèmi into "rule" instead of a milder word like "manage," seems like an attempt to support the "rule" in Genesis 3:16 as if it is legitimate activity.*
> Misleading Tactic #2

Chapter 9:

FIRST-CENTURY CULTURAL CONTEXT

Ethnic Diversity

The first Christians were Jews, and when they were persecuted, they scattered and took the faith to other cities. Also, there were devout proselytes "from every nation" who were in Jerusalem for Passover and who converted. They took the gospel home with them. These scattered Jewish believers probably first went to the Jewish communities in those Gentile cities. Paul always started in the synagogue when he went to a new city. So, it seems logical to look at every epistle in the context of the Gentile city or region where it was sent, but keep in mind that the author knows there are Jewish believers there too.

The letter to the Roman believers addresses both Jews and Gentiles and tries to help them get along more respectfully. The Jews felt superior because they were God's chosen people and they had the law. Paul spent most of the first half of Romans explaining to the Jews that those things don't matter—faith is what saves. Most of Galatians was written to encourage Jews and Gentiles to get along. Paul even mentioned correcting Peter for not being consistent in his Gentile associations. After a long history of Jews believing they were superior, we today have no idea how significant it was that Jews received Gentiles as equals. It had to be equally difficult to receive slaves and women as equals. The churches in the region of Galatia in the middle of Asia Minor received the letter that stated, "There is neither Jew nor Gentile, neither slave nor free, nor is there male and female, for you are all one in Christ Jesus." Timothy's mother was Jewish and his father was Greek. His bi-ethnicity likely aided in reaching a wider audience in his ministry. Gentiles represented several ethnicities. So, there was great diversity in the church and Paul's writings have an ongoing theme that encouraged respectful unity.

Gentile Cultural Norms and Changes

We looked at first century Jewish life for women, and will now focus more on Gentile life for women. The hundred years or so around the life of Christ (a few decades before his birth, during his 33-year life, and a few decades after) were times of great cultural upheaval for women. The next few paragraphs are a consolidation/summary of information from several sources in an effort to give my reader a sense of the times. All this information is based on approximately a hundred-year plus span, with variables regarding specific locations, social/economic status, ethnicity, particular family values, etc.

Through the early first century, women (especially Jewish women) did not have the educational opportunities afforded to men. In general, Roman females were allowed some school and then taught at home, Greek and Jewish females were only allowed to be taught at home with less education for Jews. Social norms discouraged women from speaking in civic or religious assemblies. Elite women had more privileges, especially because the family could afford education. Changes came throughout the first century, but overall, it was a slow transition happening faster in some places than others.

As we saw previously, in general contrast to Jewish women, Greco-Roman women had more opportunity and freedom to conduct business, own property, speak to men, testify in court, etc. Married women did all these things under their husband's supervision, while widows had more independence. Once married, it was expected that husbands would augment their younger wife's education, which meant husbands decided how much education wives could have and how they could use it. But those who had no husband could do as they pleased.

In the three centuries prior to the birth of Christ, there were times when so many Roman men were off to war or had died in war, women had to pick up the slack in commerce and running the estates left behind (much like what happened in the United States during WWII). Many of them became independently wealthy, which alarmed rulers who then restricted the amount women could own. They also restricted women's attire since that could be seen as a display of wealth (Sumptuary laws like the *Lex Oppia*, 215 BC). Rioting and strikes ensued, so the laws were repealed after just twenty years.

A movement started with Roman women who were rebelling against laws that restricted them in dress, property ownership, and public behavior. In protest, they cast off their head coverings, wore fancy clothes, partied, and committed adultery. They intentionally set out to do the things that the law said was allowable for men. They took education seriously, hiring their own tutors, and were known to snatch the podium in public and give speeches. This movement was called "the New Roman Woman" and covered two hundred years, a century before Christ and the first century. It had caused significant societal shifts by the time of Paul's missionary travels.

Roman and Greek cultures had various forms of shame/honor societal constructs in which women bore the burden of family and national honor by their chastity and good behavior, while men lived more as they pleased. This was also true to a lesser extent of the Jewish culture, although the double standard wasn't flaunted as much. A history of male domination led to the double standard. (I believe "the New Roman Woman" movement was a backlash, and history is repeating itself today with the radical feminist movement of the late twentieth and early twenty-first centuries. In turn, the male backlash, the "manosphere" movement, is the latest development in the gender war.)

By mid-first century, things were looking up for Roman women especially. Distinguished historian of the Roman world, Richard Saller, says this, referring primarily to the early Roman Empire, especially the first and second centuries: "Women, especially widows, could own and manage property, and estimates suggest that they held as much as one-third of the wealth in Roman society."[33]

Historian and professor Sabine Huebner has been publishing her groundbreaking research on Roman Egyptian papyri as recently as 2024. She estimates that around 30% of Roman women were single in the first and second centuries from studies of census data, funerary inscriptions, and household records.[34] Approximately 25% of households listed in census documents were headed by women.[35]

As a result of wealth and independence, Greco-Roman women began to have more influence. They became financial patrons of male politicians, the arts, social charities, and clubs. Some ran their own businesses. Surviving writings by some men (i.e. Juvenal, the Roman satirist, circa AD 55 - 128) pined for the old days when women were more restricted. Some upper-class men still took pride in the ancient

33 Richard P. Saller, *Patriarchy, Property and Death in the Roman Family* (Cambridge: Cambridge University Press, 1994), 142.

34 Sabine R. Huebner and Christian Laes, eds., *The Single Life in the Roman and Later Roman World* (Cambridge: Cambridge University Press, 2019). 40.

35 Huebner, Sabine R. *The Family in Roman Egypt: A Comparative Approach to Intergenerational Solidarity and Residential Patterns*. Cambridge University Press, 2013. 88.

luxury of hiding their women in the back half of their homes, but many households were managed by women (as a small economic system) while men congregated in public spaces and held most of the public offices. In general, Gentile women had acquired more liberty just in time to spread the gospel, but education and liberty were inconsistent, and sexism still thrived.

Head Coverings

Young Jewish women didn't usually cover their hair, but once they married, they covered in public to show men they weren't available (rooted in interpretations of Numbers 5:18 and expanded in the Talmud, e.g., *Ketubot 72a*). Especially in Roman contexts, head covering was a privilege or expectation tied to status and reflected by different types of coverings, same as the men's privileged attire. Nonbiblical, early first-century literature tells of a high-ranking, Roman figure who divorced his wife (around 166 BC) because she went out of the home uncovered. The person who wrote of it felt the divorce an extreme reaction, but it does indicate head covering was a social norm for a very long time. There are early first-century Roman art and coinage showing women with and without covering, so the rules of decorum had variances, especially considering a significant span of time. The main point is that head covering was a secular practice prior to Christianity so it was not a "Christian practice" per se. (This will become more important when we examine a NT passage that talks about head coverings.)

Because churches met in homes, some people may have felt that women didn't need to be covered since they weren't out in public, while some women may have wanted to be covered due to status and to not be thought inappropriate. Since society today doesn't have head covering as a symbol of marriage, most evangelicals do not require women to cover their heads in church. Head covering is an obvious cultural difference between Bible times and now because everyone did it, not just the Jews and Christians. Some denominations which highly value tradition or view it as a moral symbolic issue continue to practice head coverings.

Christian Women Working Within the System

Christian women in the first century attended church with men instead of following traditions like Jewish women being relegated to the outer courtyard of the temple or wealthy Greek men keeping women hidden in the back of the house. However, Paul encouraged Christian women not to stray from what was culturally acceptable.

It would be unrealistic to expect anything different than sexist, patriarchal behavior from first-century Jewish and Roman society, including Christians, since thousands of years of history ingrained it into their worldview. No doubt, many men assumed that only men would be leaders in their churches.

Regarding slaves, when Paul tells them to obey their masters and work as unto the Lord, was he endorsing slavery and not concerned about justice? No, he was only recognizing a cultural situation which could not be changed overnight. Similarly, Paul and others working within patriarchal societal norms did not mean they endorsed the system.

In most of the ancient cultures, the testimony of women was not considered as valid as the testimony of men. Evangelizing a city then, would not begin by sending a few good women to a city to speak in public, and plant and lead a church. They could be accosted or arrested in no time at all. However, it would be practical for a woman elder to travel around a city visiting homes and home churches. Typical female leadership would be women who moved in the community circle with zealous service; wealthy, educated women with large households who hosted churches; or power couples like Priscilla and Aquila, Andronicus and Junia. However, "typical" still means anything could happen, just like single female missionaries in the 1800s who went to far-off places such as China and India and had amazing ministries. They were the exceptions though.

"Why don't we see more women doing leadership-type things in the New Testament?" is the wrong question to ask. Due to the culture, what is remarkable is that we see any of them! (And we do see them if we can overcome having been taught to ignore them.)

Cultural Norms and the Epistles

Even though the NT writers were Jews and came out of the culture of female oppression, they knew of Jesus's example of respecting and including women. When they went to Gentile cities, they had no problem dealing openly with women. In fact, Paul had women ministers traveling with him, just as Jesus did. Priscilla (with Aquila) is one example, but in Paul's many mentions of women (examples, Romans 16 and Philippians 4:3) they "contended at my side in the cause of the gospel" in many places. There are (sadly) very few first-century documents preserved, but some indicate the activity of women. Clement of Alexandria (lived soon after the apostolic church fathers) wrote (circa 198 AD), the following:

> *They [the apostles] took women with them, not as wives, but as sisters, that they might be their co-ministers in dealing with women in their homes. It was through them that the Lord's teaching penetrated also the women's quarters without any scandal being aroused.*[36]

The first apostles didn't take the oppressive, Pharisaical culture with them, but they also still dealt within the existing patriarchal societal norms. It was not their goal to upend society with the lib-

36 Clement of Alexandria, *Stromata, Book 3*, Chapter 6, in Ante-Nicene Fathers, vol. 2, Alexander Roberts and James Donaldson, eds, William Wilson, trans. (Grand Rapids, MI: Wm. B. Eerdmans Publishing Company, 1951) 391.

erties of Christianity, but to upend the world with the gospel, which would then upend the injustices of society. This was a tightrope walk with three considerations: practicing what they saw with Jesus freeing women to learn and evangelize, not allowing the selfish use of Christian liberties to distract from the primary message of the gospel, and warning Christians not to cross secular culture standards for the sake of testimony.

Even though it would not have been a good strategy to send a few good (single) women on missionary journeys to start new churches, God did use women to start and care for new churches where they lived. Lydia lived in a Roman city in Macedonia where women had possibly the maximum amount of liberty, but she would still be an example of what Paul himself was comfortable doing. God told Paul in a dream to go to Macedonia. There he met Lydia, who was clearly God's choice for starting this new church. Lydia was an influential citizen in "Philippi, a Roman colony and leading city in that district of Macedonia" (Acts 16:12). She was a long way from her hometown of Thyatira across the Aegean Sea in Asia Minor, so it's likely she went to Philippi to do business. (She was a dealer of expensive purple cloth.) There is no mention of any males, only a "household" which belonged to her (*ho oikos autēs* her household). She is one of those single, property-owning, Roman women as found in the Roman census described earlier.

As a businesswoman who enjoyed freedom in society, and who chose her "religion" without consulting anyone, I do not believe Lydia would have signed on to something that held her back from taking initiative (leading) in doing good. With a group of godly women in worship at a river, she heard the truth from Paul and took the initiative to lead her household in getting baptized right then and there. Then she persuaded Paul's group to come to her home (again, no consulting anyone) and hosted them for the remainder of their time in Philippi. Luke makes a point to say Paul visited the believers in her home on his way out of town after his run-in with the civil authorities. She was clearly already a leader.

I don't believe Paul would have held church in the home of this influential, truly converted woman and then forbidden her to lead in that church. Paul was all about the spread of the gospel, not hindering it. Furthermore, the fact she was named and no one else in the city was named (not the jailer or anyone else), shows that the writer of Acts holds Lydia in esteem and feels it important to name her to his readers. That is a big clue about her being a leader that we miss if our background taught us to miss it. I have no doubt that if it were a male name, we would assume that person to be the leader of the church of Philippi.

In an interview, international translation trainer Dr. Maron Winedt emphasizes that we must pay close attention to when the Bible is at odds with cultural norms (such as only naming a woman leader in Philippi). He says when you see those anomalies, recognize that God is making an extremely important point![37] Below are just a few of the significant examples of things that happened that were unusual for the times:

- Cultural leaders and philosophers of the first century consistently held that women were inferior to men, but God said they are not.
- Jesus intentionally sent a woman as the first person to proclaim his resurrection.
- Jesus sent the Samaritan woman as the second "Messiah has come" evangelist (after John, or the first depending on how one views John's ministry).

37 Dr. Maron Winedt, "Challenges and Joys in Bible Translation," Mutuality Matters, July 4, 2024, https://mutualitymatters.podbean.com/e/challenges-joys-bible-translation-marlon-winedt/.

- None of the cultural leaders and philosophers of the first century denounced slavery, but the Bible lists slave trading among the worst sins and called on masters to recognize that their slaves were brothers and sisters in Christ.

- Contrary to the culture where everyone jockeyed for authority and position, Jesus said not to call anyone "father," not to call anyone "teacher" (because they only have one—him), and not to lord over each other or exercise authority over each other, but to be the best possible servant of each other.

> *When the Bible is at odds with the cultural norms of its day, the oddity should stand out as an important principle. However, interpreters have downplayed and hidden these oddities, elevating the cultural norm.*
> Misleading Tactic #17

Chapter 10:

SUPPOSED PROHIBITING PASSAGES

Besides the supposed "Qualification Passages" of 1 Timothy 3 and Titus 1, much oppression of women in churches has happened as a result of a poor translation of one passage sent to Timothy regarding the church in Ephesus. Perhaps some of Scripture can be read "plainly" at face value, but much Scripture needs study and context. There are passages where plain reading can cause strange doctrine or contradiction. This isn't just the case with gender-related passages. We've been taught to dive deeper and resolve those difficulties by word studies and comparing passages that seem to contradict others. But for some reason, the gender-related contradictory passages haven't received as much attention.

1 Timothy 2:11-15

The idea that this passage prohibits all women, everywhere, for all time, from teaching men is contradicted by all the passages discussed in the next chapter, but we do need to address the difficulties of this passage. The Greek is not as clear as what it appears in our English translations.

> *A woman [Footnote: or wife] should learn in quietness and full submission. I do not permit a woman [or wife] to teach or to assume authority over a man; [Footnote: or husband] she must be quiet. For Adam was formed first, then Eve. And Adam was not the one deceived; it was the woman who was deceived and became a sinner. But women [Footnote: she] will be saved through childbearing—if they continue in faith, love and holiness with propriety.*

Setting

Paul wrote the letters of 1 Timothy and 2 Timothy to guide Timothy's service in Ephesus. I had always known that the book of Ephesians was for the church of Ephesus, but it is not so easy to remember that the letters to Timothy were written regarding that same community. Because Ephesus was so important in the Roman Empire, the population included many Romans and some powerful women. Inscriptions show women in Ephesus owned businesses, ran workshops, and financed public infrastructure. However, throughout the empire, men were still dominant and Roman citizen freeborn men held exclusive right to vote on the few things one could vote on, and hold most public offices.

The Temple of Artemis (Roman name Diana), one of the Seven Wonders of the Ancient World, was central to Ephesian identity, with thriving temple, tourist, and idol industries. Women played key roles in its rituals and administration, however, so did men. There were more male high priests than female. The priestesses weren't just ceremonial figures—they managed temple finances, oversaw festivals, and sometimes advised city officials. Some scholars speculate that the Artemis Temple cult produced violent, domineering women. However, temple life was actually socially respectable. People did their banking at the temple and it was more like today's country clubs. Some records show there were quite a few priestesses, more than in temples in other cities, but some were as young as fourteen. From the description by one young woman, it seems like what we would think of as an intern year for young people who come from families who have the connections to secure the spot. The cult of Hestia Boulaia also had female leaders. Women like Claudia Trophime and Favonia Flacilla held titles such as *prytanis* (a civic priestly role) and *gymnasiarchos* (overseer of public gymnasia), indicating some civic clout.

Epistolic Context

The context of 1 Timothy is a personal letter from Paul to his mentee, Timothy. He repeatedly writes "you, Timothy" not, "to the church of Ephesus." The purpose is stated in 1:3, that Paul left Timothy in Ephesus with the charge to "command certain people not to teach false doctrines any longer." Paul gives instruction on the correct use of the law. Then he gives general instructions about how men shouldn't be quarrelsome but prayerful, the women shouldn't dress extravagantly and flaunt their wealth (behavior reflecting the "The New Roman Woman" movement), and virtues Timothy should look for in elders and deacons. Paul repeatedly returns to the false doctrine concern.

The Text

Up through verse 10, Paul is speaking in the plural, but then for 11-15, he switches to singular, making it possible that he is talking about a particular woman who needs correction. She shouldn't teach yet because she needs to learn first. And she shouldn't be domineering over a particular man, perhaps her husband. Mowczko gives three reasons why she believes it is one woman who is the troublemaker.[38]

38 Marg Mowczko, "3 reasons why it's a woman, not all women, in 1 Timothy 2:12," Exploring the biblical theology of Christian egalitarianism, August 28, 2019, https://

> *It's possible for three reasons that only one woman was being rebuked, so it's an interpretive overreach to apply this prohibition to all women for all time.*
> Misleading Tactic #19

Some scholars suggest that Christian women in Ephesus may have been too bold in the church, leading to this correction. The correction does come immediately after the instruction regarding bold attire, so that seems to fit at first glance. Their idea is that women accustomed to prominence through religious and economic avenues might have brought that assertiveness into the church and needed to tone it down. Some scholars believe that the cult of Artemis meant women were dominant in Ephesus, but there isn't enough evidence for that. Although local cities had their own social dynamics, female dominance is not really a plausible theory because Rome (highly patriarchal) would not have let Ephesus, its "crown jewel of Asia," be run by women.

As mentioned, it could be that one woman in particular was behaving badly and both Paul and Timothy knew who it was without having to name her. (Typically, Paul named the people he "handed over to Satan" but not those who still have the opportunity to repent.) We also have good reason from verse 12b to believe this woman was behaving especially badly but we'll get to that. For now, we will start from the top. There are seven phrases in this passage which will be addressed below.

1. <u>A woman should learn in quietness</u> (*hēsychia*) and <u>full submission</u>.

2. I <u>do not permit</u>

3. a <u>woman to teach</u>

---

margmowczko.com/a-woman-not-all-women-1-timothy-212/.

4. or to assume authority (NIV) exercise authority (ESV) over a man; she must be quiet.

5. For Adam was formed first, then Eve.

6. And Adam was not the one deceived, it was the woman who was deceived and became a sinner.

7. But women will be saved through childbearing—if they continue in faith, love, and holiness with propriety.

1. A Woman Should Learn in Quietness and full submission

Because of our twenty-first-century mindset, all our attention goes to the descriptor words, "quiet" and "submission." However, it is very significant that Paul says a woman should learn. In a time when it was not a priority to teach women, this was radical. Paul is **directing the woman to learn** (*manthanetō*, the verb that means learn, is in the imperative form). Some versions render it, "let the woman learn" but the verb is stronger than that.

Some translations (including NKJV) render *hēsychia* as "silent" rather than "quietly." This is a biased translation because in several other places, *hēsychia* (and closely related words) is rendered "quiet" (1 Timothy 2:2; 1 Thess. 4:11; 2 Thess. 3:12). For example, Paul says to pray for governing authorities so that believers may be able to live quiet and peaceful lives. Clearly, the word means to be calm, not silent. Inconsistently, even the NKJV renders this word as "quietly" in the same chapter (2:2).

The Greek word for "quiet" is always translated as such in the NKJV except for this passage where it pertained to women and then it was translated to the harsher word, "silent."
Misleading Tactic #2

When Paul means "silent," he uses the word *sigaō* (1 Corinthians 14:28, 30). It appears that because this is a passage about women, translators chose to use a harsher word. Once again, newer versions such as the NIV have corrected this, but the harsher rendering already impressed itself on my generation and generations before mine who taught and wrote books.

"Full submission" would be related to quiet learning, just as Jewish men would learn in quiet, full submission when sitting under a Rabbi. There's nothing especially gender-related about learning quietly in full submission. Women are typically more social and we've all probably experienced the Sunday school class or home group that is hard to reign in. I could see Paul or Timothy sighing with exasperation when calling a gathering to listen.

2. I do not permit

There is excellent reason to believe Paul's intention was temporary for this situation. Once again, the strongest work I found was Mowczko's. I'm giving my reader a summary of her work on this.

First, "the verb *epitrepō* is commonly used in contexts of localized situations, exceptions, and concessions, rather than contexts of universal norms and regulations." Mowczko lists all 16 of the other NT uses of *epitrepō* to demonstrate this. Then a footnote lists more quotations from ancient Greek texts. Ninety-five percent of the time the context is temporary. She quotes other notable scholars in agreement.

Second, the verb *epitrepō* is only used this one time in the letter, showing that it is exceptional, not usual.

> *Three factors concerning the verb for "permit" indicate that this prohibition of a woman teaching is a temporary situation.*
> Misleading Tactic #20

Third, Mowczko shows seven times in 1 Timothy where Paul uses a stronger word, *paraggellō*, to charge/direct/command someone in what to do as a more universal directive (compared to this one use of *epitrepō*). There were actually many ways Paul could have said this more strongly if one wants to list the forms Paul uses for prohibitions (i.e. Women should not teach, I urge you to not allow women to teach, etc.). Nor is "women teaching" in any list of vices or bad behaviors.[39]

This evidence seems so conclusive that I dare say if this were any other issue, the common translation would be "For now, I do not permit…"

Sandra Glahn, Dallas Theological Seminary Professor, points out that Paul says "I" rather than just stating a command. It sounds as if he's giving a personal practical suggestion rather than a "thus saith the Lord" instruction, similar to when he gives a personal opinion in 1 Corinthians 7:25. She agrees that in this passage, Paul is speaking to a specific problem which should not be universalized.[40]

3. a woman to teach

A woman is not permitted to teach (at all) at this time, because she needed to quietly learn first.

Many believe that the prohibition here is due to the fact that men had been educated, whereas women had not, so would not be capable of teaching. This might have been a factor, especially because of the imperative verb that a woman should learn, but I don't believe that is the whole story. Lack of education might have applied to Jewish women and some poor women, but not all Greco-Roman women. Since this verse appears in 1 Timothy in the context of Ephesian women and their lavish dress, I believe the prohibition is related to the particular situation in that particular church. A woman could have been educated well enough to learn but had not learned Christian doctrine yet

---

39 Mowczko, "6 reasons 1 Timothy 2:12 is not as clear as it seems," August 3, 2016, https://margmowczko.com/1-timothy-212-not-as-clear/.

40 Sandra Glahn, "The influence of Artemis on the issues of 1 Tim 2:8–15," Sandra Glahn ThM PhD, January 11, 2022, https://sandraglahn.com/blog/2022/01/artemis-of-ephesus.

> *The Greek word for "teach" in 1 Timothy 2:12 that is a supposed prohibition on women for all time, is the same word used in 1 Corinthians 14:26 where everyone (including women) is to bring a teaching.*
> Misleading Tactic #15

and needed to quietly attend to that education before teaching, even if she was leading in other areas. We will see later in this chapter where the same Greek word for "teach," *didachē*, is used in a permissive way for women (but of course, a bit obfuscated in the "plain reading").

We could go back and forth *ad nauseum* about different scholars' thoughts on each of these points. After extensive research, I prayed and asked God for clarity as I tried to decide which arguments to include here. Then, when I wasn't even thinking about it, God gave me sudden clarity. I confirmed what was revealed to me, and following is what I believe is the bottom line:

The epistle of 1 Timothy was a personal letter written from Paul to Timothy, to guide him in his ministry at the Ephesian church. In contrast, the epistle of Galatians was written to "the *churches* of Galatia" which is a *region* in the north central part of Anatolia (modern-day Türkiye). There was no city of Galatia. If we say that 1 Timothy 2 was a general principle for all places and all time, it creates contradictions with other passages where Paul very matter-of-factly refers to women teaching without prohibition. However, if we recognize that Timothy was facing a challenge in Ephesus that warranted a prohibition in a letter to him, we no longer have a contradiction, and we can also recognize that a passage like **Galatians 3:23-29, sent to a whole region of churches, is a general principle for all places and all time.** See the context:

Before the coming of this faith, we were held in custody under the law, locked up until the faith that was to come would be revealed. So the law was our guardian until Christ came that we might be justified by faith. Now that this faith has come, we are no longer under a guardian.

So in Christ Jesus you are all children of God through faith, for all of you who were baptized into Christ have clothed yourselves with Christ. There is neither Jew nor Gentile, neither slave nor free, nor is there male and female, for you are all one in Christ Jesus. If you belong to Christ, then you are Abraham's seed, and heirs according to the promise.

We are no longer in the custody of legalism but are justified by faith. All of us who were baptized into Christ and clothed with Christ are children of God through faith, with no distinction related to ethnicity, social status or gender, all one in Christ and co-heirs to the promise. Each person has a choice to make. Will you be bound or bind others by the custody of cultural law, or will you recognize that all believers are truly one in Christ? This is further emphasized in Ephesians 4:4-6:

There is one body and one Spirit, just as you were called to one hope when you were called; one Lord, one faith, one baptism; one God and Father of all, who is over all and through all and in all.

Some say, "This equality passage is just about salvation." It is about far more than salvation—being equally clothed in Christ, equal heirs of the promises of

> *It is not logical to assert that something written to an individual church leader is applicable for all places and times but then something (on related topic) written to a region of churches is for a narrow application.*
> Misleading Tactic #1

God, walking that out in life in the unity of one body of Christ, led by one Spirit. This passage supports the idea that church leaders should be appointed based on character and giftings, not based on cultural law and factors into which people were born, such as ethnicity, social status, or gender. As we saw in 1 Corinthians, the Holy Spirit does not consider those things when granting gifts.

4. or exercise authority over a man

or to assume authority over (NIV) exercise authority over (ESV) a man

Depending on how you count, there are around eight different Greek words in the NT for "authority." This particular word, *authentein* (not one of the eight) **is only used this one time in Scripture.** Various lexicons list definitions for it that range from mildly negative to violent. This one time this Greek word is used, Paul clearly means that he does not permit the woman of Ephesus to behave badly to a man. Cynthia Long Westfall examined all available ancient documents which use it and determined the following:

> *The people who are targets of these actions are harmed, forced against their will (compelled), or at least their self-interest is being overridden because the actions involve an imposition of the subject's will, ranging from dishonor to lethal force.*[41]

What is certain is that the word *authentein* does not represent the reasonable exercise of authority because there are common words for that, such as *exousia* (G1849). The ESV and NASB translate this word in 1 Timothy 2 into English as "exercise authority over" which gives the impression to the reader that it is the normal exercise of authority. The NIV rendering of "*assume* authority over" is perhaps slightly more

41 Cynthia Long Westfall, *Paul and Gender: Reclaiming the Apostle's Vision for Men and Women in Christ* (Grand Rapids, MI: Baker Academic, 2016), 292.

negative in meaning. The NKJV simply says "have authority over" which sounds quite benign.

The description by Westfall is behavior that would not be acceptable by any man or woman to another human being—something like domination or control, not the normal exercise of authority.

It is a poor translation to use the normal English word "authority" in 1 Timothy 2:12 for the Greek "authentein" which is a far more negative word.
Misleading Tactic #2

Therefore, it's more likely there was one woman or a few whose behavior Paul felt needed addressing because she was misbehaving, like men sometimes misbehaved. Again, Paul is speaking to a specific issue, writing to Timothy about the affairs of this church, not to the church at large for all time. Otherwise, this passage contradicts other passages which we will examine in the next chapter.

The word "authority" is often used in today's church setting as a broad, power word that rests with the individual who has it. The word actually means you have been authorized by someone else to do a particular thing. So, we need to ask these questions: Who authorized you, and to do specifically what? For example, a typical pastor today is authorized by the community of the church who called him, to proclaim the Word, to shepherd the church's people, even to guard them from anything seen as a spiritual danger. He is to teach principles from the Word, but he is not authorized to tell people in the church specifics like what to eat, wear, listen to, and what job to work. He doesn't have blanket authority over the lives of church members—he has *specific* authority *from others.* That authority is *exousia*, not the kind of authority associated with *authentein.*

The idea that no church gathering may choose to authorize women to lead men because of a supposed blanket prohibition on all women ever having any authority over *any* man is an exaggerated extrapo-

> *Ironically, those who prohibit women from "usurping authority" are the ones obstructing authority since God gave women authority by the same means God gave men authority: Holy Spirit filling, spiritual gifts, Dominion Mandate, Great Commission.*
> Misleading Tactic #1

lation. There are also ministry services that men and women are simply authorized by Jesus to do, not needing the authorization of a body. If men tell a woman she can't, they are obstructing her authority. It has been said so many times that women are usurpers, that people are oblivious to when men obstruct. I'm not anti-authority; I'm for not making a bigger deal about authority than Jesus did, and I'm for not reserving authority for one gender when the Bible doesn't do it.

5. For Adam was formed first, then Eve

Hierarchalists say that the reference to Genesis here indicates that the preceding prohibition is for all time. The English text with the word "For" (in all four of the major versions I compare in this book: NKJV, NIV, ESV, NASB) certainly gives this impression. It sounds like, "Women may not do this *because* (for) Adam was formed first." However, "For" is a poor translation of the word gar (G1063) which introduces more information, but **not a reason.** It is a not a synonym for "because." Mowczko has an article delving into this, with examples from all over the NT including 1 Timothy 2.[42]

The statement "Adam was formed first and then Eve" was required to refute a false teaching about women being created first. Perhaps it was being taught by this woman who needed to stop teaching and to learn. Gnosticism (Jewish-Christian heresy) reached its peak in

---

42 Mowczko, "6 reasons 1 Timothy 2:12 is not as clear as it seems," https://margmowczko.com/1-timothy-212-not-as-clear/.

the late second century, and 1 Timothy is dated late first to early second century. Various schools of pre-Gnostic teaching were emerging by the early second century, and hints like this in 1 Timothy (1:3-4) and Titus (3:9) indicate that these letters should be given a later second-century date. That the same thing was going on in Crete where Titus was, indicates this is not just an Ephesian cult issue. Jewish traditions and Gnostic-style teachings emphasized mystical lineages and esoteric knowledge. Many strange things were taught about Adam and Eve in Gnostic heresies. Some teachings claimed Eve was created first and thanked her for eating from the tree of knowledge. Even the "one mediator" principle (1 Timothy 2:5) refutes these false teachings.

It makes sense that Paul spoke about who came first in creation, not because he cared so much, but because they cared—a lot. The average church goer in the twenty-first century, who knows very little about the Ephesian cults or Gnosticism assume Paul cared a lot about creation order and who was deceived, therefore we must care—and we turn the whole thing on its head. Reading outside of context can result in coming away with the exact opposite of Paul's intent. Remember that Paul clarified in 1 Corinthians 11:11-12 that it doesn't matter who came from the other, and that neither man nor woman should claim independent superiority due to creation.

> *Interpreting one NT verse about the creation of man and woman out of context (1 Timothy 2:12) and in isolation from another text which addresses the topic (1 Corinthians 11:11-12) violates rules of good hermeneutics.*
> Misleading Tactic #9

Nevertheless, in the Lord woman is not independent of man, nor is man independent of woman. For as woman came from man, so also man is born of woman. But everything comes from God.

Who was created first is not essential to what we believe about who God is and how he operates (or shouldn't be essential). Some of the recipients of Paul's letter were struggling with some false teachings. Because their beliefs were based on Eve being created first, it had to be knocked down. If it were believed that women were superior because they came first, then naturally, women would dominate men, just like men who believe that it matters that they came first currently dominate. No one—man or woman—should dominate.

1 Corinthians 11:11-12 should be included in a discussion about who was created first. This is an example of how we need to let Scripture interpret Scripture rather than taking one verse and extrapolating meaning from it in isolation of other Scripture which addresses the same topic. Letting Scripture interpret Scripture is a basic rule of good hermeneutics.

6. it was the woman who was deceived

"And Adam was not the one deceived, <u>it was the woman who was deceived and became a sinner</u>."

The statement in 1 Timothy 2:11-15 about Eve being deceived has been used to implicitly and explicitly state that all women are naturally more gullible than men, therefore, women are less capable of hearing from God and should not lead men (but they may lead women and children under the supervision of men). After Eve was deceived, Adam ate of the fruit too, and he knew what he was doing so was in rebellion. Logically, if the events in Genesis prove all women are more gullible, then all men must be more rebellious. What is worse, sinning due to being deceived, or sinning due to rebellion? Remember, God said that rebellion is as wicked as the sin of witchcraft (1 Samuel 15:23). Who would you rather follow, someone who leans naïve and easily deceived or someone who leans intentionally wicked to the point of giving himself to Satan?

Let us test the assumption that women are more easily deceived. Satan's purpose is to steal, kill, and destroy. Which gender is more easily deceived by Satan so they feel justified in committing crimes and starting wars? Were any women involved in the crucifixion of Jesus? At least one woman (Pilate's wife) tried to prevent it. Men were deceived about who Jesus really was, despite a boatload of prophetical evidence (which some were withholding from women lest they be educated). Why have women historically attended church more, sought spiritual truth more than men, and obeyed God with less hesitation? We forget that Moses, the most revered patriarch of Israel next to Abraham, had a foreign wife who had the clarity to save his life by circumcising their son when Moses hesitated to obey God (Exodus 4:24-26). (Zipporah was quite the gutsy gal.)

Could it be we've missed the reason for the mention of Eve being deceived in this passage? Perhaps it has nothing to do with saying women shouldn't teach because they are more easily deceived. The deception reference easily goes with the creation order reference right before it, and helps counter the false teaching from Gnosticism. So, with this interpretation, here's a paraphrase of what Paul said:

"Things are pretty wild there. Therefore, I want everyone to pray for those in civil authority, that we may live quiet and holy lives. I want the men to pray, lifting up holy hands without anger or disputing. Quiet down, men! I want the women to dress modestly, with decency and propriety, adorning themselves, not with elaborate hairstyles or gold or pearls or expensive clothes, but with good deeds, appropriate for women who profess to worship God. I do not currently

> *The idea that women shouldn't lead because they are more easily deceived might sound logical but that would mean men shouldn't lead because they are more rebellious.*
> Misleading Tactic #1, 3

endorse (an?) unlearned women (woman?) there in Ephesus to teach. She should first settle down and quietly apply herself to good doctrine. Also, this woman should not dominate her husband. The Holy Scripture says the man was created first so this false teaching based on woman coming first is erroneous. Man was created first and the woman was deceived and became a sinner."

That interpretation makes sense without coming up with demonstrably outlandish statements such as, "all females are more gullible" and "all males are superior because Adam was created first," and "therefore, only men should teach." If Paul was actually saying these things, I do not think we would see all the mentions of women in ministry with him which will see coming up. Rather than believing Paul is limiting the ministry of women, I believe Paul was dismantling false teaching.

7. But women will be saved through childbearing

Let's start with the error in the second word. The Greek word, *sōthēsetai*, includes a singular, non-gendered pronoun, so it should be "she" not "women." This seems like an attempt to generalize this passage and obfuscate the possibility that one woman was causing the problem. The NIV and NASB render this incorrectly.

This last sentence in 1 Timothy 2:11-15 makes it sound like women need to stay home and have babies to please God, not run around being teachers and evangelists. Complementarians sometimes try not to say it as bluntly as this, but they have said it nonetheless, and now there are some who have become very bold about saying it. We know that "saved" can't mean your soul is saved by the act of giving birth, or even

> *"She" was translated to "women" which seems like an attempt to generalize this passage and obfuscate the possibility that one woman was causing the problem.*
> Misleading Tactic #2

that childbirth especially pleases God or all the women who haven't had children would be at a disadvantage for pleasing God. **This is yet another case where plain reading doesn't make sense, so context is everything.**

Remember, Paul is still talking about women who live in Ephesus with a culture of Artemis worship. The cult was woven into the city's livelihood and identity as the most important and "mother" city of Asia Minor. Here is the cultural, contextual explanation: In that time, more women died in childbirth than today, since they didn't have today's emergency medical help. Artemis/Diana was the Ephesian/ Roman goddess of midwifery. The following myth supposedly happened near Ephesus:

> *Leto bore Artemis first, and she, being strong-minded, leapt down to assist her mother in the birth of Apollo.*[43]

Women who could, travelled to Ephesus to give birth, thinking Artemis would take care of them. (Yet another cult-related industry besides the idol industry mentioned in Acts.) Some women didn't want to become Christian because they were afraid that they would die in childbirth without Diana's protection. So, it makes sense for the sentence by Paul to mean that if you become a faithful believer (continue in faith), and your lifestyle proves

> *Logic requires that if one must search for context for the childbearing phrase rather than accepting the "plain reading," then associated phrases about the woman teaching should receive the same inquiry.*
> Misleading Tactic #1

43 Pseudo-Apollodorus, Bibliotheca 1.4.1 (Bibliotheca is the earliest Greek systematic myth-compendium, from first or second century AD.)

you are a believer, you can depend on Jesus to save you through the life-threatening ordeal of childbirth.

Or it was a reference to Genesis 3:15, that her offspring would save humanity from sin, but we need an explanation for why Paul says something about childbirth next to being saved. If we took this sentence at "plain reading" without context, we'd be left with strange doctrine on salvation, contradicting other passages. So, why do we take the other sentences right next to it (verses 11 and 12) at face value without looking for context, even though they contradict other passages which allow women to speak and teach?

In conclusion related to 1 Timothy 2:11-15, I need to impress on the reader that I have presented curated points. If the reader encounters arguments not addressed here, they are most likely addressed in Mowczko's articles.

1 Corinthians 14:26-40

Epistolic Context

Some of the Corinthian Christians were quite selfish and proud. So a big theme of Paul's letter is how to live for others. He frequently quotes the selfish things the Corinthians are saying and then refutes them. Because first-century Greek did not have quotation marks, it can get confusing as to what is being said by the Corinthians and what Paul is saying to refute them, leading to interpretation challenges. Focusing on individual verses here and there without understanding this context (of selfishness) and interpretative challenge (of quotation/refutation) wreaks havoc with Paul's intentions.

Even though we call this letter "First" Corinthians, it is not the first letter that has gone back and forth between Paul and the Corinthian church. We're only getting a small slice of the conversation and are left to guess what Paul knows from their previous letter(s?) to him (mentioned in 1 Corinthians 7:1) and from what has been reported to him by Chloe's people (1 Cor. 1:11). Therefore, there could be times when he is correcting them that he doesn't bother to quote them verbatim because both he and they already know what he is talking about (but we do not).

In addition to letters and Chloe's people, Paul had two more sources of information. He mentions in the opening verse of his letter that Sosthenes is with him, so I researched Sosthenes and discovered from Acts 18 that he was a synagogue leader in Corinth who converted to Christianity and was beaten on Paul's behalf. Paul mentions that Sosthenes is now with him while he pens this letter, so Sosthenes apparently visited Paul and would have brought additional insight regarding the church in Corinth. Stephanas, Fortunatus, and Achaicus were also with Paul from Corinth (16:7). So, that is four sources of information (about what was being discussed and happening in the Corinthian church) to which Paul was privy, but we are not privy, leaving much to the imagination when trying to interpret some passages.

I grew up on the KJV because in the fundamentalist camp, the RSV did not exist and "mere paraphrases" were "not the real Bible." The KJV did not have any quotation marks, leading to some extreme views. For example, in 1 Corinthians 7:1, the KJV says it is good for a man not to touch a woman (no quotes) so our church leaders thought Paul was giving that command. Thus, absolutely no touching of any kind was allowed, with youth group chaperones breathing down our necks and making it impossible to just have normal fun. The NIV now translates 7:1 with quotations marks as what the Corinthians were saying, and Paul corrects them. (Furthermore, the translation indicates they are talking about sexual relations, not just casual touch.) Huge difference just due to the quote marks, regardless of what kind of touch it was.

In chapter 8, Paul quotes the Corinthians extensively about "we all have knowledge" and "we know that no idol actually exists" (so it's okay to eat food offered to idols since) "there is no God but one." They were being selfish by exercising their liberty to eat meat in any situation because of their understanding. Again, there are still no quotation marks in the KJV, but now there are quotation marks in the NIV and ESV. Translators have agreed they should be there, because Paul is quoting and then refuting.

In chapters 6 and 10, the NIV and ESV put quotes around what the translators believe that the Corinthians were saying, "All things are lawful for me" and then Paul's refutation that all things are not beneficial is not in quotes. The KJV does not have quotation marks for what the Corinthians said.

Back to the theme of exhorting against selfishness, Paul sets the example. He makes himself a "slave to everyone" rather than exercising his rights to be married and to take a salary as a preacher of the gospel. He becomes weak, becomes all things to all people, and disciplines his body—anything it takes for the sake of others (chapter 9). In chapter 11, Paul rebukes them for selfishly eating at gatherings while others went hungry. In chapter 12, Paul likens them to a body with many parts, and those parts should have equal concern and respect for each other rather than honoring some (and self) more than others. In chapter 13, Paul explains that love for each other is greater than all the ministry gifts just mentioned, because he is concerned that some people are elevated above others due to their giftings.

In chapter 14, people are acting selfishly in worship. Paul corrects them by explaining how to take turns when speaking and prophesying. Also, I will explain why I believe that men were trying to keep women from being able to speak and Paul refuted them.

The Text

This passage (14:26-39) is clearly about public worship. Let's start with verse 26:

> *What then shall we say, brothers and sisters? When you come together, each of you has a hymn, or a word of instruction, a revelation, a tongue or an interpretation.*

This passage includes female participation in public worship, and then later it seems to contain a prohibition. First comes the participation. It says "...brothers and sisters, when you *come together, each of you* has a hymn, *word of instruction*, revelation, tongue, interpretation."

Continuing the topic of good order in public worship, it talks about using interpretation for tongues, only allowing 2-3 prophecies, and taking turns. Notice that both genders are supposed to give a word of "instruction" and participate in evaluating prophecies. Then it has a somewhat concluding-type sentence, "For God is not a God of disorder, but of peace—as in all the congregations of the Lord's people" (v. 33).

Note that "brothers and sisters" is translated from the Greek word *adelphoi* which means *siblings from the same womb* (either literally or figuratively). This is the Greek word that would be used if either there were all males or it is a mixed group. Translators who are attempting to be more accurate regarding gender in Bible passages have agreed that *adelphos* (singular) or *adelphoi* (plural) should be translated to English as brother and sister or brothers and sisters (respectively) unless there is clear indication that only males are present or being addressed. The 2011 NIV led the way in this effort and received strong criticism. Then the ESV made some gender-related edits to the 2016 edition, however, the edits are extremely inconsistent, actually adding to the confusion. See a 28-page list of problems with the ESV translation—some problems representing many instances—including the category Inconsistent Gender Language in an article by translator Mark L. Strauss, *Why the English Standard Version (ESV) Should Not Become the Standard English Version* https://marklstrauss.com/articles. Be sure to read the conclusion. I feel like a version should not do any gender inclusion unless they are going to be consistent, otherwise they will mislead the reader who thinks they are reading something consistent.

Sometimes the ESV uses footnotes only at the beginning of a chapter to indicate all verses affected, but the verse where they put it doesn't have impact. Also, it's as if they created the need for it up there in order to remove it from where it really matters. I believe this is misleading. Below is an example from this passage and then we'll see another example later.

> *The ESV footnote indicating the inclusion of "sister" is located where people won't remember to apply it 20 verses later where it really matters.*
> Misleading Tactic #13

In this passage (1 Corinthians 14), starting with verse 6, the ESV switches to "brothers." They continue with some generally inclusive language but also use "brothers" in verses 20 and 26. Look again at verse 26 and notice that "each of you" is to bring a hymn, or a word of instruction (teach, *didachē* G1322), a revelation, a tongue or an interpretation. Well, we can't have women bringing instruction or teaching, can we? Nor do we want women to "earnestly desire to prophesy" (verse 39)? There is a footnote next to the word "brother" in verse 6. IF someone clicks on it, they will see, "Or brothers and sisters; also verses 20, 26, 39." This separates the footnote with some distance from when people read verses 26 and 39. I feel this is a sneaky, misleading tactic.

Also, the ESV still defaults to the masculine pronoun three times for believers in the chapter. Other passages in the NT where the ESV conceded to use "people," or "anyone" do not have any leadership implications.

> *The ESV inconsistently applies gender accurate translation, not including "sisters" when there is teaching or leadership implied.*
> Misleading Tactic #13

It is obvious throughout the whole letter that it is addressed to men and women. Back up and read chapter 14 and see all the general instructions it contains for everyone. For example, Paul says in verse 5, "I want all of you" or "every one of you" to speak in tongues, but even more to prophesy.

> *The Greek word for "teaching" in verse 6 related to Paul's activity is the same word for everyone bringing a "teaching" in verse 26. Only the NIV (out of the four compared) doesn't change the English word to something different than "teaching."*
> Misleading Tactic #15

In verse six, Paul talks about himself bringing a "word of instruction" (ESV). Other translations render it "teaching." Then in verse 26 where everyone, including women, should bring a word of instruction/teaching, (the same Greek word, *didachē*), the ESV calls it a "lesson," NIV "a word of instruction," NKJV "a teaching," and NASB "a teaching." So, the ESV and NIV call the same word used by Paul to teach, something different for the mixed crowd, and the NIV and NKJV consistently call it a "teaching." (However, the NKJV precedes it with "brethren.") With the ESV, I suppose we are to think that women bringing "a lesson" (verse 26) isn't the same authoritative activity as Paul bringing "a teaching" (verse 6). Same Greek word, same context, just slightly different in English to throw the reader off from recognizing they are the same.

> *The Greek word for "teach" in 1 Timothy 2:12 that is a supposed prohibition on women for all time, is the same word used in 1 Corinthians 14:26 where everyone is to bring a teaching.*
> Misleading Tactic #15

This is the same Greek word, *didachē*, used in 1 Timothy 2:12 where Paul says he does not allow a woman to teach (verb form). But here he is instructing all women to bring a teaching (noun form).

The ESV misleads people to believe that the activities of teaching and prophecy spoken about in this chapter belong only to men.

Women Should Remain Silent in the Churches

Here comes the seeming prohibition in verses 34-36:

> *Women should remain silent in the churches. They are not allowed to speak, but must be in submission, as the law says.*
>
> *If they want to inquire about something, they should ask their own husbands at home; for it is disgraceful for a woman to speak in the church.*
>
> *Or did the word of God originate with you? Or are you the only people it has reached?*

There are some odd things about these verses. I have read many authors and gleaned three possibilities that explain verses 34-36.

Interpolation – This is the theory that verses 34-35 were added by a scribe, because in some manuscripts, they appear in the margin or down at the end of the chapter. I've read some theories of how it could have happened accidentally, but more research showed them to be a stretch. I am not inclined to toss out verses, so interpolation is not my preferred theory. However, even some complementarians hold this belief because they are so troubled by the manuscript evidence. I include the interpolation theory here because I think this manuscript oddity is resolved by the third possibility.

Three Instructions to Be Quiet – Notice that in verse 27, Paul says that when people speak in tongues, there should be two or three people at most, they should take turns, and there should be an interpreter. If these criteria aren't being met, be quiet and stop speaking. Then in verses 29-33, there are criteria for prophesying. If they aren't being met, be quiet. You can control yourself. Verses 34-35 are along the same lines. If women (especially those who aren't educated and have questions) are holding up the exhortation with questions, it becomes a disorderly atmosphere, so they need to be quiet and wait. Along with the theme of the entire letter, people shouldn't be selfish by monopolizing the speaking time. They should let others have a turn.

None of the three "be quiet" instructions means that everyone should stay quiet at all gatherings forever. That would contradict other passages where women are encouraged to pray and prophesy in church. It is clearly situational for an orderly church service with a larger gathering of people. This interpretation has a lot of merit, but it doesn't address all of the problem phrases in those two verses, so it takes second place to my preferred interpretation.

Refutation of Error – As explained above, in 1 Corinthians, Paul is correcting many errant ideas. I think verses 34-35 should be in quotes as an errant idea (and then Paul begins refutation in verse 36). Again, the Greek doesn't have quotation marks and translators need to decide where to put them. As we've seen, there is still a lot of inconsistency with quotation marks between versions. Above, I gave an example of how the errant teaching, "It is not good for a man to touch a woman" not being in quotation marks led to misunderstanding as if it were Paul's teaching. So, there is precedence for this type of misunderstanding.

I believe that what is being said in verses 34-35 is errant teaching that should be in quotes. Following are seven words or phrases in those verses which I believe demonstrate that the speaker is in error:

1. The word "silent" here is sigaō (G4601) which means "silent" not "quiet." Complete silence is extreme for this setting of a church house gathering, contradicting for example, 1 Timothy 2:12 where Paul instructed a woman to learn in "quiet" submission. I believe this is a quotation from men who would like to see the women stay completely silent, thus it is errant.

2. The phrase, "in the churches" shows someone is trying to say this is, or should be, true of all churches. Again, we see affirmation of

women speaking elsewhere, so this is an exaggeration as if the silencing of women is happening in all the churches. It is also an extreme view that it should be happening in all the churches. Not surprisingly, there would have been men in that time (just like there are today), who would have liked to see women completely silent in all the churches at all times, so they were making their case for it.

3. The phrase "as the law says" is problematic. Where does the OT law say that women are not allowed to speak? Nowhere, so this is another error, because they shouldn't have been appealing to any law other than God's law to make a case for a spiritual or moral principle. The Greeks and Romans had laws (though fading fast) that women must learn from husbands at home and may not speak in public. There could have been some Jewish men as well, entrenched in Pharisaical "oral law." (Remember the quote from Josephus in Chapter Four, saying the woman is in all things inferior to the man according to the "law"?) Whoever it was, Greeks, Romans or Jews, some men in Corinth needed Paul's correction to understand that cultural, sexist law doesn't apply to Christian gatherings. Christian gatherings had to be unsettling for those men who were accustomed to being in spaces where slaves and women didn't have a voice or respected presence.

As we saw earlier, there is legitimate and illegitimate law, and we would do well to disregard illegitimate law. God's law that women be filled with the Spirit and speak appropriately as they are led (Joel 2:28-29, Acts 1:14-2:18 etc.) is a higher law.

4. In the Greek, at the end of verse 35, after "for it is disgraceful for a woman to speak in church" there is a single letter word (η), a disjunctive participle called an "expletive of dissociation." It can mean "What?!?" "No way!" "Nonsense!" "Can't be!" It can also mean "or." Notice, all these options are contrarian. Some versions start verse 36 with the word "Or" (which does not contribute to understanding the passage, in my opinion). The KJV is the only version (of the four considered in this book) which uses "What?" I believe Paul is using this

"expletive" to show his disdain for what was just said. (The participle is used two more times in verses 36 and 37 where it is makes sense to render it "or.")

5. In verse 36, it appears Paul is rebuking the men by shooting down what I believe is the quotation from those men who don't want women to speak:

> *(NIV) Or did the word of God originate with you? Or are you the only people it has reached?*
>
> *(KJV) What? came the word of God out from you? or came it unto you only?*
>
> *(ESV) Or was it from you that the word of God came? Or are you the only ones it has reached?*
>
> *(NASB) Or was it from you that the word of God first went out? Or has it come to you only?*

Paul appears to be telling them, "What? Do you men think you're the only ones who have God's Word, and not the women too?"

Remember from the list of translation challenges that the only time Greek grammar is completely feminine is if there are no males in the crowd. So, if Paul was correcting women and continuing to correct women, the adjective and noun for "you only" would be in the feminine. But "you only" is in the masculine. As author Seth Knorr explains:

> *The adjective which means "only" or "alone"* (monos*) is masculine in the original Greek, creating a major problem for those who want to interpret this passage as a rebuke to women rather than men.*[44]

44 Seth M. Knorr, *A Biblical Case for Women Pastors, Elders, and Deacons* (Shippensburg PA: Eleutheros Publishing, 2023), 25.

Knorr goes on to describe how some scribes undoubtedly recognized this as a problem. He believes they got rid of the problem by moving verses 34-35 to after verse 40, as seen in the western-text tradition of manuscripts. This made the masculine adjective less problematic since the end of the chapter addresses the whole congregation rather than just men or women. This explains the oddity that some are trying to address with the interpolation theory.

6. The *context of this whole letter* is that the Corinthians are selfish and focused on their own rights instead of the rights of others. The context of this chapter and the two previous chapters centers on not being selfish when gathered for worship. The *second half of this chapter* especially addresses unselfish behavior related to various kinds of speech in worship, allowing many people to participate. Paul talks about taking turns and how the person who is speaking should stop after a bit and let others speak too. So, it doesn't make sense to suddenly throw a complete silencing prohibition on more than half of the crowd. What makes good contextual sense is if Paul suddenly interjected a quotation from people who are not letting women take a turn to speak and then shoots down their errant thinking.

7. Verses 26 and 39 in the same chapter both have gender inclusivity (per *adelphoi*).

> 26 *What then shall we say, brothers and sisters? When you come together, each of you has a hymn, or a word of instruction, a revelation, a tongue or an interpretation.*
>
> 39 *Therefore, my brothers and sisters, be eager to prophesy, and do not forbid speaking in tongues.*

How could Paul talk about keeping order in public worship gatherings and include sisters in the directive to believers to be "eager to prophesy" but then tell them they can't even speak? And it wouldn't make sense five sentences later to say, "don't forbid speaking in tongues" if he had just forbidden half of the people from speaking at all.

There are seven reasons why 1 Corinthians 14:34,35 could be designated as quotes from errant men, so it should not be one of the top three passages that prohibit women in the church.
Misleading Tactic #14

Frankly, 1 Corinthians 14 is a frustrating chapter for me because I have experienced that fundamentalists inconsistently cherry pick some verses and practices as only for the first century and others as applicable for all time—whatever fits the controlling ideology. It happens with other passages as well, but this chapter especially. For example, women are to forever be quiet in church but the directive to not forbid speaking in tongues is not observed, churches don't have congregants bring a hymn or teaching (that would be out of control?), and when was the last time a prophecy was brought in church and then seriously tested by a group? None of that activity works with a pre-determined, highly controlled church service agenda that fits a cultivated brand, so we shall pretend it's not in the Bible or not for our time—oh, except for restricting women—that's there and for our time.

In conclusion, verses 34-35 regarding women staying silent in the church are so problematic, that these verses are not something on which to build a doctrine that women should be prohibited from speaking in church. I don't think those verses even make sense unless they are a quote from errant men. I believe that refutation of a wrong idea is the most plausible answer and due to the refutation in verse 36, this passage is actually one that permits women to speak.

Interpreters cherry pick some verses / practices as only for the first century and others in this same chapter (silencing women) to apply for all time.
Misleading Tactic #5

Chapter 11:

SPEAKING AND TEACHING PERMITTED

1 Corinthians 11:5

> *But every woman who prays or prophesies with her head uncovered dishonors her head—it is the same as having her head shaved.*

In this passage, we're so distracted by the head covering topic that we miss there is a matter-of-fact mention of women praying and prophesying in public worship. This activity is so well accepted that it's not the topic of contention here—head coverings is. If a woman isn't supposed to ever lead or teach any man, not even her own husband, what is she doing praying aloud (leading in prayer) and prophesying in public worship (men present)? Many complementarian churches do not allow women to lead a mixed gender congregation in prayer, but "soft" complementarians do allow it. This doesn't make sense to me. Either women are allowed to spiritually lead, exhort, and teach, both in public and private, or they are not. Arbitrary positions such as "prayer is okay but not preaching," or "private teaching is okay but not public," does not help clarify doctrine, it muddies the water.

Teaching and prophesying (with the definition of exhortation/truth-telling by impression of the Holy Spirit) have overlapping goals. Teaching is instruction and exhortation from the Word for edifying the body (Ephesians 4:11-13, 2 Timothy 3:16-17, etc.) 1 Corinthians 14:1-26 and 31 below includes helpful descriptions of prophecy, shows that its purpose overlaps with teaching, and that it is not practiced by men only (bolded emphasis mine):

> 1 *Follow the way of love and eagerly desire gifts of the Spirit, especially prophecy.* (Prophecy is the most desirable gift.)
>
> 3 *But the one who prophesies speaks to people for their* ***strengthening, encouraging*** *and* ***comfort****.*
>
> 12 *So it is with you. Since you are eager for gifts of the Spirit, try to excel in those that* ***build up the church****. (This was not directed to just the men.)*
>
> 26 *What then shall we say, brothers and sisters? When you come together, each of you has a hymn, or a word of instruction, a revelation, a tongue or an interpretation. Everything must be done so that* ***the church may be built up****.* (Notice, it doesn't say women may only sing and then only prescribed songs such as from the hymnbook. There are churches with this policy. It communicates to women that God doesn't want to hear from us as much as he wants to hear from men.)
>
> 31 *For you can* ***all prophesy*** *in turn so that* ***everyone may be instructed and encouraged****.* (ESV, NKJV, and NASB have "... everyone may learn.") (Notice that prophecy results in instruction and all may prophesy.)

Among the gifts listed in Romans 12:6-8 and Ephesians 4:11, prophecy or prophets are listed before teaching or teachers. In the following list, prophets seem to be above teachers.

And God has placed in the church first of all apostles, second prophets, third teachers, then miracles, then gifts of healing, of helping, of guidance, and of different kinds of tongues. (1 Corinthians 12:28)

There are five important observations: Prophesying women are endorsed by Paul; everyone in the church may bring instruction; prophecy can contain instruction; prophecy has some of the same outcomes as teaching; and prophesy is esteemed higher or more desirable than teaching (if indeed Paul is ranking them—prophecy is definitely not below teaching).

Contrary to popular teachings, there is a matter-of-fact mention of women praying and prophesying in public worship; teaching and prophesying are equal or prophecy is above teaching.
Misleading Tactic #16

Therefore, the idea that teaching is somehow above prophesy and thus reserved for those with higher authority is an extra-biblical (outside of the Bible) construct. Obviously, more training and familiarity with the Bible can (not will) help one person teach better than another, but the Holy Spirit is the biggest factor and can level the playing field. (Familiarity with the Bible also helps prevent false teaching.) When everyone brings what God is teaching them and engages in conversation, it is motivating for personal study and more beneficial to everyone. Conversely, when one person (a preacher) does all the studying and presenting, it benefits that one person the most, and the others will probably quickly forget what was presented. Also, group engagement offers the opportunity for prophecy.

A few years ago, I heard a sermon by a well-known complementarian describing how standing behind the pulpit and proclaiming God's Word after having studied it for preaching is the highest and holiest gifting and responsibility, above that of teaching in any other setting. Besides the unlikelihood that very early churches had pulpits, it appears that he is conveniently overstating the value of his own gift. I have the gift of teaching, but believe it would be wrong to say it is higher than someone else's gift.

I suspect that if Jesus were here today, he would be flipping some big pulpits over and saying, "You will not do that in my house. My house is a house of prayer, not a place to lord your gift over the gifts of others." (This is not to say every preacher is lording their gift, but there is lording going on.)

According to 1 Corinthians 11:5, 1 Corinthians 14:26, and passages which list gifts and include all believers, women may pray aloud, prophesy, teach, etc. in the company of men in public worship. This is another reason why the prohibition on a woman teaching in 1 Timothy 2:12 must be related to the particular situation in Ephesus, and why we should be cautious about making one verse the rule.

When God Speaks to Women

Does God only speak to or through men? I hope this seems like a rhetorical question. After the obvious answer, "No," comes the real question, "When God speaks to women, are they supposed to keep it from men?"

God spoke directly to Isaac's wife Rebekah and told her about the future of the twin boys in her womb. Should she not have told her husband about it because telling him would mean she's somehow instructing or informing him with a message from God? If Isaac had listened to her and determined to give Jacob the elder son blessing, it still would have been difficult, but perhaps there would have been less division in the family. Isaac saw enough in Esau's life to confirm the prophecy given to Rebekah. God directed Moses to record this revelation to Rebekah in Scripture. Do we think God speaking to the woman was an anomaly?

Ruth, the Moabitess, spoke faithful words that have been immortalized in Scripture as an inspiration to millions of believers throughout the centuries. No doubt she was led by God and the author of the book of Ruth was inspired to quote her. Notice that Ruth is the central figure in the book, not Boaz, even though he was the kinsman redeemer and picture of Christ. God chose to honor this woman.

> *There are examples of God speaking to and through women all throughout the Bible, yet today, women communicating messages from God (teaching) is considered not authorized by God.*
> Misleading Tactic #16

A "wise woman" in the city of Abel Beth-Maacah negotiated peace between Joab and the city leaders, saving the city (2 Samuel 20).

All of Proverbs 31 is the words of a woman. I dare say many men have learned from it. It begins as follows:

> *The sayings of King Lemuel—an inspired utterance his mother taught him. Listen, my son! Listen, son of my womb!*

Elizabeth and Mary heard from and spoke through the Holy Spirit as recorded in Luke. Should men not read their words lest they be taught something? (More examples of women hearing from God are in the chapter on women prophets.)

The Women of Romans 16 and Other Passages

So far, we have spent all our time in letters related to Ephesus and Corinth. Now we move on to Rome, where the culture is even more pronounced.

In Chapter 1 where I discussed creation order and the interdependence of men and women, there is a cited article about how Christianity was denigrated for having so many slaves and women.

This article also explains that the population of the Roman Empire was two-thirds male. (I believe this could only happen if female babies were discarded due to the cultural preference for males.) However, the early church was made up of two-thirds women. Logistically, it seems obvious that there MUST have been women leaders, considering the sheer outnumbering of women to men.

There were tensions between Jews and Gentiles in Rome at the time Paul wrote the letter. One of Paul's primary concerns was unity. (Note the many references to nationality and the explanation of God's eternal plan concerning Israel.) A priority regarding unity fits with Paul's mention of many women, including the way he interspersed them with the men in Romans 16 instead of a separate list which could be more expected in that time.

Phoebe

Romans 16:1 introduces the female deacon, Phoebe. She was a deacon in a specific church that is named. The ESV committee decided to translate *diakonos* as "servant" rather than deacon even though they translate the same Greek word as "deacon" elsewhere when they believe it refers to men (Philippians 1:1, 1 Timothy 3:8, 1 Timothy 3:12). What is their justification for doing this? Because Phoebe is female, surely Paul didn't mean she was a deacon? That kind of thinking is letting one's theology affect one's translation work, rather than letting the translation affect theology. This is an example of translation that is intentionally misleading.

> *The same Greek word (diakonos) is translated into a different English word based on whether it seemed to refer to men (deacon) or women (servant).*
> Misleading Tactic #15

When I first read the speculation that Phoebe carried the letter of Romans from Paul to the believers in Rome and probably even explained it to them, I thought it farfetched and dismissed it. It took several readings of Romans 16:1 (in different versions) for me to see the clues I had been missing due to many years of training in dismissing such possibilities. Here are the clues:

Paul says "I commend to you our sister Phoebe." This is an introduction, like "I would like to respectfully introduce our sister Phoebe to you." He then gives her credentials as part of the introduction. One of the reasons I thought it unlikely that Paul was introducing her as the carrier of the letter to the Romans is that the introduction happens at the end of the letter (our last chapter, 16). Who does that? Who brings and reads a long letter and then near the end says, "Oh, here's the introduction of me from the letter writer." (There's my twenty-first-century assumptions projected onto the first century!)

But after pondering how long it would have taken Paul to write this letter, it occurred to me that he may not have decided who would deliver it until he was finishing. Authors didn't have the luxury of "word processing" where they could go back a month into writing and insert something into the beginning. As expensive as materials were, writing was a "one and done" endeavor. Or, it could have been well-planned, but introductions and individual greetings at the end is just how they did things. Regardless, chapter 16 is the letter wrap-up, and it begins by introducing Phoebe, with her credentials, and the recipients of the letter are instructed to give her any assistance she may need because she is from out of town.

Her credentials are more significant than I previously realized. In part because I read "servant" for many years when I should have been reading "deacon," and also because I didn't understand the significance of the word "benefactor" (v. 2). However, after all my reading about patrons, it dawned on me that "benefactor" meant a financial patron (at least). The fact that she was a benefactor "of many, including me" means she had significant wealth and resources.

I had no idea from where people got the idea Phoebe might have carried the letter, because I had never before bothered to look up where Cenchreae was (near Corinth on the east side of Greece), to see that it is a long way from Rome (requiring a ship journey), which now led me to wonder what could have taken her so far from home. Because I missed the fact of the introduction, I had assumed Paul was just mentioning a woman already in Rome that he wanted to commend. Now that I realize he's introducing her, and she has come to them from far away, the purpose of bringing the letter to them makes sense. We need to remember that Paul does not have us in mind when writing this, so he is not going to waste ink and space saying the obvious, "she's bringing this letter to you" because she would be standing there holding it.

I mentioned earlier that sending women on a journey was not a practical thing to do, another reason her mission didn't make sense to me. Unless she was a wealthy woman like Lydia who travelled to major cities to do business. After learning how Lydia was from a city (Thyatia) 300 miles away over land and sea, but was living in Phillipi in Macedonia as part of her purple cloth trade, the theory of Phoebe makes sense. She would have had an entourage to keep her safe. She's not travelling to a new place to establish a church where she might get into trouble by speaking in public, she's on a mission from Paul to another church.

I read someone dismiss the whole idea with, "Who cares who dropped off the package?" Again, this is projecting twenty-first-century life onto first-century life. Today, there are dependable delivery services which have accountability and motivation for employees to deliver packages safely. Back then, all packages had to be delivered by someone you knew and trusted, or else your package would simply disappear.

Let's review all the clues that Phoebe brought the letter from Paul:

- She is a wealthy woman who travels, which means she is educated; therefore, she can read.
- She is an appointed leader in the church of Cenchreae.
- Cenchreae is near Corinth where Paul is staying.
- She is *introduced* (not greeted) to the Roman church at the top of the chapter which contains all the personal greetings.
- She is introduced with credentials.
- The Romans are instructed to assist her if she needs anything.
- No one else is mentioned in the letter as a possible delivery person.

These clues amount to an excellent probability she delivered the letter. If she is delivering the letter and can read, she will probably read it to them and explain it to them. Again, I thought the explaining part was a stretch. But then I remembered learning with my children in homeschool about the great orations of the Greeks and Romans, such as Cicero. We have copies of those speeches, like the biblical epistles, because they were read aloud to crowds. How one delivered the speech was extremely important. I instructed my high school speech students about the importance of delivery countless times. Pauses, and which word receives the inflection in a sentence, can change the entire meaning! We would go through famous speeches and our own speeches with colored pencils to decide which words to emphasize, where to pause, and so on. Those decisions can't be made without understanding the content. That's why I'm narrating my own book!

No doubt, if Paul sent someone with his letter to read to a crowd, he explained how it should be read, made sure they understood it so they could answer questions, and had them rehearse. Because the Greek language didn't have quotation marks, the reader's inflections would clue in the crowd that something is a quote, and then comes the refutation, etc. That was just how things were done. It was important that there be no misunderstandings, and as we know, the written word can be misconstrued, so having an in-person interpreter was crucial.

Having a female interpreter went along with the unity Paul was asking of the Roman believers. It's clear from the content of the letter that there were questions regarding Jews and Gentiles that were affecting unity between those believers. If they could accept a female instructor from Paul, surely the Jews and Gentiles could practice humility and accept each other.

> *There are plenty of clues that Phoebe instructed the church in Rome but those clues are ignored by otherwise diligent scholars.*
> Misleading Tactic #17

After considering all these things, I am now comfortable that it is a very plausible theory that Phoebe delivered this extremely important thesis of Christian doctrine to the church in Rome and explained it to them (which is teaching). When I read commentaries, I see many widely accepted conclusions about many things drawn from far fewer clues. The reason we don't hear this valid speculation in conservative circles is because it means a woman would have been instructing the church. Of course, she would have done it as an understudy of Paul, but weren't they all? Aren't all teachers today an understudy of Paul?

Junia

In Romans 16:7, Paul commends a man and wife couple and calls them apostles.

> *Greet Andronicus and Junia, my fellow Jews who have been in prison with me. They are outstanding among the apostles, and they were in Christ before I was.*

The wife's name is Junia. It was used around forty times in first-century secular texts and on hundreds of inscriptions--and it was always female. Also, over a dozen early church and medieval scholars took her name to be feminine. Most translations continued with the feminine until the late 1800s (while women's suffrage was controversial). A thorough history of which versions used which gender, which popular theologians wrote about women, and when the name was switched back to feminine (mostly recently, since the year 2000) is in this article on the Christians for Biblical Equality website: https://www.cbeinternational.org/resource/junia-female-apostle-examination-historical-record/.

> *For the last 150 years, Junia's name was obfuscated to appear male in order to hide the fact that she was a woman who was equally recognized as an apostle with Andronicus.*
> Misleading Tactic #12

Junia was serving with Andronicus and earned the title of apostle as well as he. Because the ESV committee can't believe that a woman was identified as an apostle by Paul, they chose to translate as follows: "they are known to the apostles." The preposition commonly means "in" or "among," seldom "to." Also, "to" does not make good sense. Apostles ("sent one" G652) knew many people, so it's not very special to identify someone as simply being known to them. Furthermore, the meaning of the word they translated to "known" has a much stronger meaning of notable, highly esteemed, or remarkable.

> *Translators further tried to obfuscate Junia's apostolic ministry by translating "outstanding among the apostles" as "known to the apostles" instead.*
> Misleading Tactic #15

Junia was not just tagging along with her husband, she was recognized as half of the team, like Paul and Barnabus. Paul referred to them both as having been in prison with him, so Andronicus wasn't out there preaching while Junia stayed home ironing his shirts.

Note that the word "apostle" occurs several times in the NT not associated with one of the original twelve. I was told growing up in church that "apostle" is a special term reserved for the original twelve. Certainly, they were the foundational apostles, but I now know that the word was used more broadly, and in Romans 16, it was used for a woman. I find it odd that the word "pastor" is used in the Bible only once (a few more times if "shepherd" is counted), but it has been greatly used by evangelicals. It seems only black churches use "apostle" and white people cringe to hear it although they are the ones ignoring biblical usage. They fear granting too much prestige, but they grant it elsewhere. So, maybe they fear that "apostle" was used for a woman.

Because apostle means "sent one" I take that to mean that someone of status or a body of believers officially sent them. Today we would call that ordination. A person is "ordained" or given an order or command to do something. The Latin was *ordinare*: "to order, arrange, appoint." The SBC is making a huge deal out of only men being ordained. Yet in Romans 16, a woman is called a "sent one" or "apostle."

Priscilla (Prisca)

Paul greeted Prisca and Aquilla in Rome. Luke mentions in Acts 18 that Priscilla and Aquila taught Apollos. Complementarians have dismissed the significance of this by saying it's all right for women to teach one man in private. Why do they think they can split hairs about the number of men being taught or whether the teaching happens publicly or privately? Is there a different Greek word for "teach" if it's just one man versus a room full of men? No. Does the Bible differentiate between public and private teaching? No. In fact, most teaching in the first century happened in home gatherings which would be considered "private" by us in the twenty-first century, and yet that was the church. There were no big Christian buildings with platforms and pulpits. The idea that it matters if teaching happened with one man in private is extra-biblical. The contortions used by complementarians to explain away evidence contrary to their belief are astonishing! Some have argued that the Greek word for Pricilla and Aquilla's teaching is not the usual verb for teaching. Mowczko has an article comparing all the words used for Paul's teaching (https://margmowczko.com/did-priscilla-teach-apollos/), showing this word is equally valid.

> *The order of Barnabus and Paul's names change as Paul becomes the lead teacher, yet we are supposed to ignore that Paul mentions Priscilla first in every teaching context. Misleading Tactic #17 Some copyists reversed order to obfuscate this honor.*
> Misleading Tactic #15

Notice that in the context of teaching, Priscilla's name is mentioned first. She is mentioned first four times by Luke and Paul, in context of teaching ministry. Aquila is only mentioned first when Paul first met them (Acts 18:2) and when Paul mentions their greetings to the Corinthians (1 Corinthians 16:19). Why does the order matter? Barnabus and Saul were listed in that order in Acts repeatedly until Paul (no longer called Saul) gave his first sermon. Once he became the more highly regarded teacher, he was listed first. That precedence implies Priscilla was the better teacher! However, a copyist reversed the order in Acts 18:26.

The husband-first word order occurs in a particular manuscript copy around AD 400 that was then used in a Greek text used by KJV translators. Today, fifteen translations on BibleGateway.com give first-mention honor to the husband. Of the four versions compared in this book, the NKJV in Acts 18:26 is the only offender (which doesn't recognize the preponderance of manuscript evidence, because the

KJV was translated with limited manuscripts available). Bias has infiltrated the church in big and small ways, making it difficult to understand the full impact.

Priscilla was a significant church leader. Here are the reasons:

She is associated with churches in Corinth, Ephesus, and Rome, indicating a traveling ministry—a trait of apostolic leadership. She and Aquila traveled with and without Paul to start and shepherd churches.

It appears that because a woman is involved in the teaching, the ESV and NKJV contributed to interpreters downplaying the teaching in Acts 18:26 as if a single, side conversation.
Misleading Tactic #15

We already mentioned that Priscilla was mentioned first, before Aquila, in contexts regarding teaching.

In Acts 18:26, Priscilla taught Apollos, himself a gifted teacher/preacher. Some propose that she and Aquila just merely "took him aside" (that's how the NKJV and ESV render it) at a gathering and spoke to him for a few minutes. This is not how you teach someone solid doctrine "more adequately/accurately." It also wouldn't earn a mention by Paul. The KJV says "took him unto them," and the NIV says "invited him to their home," which makes the most sense. This is not a huge translation difference, but it contributes to interpreters downplaying a woman's teaching.

Romans 16:3-5 mentions the church that meets in their house. Considering the other points made here, they were no doubt the spiritual overseers of this church in their house. (This also lends to understanding that others who host churches are most likely leaders.)

Paul refers to Priscilla and Aquila as "co-workers in Christ Jesus" (Romans 16:3), a term he uses for ministry partners, including leaders like Timothy and Titus.

Romans 16:4 says they "risked their lives" for Paul, suggesting deep involvement in missionary work and leadership, not just hospitality.

Terran Williams points out that the New Testament does not name any male pastors or elders, which challenges the assumption that leadership was exclusively male and causes Priscilla's visibility to stand out in contrast. He says she's "hidden in plain sight." I believe we've been trained to ignore the leadership of women in Scripture.

Other Women

Marg Mowczko has a list of all 29 people mentioned in Romans 16:1-16 with an analysis of each mention. The article is well worth the read, including the footnotes: https://margmowczko.com/list-of-people-in-romans-16_1-16

Here is her summary:

> *Of the twenty-nine people, ten are women. What is especially interesting, however, is that seven of the ten women are described in terms of their ministry (Phoebe, Prisca, Mary, Junia, Tryphena, Tryphosa, Persis). By comparison, only three men are described in terms of their ministry (Aquila, Andronicus, Urbanus), and two of these men are ministering alongside a female partner (Aquila with Prisca, Andronicus with Junia). These are numbers worth remembering.*
>
> *It is apparent that women were active in significant ministries in the church at Rome. It is also apparent that Paul has no problem with these women. Rather, he affirms them and their ministries. Did Paul make a point of affirming these women in an effort to ease tensions caused by some Roman Christians who had a problem with ministering women?*[45]

---

45 Marg Mowczko, "A List of the 29 People in Romans 16:1-16," Exploring the biblical theology of Christian egalitarianism, May 18, 2019, https://margmowczko.com/list-of-people-in-romans-16_1-16/.

Chloe

One example of second-century criticism by Celsus was that Christians met in homes (where women were in charge) rather than out in public (where men were in charge). The NT talks about the believers fellowshipping house to house, less out in public where more meetings normally took place.

Paul mentions somewhat offhandedly that people from the church in Chloe's house have reported quarrels to him. We would expect Paul to refer to a church by the main leader of that gathering of believers, such as "Simon's gathering." If it's a church that meets in someone's home, the man who owns the home would be referenced. Two examples of this are the men, Aristobulus and Narcissus, mentioned separately in Romans 16. Therefore, mention of Chloe herself is significant as the most likely leader of that gathering/local church, similar to the church which continues to meet in Lydia's house after Paul leaves. It is likely that both these women led the churches or at least co-led the churches with other believers.

Nympha

Paul writes in Colossians 4:15: "Give my greetings to the brothers and sisters at Laodicea, and to Nympha and the church in her house." Nympha is recognized as a house church leader, hosting a congregation in her home, whom Paul called by name and no one else. (It is doubtful that a mere host would be called by name without greeting the leader.) With there being "brothers and sisters at Laodicea" besides her home, there could have been a network in the region with her location being the most prominent.

The same thing was done to her as to Junia, masculinizing her name. The KJV still has her name masculinized (NKJV with footnote) and the pronoun "his" house but the other major versions are corrected. To read the whole story and the importance she was given while commentators thought she was a man, see the article by Marg

Mowczko titled, "Nympha: A House Church Leader in the Lycus Valley (Col. 4:15)," https://margmowczko.com/nympha-house-church-colossians-415/.

How many of us who grew up in the church know of Nympha and the church in "her" house?
Misleading Tactic #12, 17

Lois and Eunice

Paul said in 2 Timothy 1:5, "I am reminded of your sincere faith, which first lived in your grandmother Lois and in your mother Eunice and, I am persuaded, now lives in you also." Then, "Continue in what you have learned and have become convinced of, because you know those from whom you learned it, and how from infancy you have known the Holy Scriptures" (3:14-15). Some say that these women only taught Timothy as a child, as an example of how women today should only teach children. I find that a bit silly because my children wouldn't remember much of the Scriptures if we stopped teaching them at say, age twelve. They would have rote memory training but not good understanding. Paul thinks the women passed on true faith to this young man, indicating ongoing discipleship in Christianity. I imagine they also spoke with his friends and others.

We already mentioned Lydia as the only person named in Philippi. This is not an exhaustive list of the women named in the NT who could have been leaders. When the epistolic authors wrote letters, they wouldn't have just rattled off the names of anyone and everyone they knew because it would be too many to mention. It was the people to be most commended to their readers.

Did the Bible Endorse Slavery and Patriarchy?

We take mentions of slaves in the Bible into cultural context. We recognize that slavery was commonplace in that culture even though today, we would never consider slavery to be acceptable under any circumstances. So, do we say the Bible was endorsing slavery? No, we say the Bible was just recognizing that bondservant (debt payoff) slavery was happening and advising indentured servants to make the best of it to keep their testimony. As noted earlier, kidnapping and owning people was strongly condemned.

I am not equating the cruelty of slavery to the discriminatory treatment of women. There is, however, a parallel between them: failure to consistently recognize cultural context in the Bible. Women had fewer rights than men in this society, so both Jesus and the epistolary authors encouraged women to keep a subdued and respectful manner, while at the same time they permitted practices in the church and marriage that were radically countercultural without being overt enough to cause riots.

We should consider that passages about women have a cultural context and not everything described is a prescription for all time. The question should be how both Jesus and the writers of the epistles handled the realities of their day. They pushed against unjust realities while not letting them overshadow the church mission.

In Jewish law and custom, the firstborn son received a double portion of the inheritance and the remaining inheritance went to the remaining sons. Daughters could receive the inheritance only if there were no sons or the father created an exception. Primogeniture was still upheld in rabbinic law during the Second Temple period and into the first century. This is why several verses describe our spiritual inheritance as being adopted as a son (not a daughter). Only the referencing of a son's inheritance could portray the benefits of believers in Jesus with all the rights and privileges of sonship (Romans 8:15, 8:23, 9:24; Galatians 4:5, 4:6; Ephesians 1:5).Today, if a person dies without a will that specifies otherwise, the inheritance from a deceased parent goes equally to sons and daughters, so we miss the significance of female believers being told they had the spiritual rights of sonship.

Do Christians today say that only sons should receive an inheritance because the Bible endorses that? No, we recognize that was the culture of the day. Likewise, we recognize that the opportunities of women were limited in that time, and we shouldn't continue those limitations now, any more than we should endorse slavery and gender-limited inheritance because they had some mentions in the Bible without condemnation.

Interpreters fail to communicate the significance of women being included in the same spiritual inheritance of sonship. Paul was demonstrating that the patriarchy of that time was changed to equality in the present Kingdom of God.
Misleading Tactic #17

Martin Luther King, Jr. pointed out that Sunday morning at 11:00 a.m. was the most segregated hour in the country. Today, the church may say, "Women are equal in God's sight" but it continues to find ways to add, "but not functionally," and Sunday morning at 11:00 a.m. is the most sexist hour in the country, especially within most Baptist churches, the Lutheran Church – Missouri Synod, and the Presbyterian Church of America (to just name the largest non-egalitarian denominations). The SBC broke away from northern Baptists in 1845 due to what the SBC claimed was biblical support for slavery. Do they want to make another mistake in failing to recognize the Bible's support for gender equality?

A Teachable Spirit

A result of the dogma that women should not teach men is the implication that men cannot learn anything from women, or that it's shameful for men to take instruction from women. Proverbs instruct the son to learn from father and mother in at least six verses. At what point does a son suddenly become unable to learn from her? Or, at what point does it become wrong or inappropriate? I've seen churches establish an arbitrary age where boys may no longer attend a Sunday school class taught by a woman. Or homes in which the father tells the mother that the son is of the age where if he needs instruction, only the father should do it. It is disrespectful to train a son not to be teachable by his mother or adult women, and it sets him on a course to have marital difficulties. The Bible doesn't set a particular age of emancipation, and many ancient cultures expected children (includes sons) to obey parents (includes mothers) their entire lives. (Not that I agree with that, I'm just arguing there is no support for not listening to one's mother at any point in one's life.)

If a son can always learn from his mother over his entire life, why can't other men learn from mature women? Why can't a husband learn from his wife as well as a wife learn from her husband? The dogma that women should not teach men contributes to a man feeling disrespected if a woman gives any instruction, or requests that he do something, or suggests that he do something a different way. I have personally seen this sensitivity in some men, where it seems to threaten their manhood if they're asked to do something by their wife or a woman in ministry. I know that some men do not give a response (yes or no) to a request because it feels that they might be receiving direction. The wife is left to guess whether the husband will do what was requested and mind games ensue as time passes, adding to communication challenges and marital difficulty. The pressure to be completely adequate by himself is a terrible burden for a man to carry.

John Piper, *et al* have cultivated this sensitive attitude with illustrations of how no woman should ever instruct any man in any way in *Recovering Biblical Manhood and Womanhood,* a book edited by Piper and Grudem. In one example, George Knight III says that if a man asks a woman for directions, she should not say, "Turn here and then go there" because that would be instruction. She should say, "If I were going there, I would turn here and then I would go there."[46] This kind of teaching encourages men to be thin-skinned and prideful, worried about whether a female is instructing them instead of focusing on cooperation.

Another instruction Knight gives in the same chapter titled, "The New Testament Teaching on the Role Relationship of Male and Female," is that the closer a relationship, the less direct a woman's instruction should be. His example is that if a woman designs a traffic light, a man can stop at it because there is distance in the relationship, but if a married woman wants to give instruction, she must be extremely indirect to the point of not giving it at all.[47] I trust the reader can recognize that this kind of teaching leads to dysfunctionality and precludes an honest and humble relationship. It also disrespects the Holy Spirit in a believing wife. Some complementarians take this proximity rule to mean that it's all right for a man to learn from a woman by reading a book or listening to a podcast, but not in person. So, real relationships don't get the same dignity, and men might learn something from another man's wife that the husband himself can't learn. So bizarre.

Billy Graham was asked who was the greatest theologian he knew. To everyone's surprise, he said that would be his wife, that even though he was a good speaker, she had a much better grasp of the Scriptures and was a great help to him.[48] Apparently, he was teachable by her. He had a humble (godly) attitude to acknowledge that he wasn't necessarily "right" about all things theological or spiritual just because he was the man/husband and had been ordained by other men. Years

---

46 John Piper and Wayne Grudem, eds., *Recovering Biblical Manhood and Womanhood: A Response to Evangelical Feminism* (Wheaton IL: Crossway, 2021), 150..

47 Ibid, 150..

48 Anne Blue Wills, "Mama was 'a real theologian,'" Christian History Institute, Accessed September 15, 2025, https://christianhistoryinstitute.org/magazine/article/mama-was-a-real-theologian/.

later, he would say that his daughter, Anne Graham Lotz, was "the best preacher in the family."[49] Here was a man who could see what was obvious in front of his eyes, whereas others are blind to reality because of bias. I believe that humble spirit is why his ministry was so fruitful.

49 "About Anne Graham Lotz," Anne Graham Lotz, Accessed September 15, 2025, https://www.annegrahamlotz.org/about-anne-graham-lotz/about/.

Chapter 12:

WOMEN AND PROPHECY

There are three significant reasons women are approved by God to teach all people: the words and examples of Jesus, the matter-of-fact inclusions and commendations by Paul, and the existence of female prophets in both the OT and NT. In chapter 11 we saw that teaching and prophecy have similar purpose and value. Here is how the Bible describes prophecy:

- purpose is to speak to people for their strengthening, encouragement, and comfort – 1 Corinthians 14:3

- comes from a person who hears the words of God, who has knowledge from the Most High, who sees a vision from God, and whose eyes are spiritually open – Numbers 24:16

- revelation of God's plans – Amos 3:7

- performed by the outpouring of the Lord's Spirit on all who are the Lord's servants, young and old, male and female – Joel 2:28-29

- speaking for God while being carried along by the Holy Spirit – 2 Peter 1:21
- able to fathom mysteries and knowledge – 1 Corinthians 13:2
- the most desirable gift of the Spirit – 1 Corinthians 14:1
- a sign for believers – 1 Corinthians 14:22
- can bestow a spiritual gift – 1 Timothy 4:14
- gives testimony to Jesus – Revelation 19:10
- not to be treated with contempt but tested – 1 Thessalonians 5:20-21

There is nothing in all these descriptions that limits prophecy to a particular time in history or to a particular class or gender of people—on the contrary, it is described broadly.

Below are five women prophets in the OT. These mentions of female prophets are so casual and incidental, that it seems likely it was a common thing and that there were more than these five. Also, note that most were married, so having a husband neither elevated him or disqualified her.

Exodus 15:20
Then Miriam the prophet, Aaron's sister, took a timbrel in her hand, and all the women followed her, with timbrels and dancing.

Judges 4:4
Now Deborah, a prophet, the wife of Lappidoth, was leading Israel at that time.

2 Kings 22:14, 2 Chron. 34:22 (Very similar passages—King Josiah sent a delegation of important men to inquire of Huldah. It shows great respect that he didn't summon her to his presence.)

Hilkiah the priest, Ahikam, Akbor, Shaphan and Asaiah went to speak to the prophet Huldah, who was the wife of Shallum son of Tikvah, the son of Harhas, keeper of the wardrobe. She lived in Jerusalem, in the New Quarter.

Nehemiah 6:14
Remember also the prophet Noadiah and how she and the rest of the prophets have been trying to intimidate me.

Isaiah 8:3
Then I made love to the prophetess, and she conceived and gave birth to a son.

Following are mentions of women prophesying in the NT:
In Luke 2:36-38 Anna is called a prophetess, using the same Greek word that is used in the Septuagint (Greek translation of the Hebrew OT) for prophet. She is led by the Holy Spirit to speak about Jesus as Messiah. The masculine gender of the signifiers describing her audience indicates Anna prophesied to both men and women.

...to all who were looking forward to the redemption of Jerusalem.

Acts 21:8-9 mentions Philip's daughters. Philip was one of the seven Greek-speaking men who were selected to be deacons for the Greek-speaking widows in the Jerusalem church. By the end of the book of Acts, he was living in Caesarea.

Leaving the next day, we reached Caesarea and stayed at the house of Philip the evangelist, one of the Seven. He had four unmarried daughters who prophesied.

Acts 1-2 includes women believers who fulfilled the prophecy of Joel 2.

1:14 They all joined together constantly in prayer, along with the women and Mary the mother of Jesus, and with his brothers. 2:1

When the day of Pentecost came, they were all together in one place. 2:4 All of them were filled with the Holy Spirit and began to speak in other tongues as the Spirit enabled them. 2:14, 16-18 Then Peter stood up with the Eleven, raised his voice and addressed the crowd...This is what was spoken of by the prophet Joel: "In the last days, God says, I will pour out my Spirit on all people. Your sons and daughters will prophesy...even on my servants, both men and women...."

First Corinthians 11:5 has a casual mention of women prophesying in a church gathering—so casual that the topic is something else (head coverings).

But every woman who prays or prophesies with her head uncovered dishonors her head.

We saw in the last chapter that the words of other women were also included in the Holy Scriptures, so they could reasonably be classified as prophets.

Because the Bible identifies female prophets, complementarians employ three strategies against women. (I read about it in a well-known man's doctoral thesis.) The strategies are as follows: claim prophecies have ceased so those women were an exception; downgrade prophecy to lower than teaching; claim that if prophecies have not ceased, women are barred from the testing of it. For the sake of brevity, I will only curate some of the reasons why those teachings are wrong.

1. The claim that prophecies have ceased

- There is no clear teaching in the Bible that says prophecies will cease (at least, not before other things cease as well—things which have not ceased).
- Peter said at Pentecost that what people were seeing was the fulfillment of "the last days" prophesied in Joel 2:17 that God would

pour out his Spirit on all flesh. If that was the beginning of the "last days," we are now even later in the "last days." Why would anyone be forbidden to prophesy if "Christ gave" (Ephesians 16:11) those giftings back then, and we're to expect an even greater measure of them in the "last days"?

2. The claim that prophecy is not on the same level as teaching

- The aforementioned renowned preacher says prophecy is merely what people think based on Scripture, by common inspiration, not "intelligent study" in preparation and delivery of a sermon. The work of the Holy Spirit is far more expansive than formal teaching. Or else, we would have to remove John chapters 14-17 and 1 Corinthians 2:15-16 out of our Bible! This claim not only limits women, but all men who do not have a pulpit. Of course, a great amount of study in the Word can help with knowledge and wisdom, but the primary requirement for being Spirit-led is surrender to the Spirit. Every time a believer exhorts another believer by the power of the Spirit, impact happens.

- The purpose of prophecy and teaching is the same--to equip for works of service and to build up the body of Christ. (The mission of apostles, evangelists, and pastors is also the same as prophets and teachers.) Ephesians 4:11-12 says,

Christ gave the apostles, prophets, evangelists, pastors and teachers to equip His people for works of service, so that the body of Christ may be built up.

- If there is any list that ranks the gifts, it would be 1 Corinthians 12:28:

And God has placed in the church first of all apostles, second prophets, third teachers, then miracles, then gifts of healing, of helping, of guidance, and of different kinds of tongues.

Other lists also have teaching listed after prophecy and not even as high on the list as this one. Then, all of the gifts are ranked lower than having love (1 Corinthians 13). There is also extensive teaching in 1 Corinthians on the honor and value of every part (person) of the Body of Christ. So, claiming that speaking from behind a pulpit is higher than the exercise of the other gifts is a vain enterprise.

3. The claim that women are barred from evaluating prophecies

- First Corinthians 14:29 and 1 Thessalonians 5:20-21 are the only passages that describe this procedure. Paul could have specified that men make those evaluations, but he did not. Again, some translators have made it appear men were specified in 1 Corinthians 14:29 (see Chapter 10) by using masculine generics when the text is neutral.
- Those who make this claim base their reasoning on foregone conclusions about the disqualification of women that are refuted elsewhere in this book.

Prophecies today should not claim to be on par with Scripture or confidently claim "thus saith the Lord." They should have the same standard of agreement with Scripture that teaching has and be carefully weighed by other mature believers. It appears to me that a great error in restricting prophecy is happening as part of an effort to restrict women.

> *Because the Bible identifies female prophets, complementarians employ three strategies to downplay prophecy: claim it has ceased or downgrade it to lower than teaching or bar women from the testing of it.*
> Misleading Tactic #16, 17

Chapter 13:

EXTRA-BIBLICAL EVIDENCE FOR FEMALE LEADERS

Comments by early church fathers about women in ministry are mixed, similar to today. They also disagreed about what Paul meant in 1 Timothy 2:11-14 (we'll look in detail at that passage in the next chapter). Their writings were primarily intent on apologetics—defending the Christian faith from attacks from the empire and attacks from within regarding various heresies. Thus, they didn't write much history about who went where and did what, but we have the book of Acts and mentions of women in ministry by Paul.

In his book, *Tell Her Story* (2023), highly accomplished scholar Nijay Gupta connects New Testament mentions with clues from Scripture and other documents to open our eyes to the important role women played in the early church. If my reader has never heard of Damaris and Nympha, his is the next book to read. Gupta tells about his own journey from complementarian to egalitarian in his blog post, "Why I Believe in Women in Ministry," found on the website Patheos:

The following is a short sampling of evidence of female leaders in the first 300 years of the church.

During the reign of Emperor Trajan (AD 98-117) Pliny (the Younger) was a provincial governor of Bithynia, what is now modern-day Türkiye. He wrote a letter to Trajan asking what to do about the Christians, describing his persecution of them and his extensive questioning about their practices. His letter is included in the book, *Documents of the Christian Church,* and includes the following sentence:

> *I thought it the more necessary, therefore, to find out what truth there was in this by applying torture to two maidservants, who were called deaconesses.*[50]

Pliny's letter was in Latin. The word "deaconesses" was the Latin *ministrae* per Bettenson's footnote. That is the feminine plural of ministers. Pliny had leaders in custody.

One can find many more examples by searching the category, "Women in Ministry" on Mowczko's site but I will list four here:

In the following blog post, "A Female Teacher and Deacon in Antioch (AD 360s)," Marg Mowczko references Theodoret of Cyrrhus's Church History in which there is an interesting story of a brave woman. https://margmowczko.com/female-teacher-deaconess-4th-century/.

In the following blog post, "A Christian Lady Teacher in Egypt in the 300s AD," Marg Mowczko writes about SB 14 11532, a papyrus letter, possibly written in the early AD 300s. The letter seems to have been sent from an unnamed Christian woman who is a teacher, and it was to be delivered to a man named Philoxenos who was himself a teacher. https://margmowczko.com/lady-teacher-papyrus-sb-14-11532/ .

---

50 Henry Bettenson and Chris Maunder, eds. *Documents of the Christian Church* (3rd ed.) (Oxford: Oxford University Press, 1999), 4.

Mowczko cites Ute E. Eisen, who wrote Women Officeholders In Early Christianity, Epigraphical and Literary Studies. Mowczko writes about Eisen's findings:

> *Three men and three women are clearly identified in what remains of the letter. Ute Eisen observes that "The high percentage of women—relative to literary texts—is characteristic of Christian papyrus letters."*[51]

Ignatius of Antioch likely lived around AD 35–50 to approximately AD 110. He served as bishop of Antioch in Syria and is considered one of the Apostolic Fathers, meaning he had direct contact with the apostles or their immediate circle. While he does not explicitly endorse or reject women in formal leadership, his greetings and references suggest that certain women held influence, particularly in hosting and supporting house churches. For example, in his *Letter to the Smyrnaeans 13.2,* he writes, "I salute the house of Tavia, and pray that it may be confirmed in faith and love, both corporeal and spiritual."

Because the church started out as a movement mostly of women and slaves, I believe they would have continued to evangelize their own and be the primary movers and shakers at the grassroots level.

Hence, an up or down opinion regarding women in leadership from church fathers (especially those after AD 400), the Reformation leaders, the early American-era preachers, or the big-name preachers of today is, to me, irrelevant. It is important to recognize great thinkers and carry on conversations over the centuries about significant ideas applied from biblical principles (such as Augustine's Just War Theory), but because one of these great thinkers wrote something does not make it truth. They had some easily identifiable errors too.

51 Ute E. Eisen, *Women Officeholders In Early Christianity, Epigraphical and Literary Studies* (Collegeville, MN: Liturgical Press-Michael Glazier, 2000), 90.

Chapter 14:

DENOMINATIONAL POSITIONS ON WOMEN

The Slippery Slope Fallacy

A common belief is the fallacy that if a denomination ordains women, other decisions will necessarily follow which are unbiblical, especially regarding sexuality. The most important factor to any decision is belief in whether the Bible teaches the principle. It is a fallacy to assume one decision must lead to another. There are examples of both cases, where the decision to ordain women was followed by sexually liberal decisions, and at least ten significant denominations where the decision to ordain women was never followed by sexually liberal decisions, even after many decades (or over a hundred years like Quakers, Wesleyans, Salvation Army, and Nazarenes). Pentecostals were egalitarian a hundred years ago and moved less so as they became institutionalized. By my count, there are more egalitarian denominations which are not LGBTQ+ affirming than those which are affirming. Conservatives engage in scaremongering by linking egalitarianism with other progressive issues. For example, American Reformed denominations are engaged in major internal debates about social justice, distinct from concerns about gender roles in leadership.

"Men Won't Step Up" Fallacy

I've always heard that if women are allowed to lead, men won't step up. I'd like to see actual studies for that theory. For over two years, I attended a mutualist church whose elder board consisted of married couples. It's been operating for 12 years as of 2026. It's a member of a group of similar churches and seems to be a healthy church in many ways. Every so often, an elder couple speaks on Sunday morning. The men start and introduce their wives who then finish the sermon, or they present together in a conversational format. They often explain how they developed their subject matter both together and separately. It's a beautiful thing to behold such cooperation and mutual respect. Rather than men failing to step up, there is a male majority in the prayer meetings (more than I've seen in churches that forbid women to lead prayer in church services), and a male majority in the service activities that I attended.

Not only are women encouraged to publicly exercise their gifts in this church, but the lead pastor couple is blessed and encouraged by the congregation to an extent I have never seen before, and people openly encourage each other like I've never seen before. There is a spirit of gentleness and respect by both genders to each other that truly reflects the fruit of the Spirit of gentleness, rather than just the women instructed to be gentle. I've been a regular church attender all my life, and as soon as I entered this church, I sensed something unusually positive. After I learned of the elder board and saw the mutualist practices, I understood what I sensed.

I appreciate that soft complementarian churches are trying to include women more. They have women give announcements and sometimes pray or read Scripture. They invite women to give input at some meetings. That's nice, but it's token. Eve was essential to Adam. How are we fleshing that out in life and in the church?

Protestants in the USA

Today's American Protestant church denominations are divided into "Mainline" and "Evangelical." And then there are the ultra-conservative, "Fundamentalists" who mostly eschew denominations, but have some "fellowships" (networks), or they are completely independent churches. Mainline denominations tend to be more theologically and socially liberal/progressive, emphasizing ecumenism, social justice, and historical traditions. Evangelical denominations tend to be theologically and socially conservative, emphasizing the inerrancy of the Bible, evangelism, and missions. Most of the Baptist denominations land in the Moderate/Conservative range, with some being Fundamentalist/Conservative. Presbyterian denominations from mainline to most conservative would be Presbyterian Church USA (PCUSA), then Presbyterian Church in America (PCA), to Orthodox Presbyterian Church (OPC). Lutherans, Methodists, and Anglicans have some denominations in each of the Liberal/Mainline, Moderate/Mainline, Moderate/Conservative, and Conservative categories.

Here's why this is important: It used to be that only the most conservative denominations or churches restricted women, but the complementarian movement with male-only leadership has made major inroads into Moderate/Conservative evangelicalism. It's become almost as distinguished as evangelism and missions. The Danvers Statement (DS) was published in 1988 as a response to rising egalitarianism, and a marketing campaign ensued. Shortly after, many PCA leaders, T4G (Together for the Gospel), and The Gospel Coalition—publicly affirmed the DS. Although the PCA itself did not formally adopt the DS, its language began to appear everywhere: publications, seminary curricula, and parachurch networks. It shaped the tone and theological framing of pastoral statements, seminary teaching (remember the Systematic Theology textbook with EFS), and denominational debates. Similarly, the SBC did not formally adopt the DS, but they revised their statement of faith (The Baptist Faith and Message) from the 1963 version to the 2000 version that states the husband is the leader of the home and the office of pastor is limited to men. Also, top leaders affiliated with the CBMW and additional DS language showed up everywhere, including SBC seminaries, just like in the PCA. **The movement successfully turned the tide within evangelicalism.**

SBC leaders linked "complementarian" teaching to the inerrancy and authority of the Scripture. It is odd, because back during the Reformation, Baptists (originally Ana-baptists) had the following distinctives from the other Protestant reformers: separation of church and state, differences regarding communion/eucharist, egalitarianism, and believer's baptism. Yes, Baptists actually had an egalitarian heritage! (See article on my website.) Today, they would have us believe that male-only leadership is how it has always been, but they have forgotten their heritage. Today's Baptists think egalitarianism is "liberal and progressive."

It is fine if a denomination like the SBC wants to come up with an "office" like pastor and elevate it for their own purposes as the highest office in their denomination's churches—they can do whatever they want to do. However, they should not say, "The Bible says women should not be a pastor." That is misleading. Do your own experiment and ask people who attend SBC churches if the Bible forbids women being pastors, and they will all say, "Absolutely, the Bible forbids

> *Baptist leaders who know anything about their history, know that Ana-baptists were egalitarian. But today's leaders would have us believe that male-only leadership is how it has always been.*
> Misleading Tactic #17

it" because that is what they've been taught. Ask if they think female pastors is "apostasy" and see how many affirm that it is. The SBC has come up with its own definition and qualifications for one word in the Bible and is passing it off as a biblical teaching rather than what it truly is—a denominational construct. That is deceptive and destructive. If you aren't convinced that is what they are doing, here is a quote from Mike Law who authored the *SBC Law Amendment.*

> *Over a year ago, I realized that five Southern Baptist churches within a five-mile radius of my congregation had women serving as pastors, including senior pastors. When an unbeliever looks for a Southern Baptist church in my area, we want them to find a church that holds the Bible's teachings and our convention's beliefs.*[52]

Excerpt from "Article VI, The Church," Baptist Faith and Message 2000:

> *Its two scriptural offices are that of pastor/elder/overseer and deacon. While both men and women are gifted for service in the church, the office of pastor/elder/overseer is limited to men as qualified by Scripture.*[53]

The SBC confidently says there are only two offices: pastor/elder/overseer are the same office, and deacon is the other. They claim Scripture is clear that only men qualify for pastor/elder/overseer, so

---

52 Leonardo Blair, "SBC amendment to permanently ban women pastors falls short," The Christian Post, June 12, 2024, https://www.christianpost.com/news/sbc-amendment-to-permanently-ban-women-pastors-falls-short.html See also: Brandon Porter, "Mike Law says constitutional amendment meant to provide clarity," Baptist Press, September 7, 2023, https://www.baptistpress.com/resource-library/news/mike-law-says-constitutional-amendment-meant-to-provide-clarity/.

53 "Baptist Faith and Message: Article VI, The Church," *Southern Baptist Convention,* accessed August 1, 2025, https://bfm.sbc.net/bfm2000/#vi.

it appears they are fine with female deacons. (I don't believe this is widely known, and it would be interesting to see just how many SBC churches have female deacons. I suspect it is an extremely low number.) So, the spirit of Article VI is that they believe the Bible limits the highest office to men (which again, is their right to decide).

However, there are/were local churches in the SBC (such as Saddleback) which have elders as a higher office than pastors and restrict women from the higher office of elder, yet the SBC still expelled them. So, the issue is not about the spirit of the law (what they believe the Bible means--that the highest office/authority should not be held by women), it is about the letter of the (their) law, that their preferred office name is to be held sacred, regardless of what the Bible says or means. While claiming great concern about the inerrancy of the Bible, this issue is really about their own organizational law, plus they take liberties with interpreting Scripture by emphasizing one rarely mentioned "office" (pastor, a gifting, see Chapter 7) and lumping all (supposed) offices together with it except deacon.

> *The SBC claims Scriptural support for a hierarchical construct (which prefers a rare "title") instead of recognizing it as a denominational preference.*
> Misleading Tactic #16

Remember the section in Chapter 4 on legitimate and illegitimate law? Jesus described in Matthew 23 how the Pharisees broke the spirit of the law while keeping the letter of the law. Today's Pharisees not only break the spirit of God's law (that in the last days women would participate in ministry in every way), but they break the spirit of their own laws (that men should have the highest office) if it transgresses their organizationally preferred title. This whole issue regarding titles and offices is far afield from what Jesus described. No wonder Jesus basically said, "Just don't do it at all."

What would happen if local churches didn't have buildings and staff salaries to support? Would pastors have far fewer things to worry about (like platform performance and other performance, attendance, size of offerings, managing staff as the "boss," whether to confront a contentious man who gives a lot of money, etc.)? Reports suggest over two-thirds of pastors consistently feel "burnt out."

Space in this book does not allow for a deep dive into this, but I recommend Lance Ford's 2024 book, *The Atlas Factor: Shifting Leadership Onto the Shoulders of Jesus.* I also recommend The KC Underground Podcast, which is hosted by different leaders of the KC Underground network of microchurches. This is not theory in a book; this is real people living the real thing of no hierarchy. They frame things in the language of family, pointing out that Paul called Timothy "my son" in the beginning but later "my co-worker." "Elders" are those who shepherd others into becoming shepherds and elders themselves, so the multiplication of disciples is exponential.

The model explicitly affirms both complementarian and egalitarian stances, allowing for a wide range of theological convictions within the microchurch ecosystem. Women lead microchurches and disciple others. Mission stories on the website feature all types of ministry outreaches. The model emphasizes ordinary people living out the mission of Jesus, regardless of gender, age, or background.

Who Will Lead, the Church or the World?

Because the American culture today recognizes the principle of equality as a given, we miss the upending significance of Jesus and Paul stretching the limitations on women. Hence, when we read the Bible with its more restrictive culture, we take the opposite meaning from what we see. The "you have heard it said...but I say" teachings of Jesus, were, and still are, up-enders, because they go to the heart of the matter. The spiritual and practical equality of women in partnership with men in ministry and marriage also goes to the heart of the matter. The examples that contrast *the heart of God* with cultural norms should make us sit up and take notice because they are huge!

Is today's church ready to show the world God's heart, or are we going to let the world lead in this matter? The world leads poorly in this matter because it leads from an angle of equal rights rather than equal service. When Christian men show sacrificial love, respect, and partnership by sharing power with women, there is no need for women to protest for equal rights, so it pulls the rug out from under the anger and resentment of the world's women. When Christian men act authoritatively or with condescension because they don't truly believe in equality, not only is it in direct violation of Jesus's commands, but it misrepresents the heart of God and impedes the service of women.

It is ironic that the church was in contradiction with cultural norms back in the first century by having women leaders, but now the culture and the evangelical church have flipped positions. The church should have held its position and resisted thousands of years of societal pressure. The church needs to recognize that the world has finally thrown off patriarchy (for the most part), and is no longer offended by women leaders, rather, it is offended if equality for women is not acknowledged. The church needs to recognize it is hurting the cause of the gospel by continuing to restrict women without solid biblical reason.

> *In the Protestant church, 83% of women's ministry leaders are volunteers or unpaid staff and only 5% of them participate in planning alongside church staff.*

LifeWay Research conducted an excellent survey in 2023 of female Protestant churchgoers and female church leaders. They discovered that only 5% of women's ministry leaders participate in planning alongside church staff. They are not included in visionary and planning meetings with other staff members. This is possibly partly because meetings are not held when they can attend since 83% of women's ministry leaders are volunteers or unpaid staff members.[54]

Lifeway Research recommended that SBC churches have "more intentionality and investment in building the [female] leader of a ministry that likely reaches over half of a church's attendees." – Becky Loyd, Director of Lifeway Women. The report acknowledges that some of the most successfully planned and consistently attended church events are in ministry to women, yet it questions whether there are adequate attention and investment of time and finances given to women's ministry. The report explores how to train and encourage female leaders as an item of stewardship concerning their gifts and talents. It encourages churches to "Bring women's leadership into the directional, planning conversations and listen to them to gain a whole-family and a whole-church perspective."

This sounds great, but until the denomination recognizes spiritual equality and is willing to bestow equivalent titles to male and female leaders (i.e. "pastor") there will be no equality in funding, attention, and leadership voice. They are undermining themselves by creating a culture of "less than" while wondering what is wrong. Notice that the report is about ministry to women. What about the many other ministries in a church which need leadership? Women may not be allowed to lead them and if they are, they must avoid the title of "pastor" since that implies spiritual

> *Churches call women leaders "Coordinators" or "Directors" as if it is an administrative job, but then want them to care for people like a pastor –providing mixed messaging.*

54 "State of Ministry to Women," LifeWay Research, Accessed September 15, 2025, https://research.lifeway.com/state-of-ministry-to-women/.

leadership. Do we not want women to lead others as a shepherd? Do we really want them to be "Directors," approaching it like a secular admin job (but then telling them to be spiritual about it—a mixed message)?

While talking about helping women feel valued, they are fostering concerns about whether a woman's voice is inappropriately filling a meeting room or having too much influence on a decision. They are withholding a spiritual gifting title that acknowledges shepherding. They are leaving leader and volunteer positions unfilled because there are males who are uncomfortable being led by a woman due to the church's teaching. Is this always obvious? No, it's rarely said out loud. It's the elephant in the church building that no one will name. It's the boat that needs to be rocked so some baggage can fall out.

Right now, the SBC and many other denominations are imbalanced. Women need to see and hear from women, but they cannot on Sunday morning in these churches, and seekers don't usually come to weekday meetings—they start by coming on Sundays.

It might seem that I'm coming down hard on the SBC, but they are the largest Protestant denomination in the USA and nearly one in five seminarians in the USA attends one of the six SBC seminaries. Some other Baptist denominations and many baptistic non-denomination "Bible" churches are similar to the SBC in gender practices and if they are all counted together, Baptists are the second largest Protestant denomination worldwide (after Pentecostals), so have significant influence. (There are six smaller Baptist denominations that are egalitarian and four that are mixed.)

Chapter 15:

ABUSE-OF-POWER CRISIS IN THE CHURCH

Citations are not provided for many examples in this section because documentation is readily found online. I struggled with whether to include names and other specifics in this chapter and decided to do so for the following reasons: The stories don't seem real without names and specific details. I believe the details are necessary for readers to be rightfully shocked and indignant, especially about those who are still leading ministries or led them for decades while abusing others. I believe the details are necessary for readers to even begin to grasp the broad range of abuses. First Timothy 5:19-20 says,

> *Do not entertain an accusation against an elder unless it is brought by two or three witnesses. But those elders who are sinning you are to reprove before everyone, so that the others may take warning.*

Everything I write about has been "brought" by multiple witnesses and the sin needs to be exposed to "everyone" so others may think twice before doing the same things. Ephesians 5:11 says to expose the deeds of darkness so we can grow in wisdom and understand God's will.

Have nothing to do with the fruitless deeds of darkness, but rather expose them.

What is Abuse of Power?

I believe God is at work to purify the American church of the sins of abusive leadership. Some would say there is a rash of sex scandals, but those revelations are just one manifestation of abuse of power. Sex scandals cross a line where men get fired, but a line that has been danced upon with rare consequences is non-sexual abuse of power. This is where spiritual leaders use influence and authority to intimidate, bully, manipulate, shame, use, and control others for personal gain (i.e. power of position, financial gain, or narcissistic gratification). I believe that patriarchal theology has given perpetrators an excuse and a smoke screen to hide behind until their actions become so egregious they must be called out. Until then, a lot of low-level abuse happens under the guise of "biblical authority" or because church leaders don't want to lose a pastor who seems essential to the church's branding.

Where is it?

Abuse-of-power corruption has infected major denominations, independent and nondenominational churches; megachurches, mid-size, and small churches; mainline, evangelical, charismatic, Pentecostal, Baptist, liberal, and conservative churches; and even parachurch organizations. It's like a disease spreading throughout the body of Christ. If anyone doesn't believe the church is scandal-ridden, check out the litany of verified news reports on ChurchLeaders.com and the Roys Report at JulieRoys.com. There were always big revelations of scandals in the 80s, 90s and 2000s, but nothing like the avalanche of revelations since 2018.

Is it new?

Is there a new level of corruption in these times, or is there just a new level of exposure? I believe it's the latter. In decades past, women didn't have the means or courage to speak up because they had so few resources and little ability to support themselves financially or emotionally. I believe that the 2017 secular #MeToo movement gave courage to women who had been abused by religious authorities, so the #ChurchToo movement began. Then others began to connect the dots between abuse of power in sex scandals to the abuse of power in broader terms.

How is abuse being exposed?

The seismic exposure of corruption seemed to start in January of 2018 by whistleblowers at Moody Bible Institute who then also exposed James MacDonald at Chicago's Harvest Bible Chapel and eventually started The Roys Report Newsletter and Podcast. With social media, the ease of podcasting, and more time to launch podcasts in 2020 when people were stuck at home, there's been an explosion of programs talking about abusive behavior everywhere from Christian colleges, parachurch organizations, particular movements or denominations, and stories of pastors and untrained church staff who gave destructive "biblical counseling."

In addition to The Roys Report, there are countless podcasts focused on various aspects of abuse within the church. The Preacher Boys Podcast was started in 2020 by Eric Skwarczynski who noticed expensive shoes on big-name preachers. The podcast quickly amassed over three million downloads. Preacher Boys and Leaving Eden Podcast with Sadie Carpenter specifically call out abuse by Independent Fundamental Baptists (IFB). Their podcasts highlight the fact this crisis is not new, because they have copious adult testimonials from the 1970s through the present. The Untangled Faith Podcast was started by someone who had a front row seat to bullying behavior in a Christian organization and aims to help others who are disillusioned to hold on to their faith. Heaven Bent Podcast exposes failures in the Pentecostal and Charismatic world. Bodies Behind the Bus Podcast focuses on spiritual abuse survivors, particularly those affected by the Acts 29 network. The Flying Free Podcast was launched by Natalie Hoffman who was excommunicated from John Piper's church, Bethlehem Baptist, because some elders thought she should reconcile with her abusive husband since they thought he was repentant, even though she could see that he wasn't. This podcast expanded into a website and support groups for women. Church Disrupted Podcast, produced by the Spiritual Abuse Institute, features Pastor Jeff Cochran who critiques sermons containing abusive misapplication of Scripture. He did two episodes in 2025 about the Association of Related Church's sham church governance that claims accountability but runs everything in a circle back to one power center. These are just a sampling of the podcasts on the religious abuse topic.

There are also websites such as LeavingtheNetwork.org dedicated to churches leaving a group/fellowship/network that has shown itself to exercise abuse of power, and Facebook has numerous pages for people leaving various ministries, such as Stories of the Survivors of the Harvest.

A 19-episode podcast, The Rise and Fall of Mars Hill, funded by Christianity Today, took a deep dive into the church-culture catastrophe of Mark Driscoll and the Acts 29 church-planting organization (of which he was co-founder). Acts 29 did tell Driscoll to leave and get help, and they did some hard work to clean up their own act. To their credit, they (and President Matt Chandler) even handled an indiscretion by Chandler well. The organization seems to be doing better, although there are still some voices saying the reforms are only skin deep. Time will tell.

Another church planting organization which helps churches "launch large" with slick marketing, professional worship, and quality childcare, is the Association of Related Churches (ARC). It has a track record of covering up abuse and quickly "restoring" abusers, some in as little as six weeks, in spite of multiple offenses. Robert Morris, disgraced pastor of Gateway Church in Dallas metro-plex, was an "overseer" within ARC, and Gateway was one of the first churches to platform Driscoll after his fall with Mars Hill. Pastor Chris Hodges, a co-founder of ARC and senior pastor at Church of the Highlands, mentioned in 2021 at their Gather conference that he and the ARC executive director were involved in about 20 cases of pastoral moral failures or restorations at the time (most of these documented on The Roys Report). Hodges emphasized that restoring pastors was something he wanted to be known for, even though he preferred preventing moral failures rather than addressing them after the fact. Isn't something wrong when shepherds who betray the flock get to go back to shepherding? Why are church standards lower than, say, banks or pharmacies which don't allow those who broke trust to ever again work in the industry?

Several online and social media programs turned into conference events with people who are calling out spiritual abuse or trying to help people understand it, heal from it, and prevent it. Some podcast hosts lost their faith (including some listed above), but most seem to work at helping people retain their core faith while sorting out what was unbiblical about the behavior of offending Christians. JulieRoys.com professes the purpose of purifying the church. It has expanded beyond reporting on church scandals to providing resources for churches seeking transparency, accountability, and reform. While its primary focus remains on investigative journalism, the platform also holds discussions on best practices for church governance, financial integrity, and abuse prevention. They also hold an annual conference for abuse survivors.

Some offenders exposed for abuse of power without sex scandal were leaders at Moody Bible Institute and Harvest Bible Church in Chicago where James MacDonald slandered the primary voices in outing him (including calling Julie Roys a "gossip slut") as a means of intimidation. Some did their best to hide and downplay the guilt of abusers. Others said that anyone interested in such reports is "engaging in failure porn." As punishment for daring to call them out, abusers systematically accuse their victims of slander and false accusations and attempt to ruin their lives and reputations or at least cause them considerable distress (financial or otherwise). Often church members (even deacons and elders) just get the boot when they bring concerning evidence forward. Revelations are frequently attributed to attacks from Satan.

ChurchReformInitiative.org has produced shocking documentaries (many witnesses) of abuses of power by names that would surprise my readers. On sites like ChurchLeaders.com, MinistryWatch.com, and TrinityFi.org one can find:

- takeovers of large churches by stealthy document changes
- church leaders who wouldn't fire or retire a lead pastor even after one or more third party investigations concluded abusive behavior
- high-profile pastors who are so entitled that after damaging their churches, they demand exorbitant retirement packages
- big-name speakers compensating each other with tens of thousands of dollars per speaking engagement at each other's churches without disclosing the income to their congregations (because it's "personal income") effectively fleecing the flock for their own profit

- church pastors on each other's boards, protecting each other from scrutiny and accountability by people who actually work with them

Examples of How Patriarchy Plays a Role

An example of how patriarchy plays a role in the wider picture of abuse of power is the character of Mark Driscoll. He berated and goaded the men in his church to be dominant in their homes. He paraded as a macho man with strong language, gaining a cult-like following. He abused staff and members alike. This scenario demonstrated that when men in a congregation are taught to be spiritual abusers, they are being groomed to be spiritually abused themselves. If their wives are not to question their behavior, then they are not comfortable questioning the behavior of their macho leader. Many men have testified that they were left devastated by Driscoll's influence. When Driscoll's megachurch (Mars Hill) in Portland came crashing down in 2014, he left and eventually started a new megachurch in Arizona where he is currently repeating the abusive pattern. People leave the church and chronicle jaw-dropping stories of bullying. In spite of this, other pastors and radio and podcast personalities continue to give him a platform. His social media content seems powerful and often on point, but unless people check into his past, they don't realize his insidious techniques.

Another example of patriarchy leading to abuse of power is the ministries of the late, well-known Pastor John MacArthur (Grace Community Church in Sun Valley, CA and The Master's University and Seminary). MacArthur saw feminism behind every bush, seemingly as the evil behind every evil, calling it out at every opportunity and even sometimes without opportunity (no context or reason). To be fair, some feminists believe patriarchy to be the underlying evil of all evils—and we call them "radical." God did include male dominating behavior in the top three griefs when he informed Eve what she would suffer, so I believe God sees the imbalance correctly.

MacArthur created a firestorm with his "go home" comment about Beth Moore in 2019 and follow-up rant about how women just want the ultimate power position of lead pastor (a revealing perspective on pastoring). He purged his organizations of any female leadership, down to the final firing of a librarian because she had two males under her. The sexism was so obvious that she won a wrongful dismissal lawsuit.

MacArthur is an example of using the word "feminism" to shame egalitarians, mutualists, or women who would dare stand at a pulpit even at the invitation of a church's pastor and elders, even to stand alongside her husband. In 2023, MacArthur told his seminarians not to speak at conferences which allow women speakers. His own annual (since 1980) Shepherd's Conference does not allow female attendees because according to the website, "it is designed for pastors, elders and church leaders." Notably, the Master's University and Seminary were placed on probation by their accrediting commission in 2018 for numerous ethical violations including intimidation of whistleblowers. Then, the University and Seminary pre-emptively withdrew from the Council for Christian Colleges and Universities (CCCU). They were so busy policing women who want to serve God that they forgot to police themselves.

Ultra-conservative, cult-like organizations such as the Institute in Basic Life Principles (IBLP) have shown themselves to be all about abuse of authority wrapped up in patriarchy. My family lived in a Chicago suburb and my pastor father took us to the IBLP conferences where we heard days-long teaching on "principles of authority," not teaching on Jesus. Of course, authority of husbands was second on the list after pastors. I'm sure plenty of well-intentioned men used the teaching to try to become better husbands and fathers. However, the teaching is attractive to men who relish the authority that comes with the titles of "pastor" and "head of home."

In our home, every IBLP event we attended was followed by authoritarian tyranny. It is not surprising to me that the founder (Bill Gothard) was grooming girls and abusing young people at campuses and mission trips (i.e. locking them up in solitary confinement for minor infractions). Hundreds of thousands of families have attended IBLP conferences. Although I'm sure many children stayed in the faith, there are countless chronicles of those children losing faith and becoming "exvangelicals." I struggled myself, trying to understand how supposed Holy Spirit indwelling could be a cover for tyranny.

The amount of damage from just this one organization is incomprehensible. Shockingly, as of this writing, the IBLP is still operating in spite of several lawsuits and negative publicity from the Prime docuseries *Shiny Happy People: Dugger Family Secrets*. Between the statute of limitations and the government not being able to rule on religious teaching, it seems there will be no accountability.

The alleged debauchery and serial sexual abuse by David Hyles and coverup by leaders at First Baptist Church of Hammond, Indiana, and Hyles Anderson College, happened in the 70s when my family had some affiliations, but wasn't exposed until 2020! A class action suit failed due to the statute of limitations so Hyles still leads a ministry. The church and college have always had rigid patriarchal theology. Thousands of other churches were styled (mostly by graduates) after the authoritarian Jack Hyles, Sr. and the manuals produced by Jack and David. Again, the influence is astronomical. Unrepentant himself, David Hyles's "Restoration" ministry for fallen pastors is accused of minimizing harm, failing to acknowledge victims, and recycling disqualified leaders back into ministry without transparency or accountability.

Patriarchy contributes to these atrocities by fostering a sense of male entitlement supposedly established by God himself. The wreckage left in its wake isn't measurable by news stories.

"Leadership" Power and Cover-ups

The Global Leadership Summit (GLS) (formerly Willow Creek Association), hosted by Willow Creek Community Church northwest of Chicago, began in 1995 to equip church leaders with practical tools for ministry and leadership. The church had become famous for its "Seeker Church" growth model. Founded by Bill Hybels and the church leadership team, the GLS, for ten years now, has been drawing over 250,000 participants annually across hundreds of host sites in more than 100 countries, making it one of the largest leadership training events in the world. In 2018 and 2019, at least ten women (including Hybel's secretary) came forward with credible allegations that Hybels had sexually harassed or abused them. He resigned but never apologized, both he and other leaders calling the women liars and colluders. Eventually the entire elder board and two other pastors resigned due to grossly mishandling the situation.

The GLS events and the authors that frequented its stage have had a mantra of "leadership" and how everything rides on it for church growth. The GLS was called "the best business summit there is" even for non-Christians. International business leaders speak at it. Pastors have gobbled up everything offered for three decades. There probably isn't a traditional pastor in the USA without a book peddled at the GLS. The influence on today's churches is incalculable. Of course, it's not all bad, but there's a systemic rot in the "leadership" model. Once in a while "servant" is added to the front of the word "leadership" but it's still not what Jesus taught.

James MacDonald (Harvest Bible Chapel, a megachurch in Chicago), Mike Pilavachi (co-founder of Soul Survivor with Matt Redman who has given extensive testimony), and several Hillsong pastors are other examples of powerful leaders who allegedly engaged in psychological, sexual, financial, and spiritual abuse of staff for many years while others covered for them.

Severe disappointment and disillusionment resulted as highly respected leaders such as Ravi Zacharias (apologetics evangelist), Reggie Joiner (Orange curriculum founder), Mike Bickle (International House of Prayer founder), Johnny Hunt (two-term Southern Baptist Convention president), Paul Pressler ("engineer" of the SBC Conservative Resurgence) were just a few of the high-profile leaders exposed as sexual predators. Their organizations protected them at first, refusing to allow independent investigations. Then-president of the SBC Southeastern Seminary, Paige Patterson, said "I want to break her down and destroy her" about a woman who asked for her campus sexual attacker to be held accountable, eventually leading to Patterson's firing in 2018. It took extreme courage and perseverance by many victims for the truth to come out in these and other cases. Some victims were too naive to view themselves as victims at first. They didn't understand the psychological dynamics of a power differential or predatory leaders who excel in grooming, so considered themselves equally at fault for an "affair."

Other high-profile churches, such as Highpoint megachurch in Memphis, mishandled the revelation of a pastoral assault, and Sovereign Grace Churches have been in trouble for failing to respond to sex abuses. Some big-name leaders were demoted in 2025 due to knowing for decades that other big-name leaders were guilty of sexual assault and doing nothing. It seems as if there's another pastor of some rank (senior, associate, youth, or music) charged with a crime most days of every week. (See Julieroys.com.) Statistical multipliers of 10 to 30 times higher are commonly used in public health, fraud detection, and abuse research to estimate true prevalence that goes underreported. I intentionally included some older scandals in this chapter's relatively brief listings because I believe it's always been this bad, at least during my lifetime. Social media and other alternative platforms have vastly improved the ability to spread information, women (and some men) are gaining the education and courage to enable them to speak up and I believe God is using these factors to clean house.

A disturbing statistic from the Barna Research Group indicates that 57% of pastors and 64% of youth pastors self-disclose as struggling with porn either currently or in the past.[55] The answer to this problem has been to direct men to books like *Every Man's Battle.* (See the problems with this book and how it contributes to wrong ways for men to view women: https://www.wildernesstowild.com/blog/does-every-mans-battle-enable-abuse.) Without getting sidetracked on the porn issue, it should at least be acknowledged that porn objectifies women rather than seeing them as sisters in Christ with important spiritual contributions. I believe that religious teachings that women can't be trusted as leaders or with God's Word, and that men deserve respect regardless of their behavior because God has given them a superior position, contribute to the low view and objectification of women.

New Systems for Accountability

Praise God, the results of all this exposure have been new developments for accountability:

- There are new state "clergy abuse laws" in order to prevent clergy from using their influence to victimize other adults and then hide behind "consensual." More states need to pass these laws.

- There are a few new state laws to extend the statute of limitations for child abusers and those who protected them. It's imperative that other states follow suit.

55 Sam Louie, "Pastors and Porn," Psychology Today, January 30, 2020, https://www.psychologytoday.com/us/blog/minority-report/202001/pastors-and-porn.

- The CCCU stepped up investigations of abuse of power and suspended the membership of offending colleges.

- There is new pressure for ministries to use genuine, third-party investigators to look into what happened instead of using law firms that are primarily interested in protecting the institution over protecting victims. Examples of good investigators are GRACE (Godly Response to Abuse in the Christian Environment) and Guidepost Solutions.

- There are new media platforms which publicly expose serious offenses, not only primary offenders, but those who supported and protected offenders. This is biblical (1 Timothy 5:20).

- There are new advocacy groups and resources to support survivors and help them speak out. For example, there is a movement to make Non-Disclosure Agreements (NDAs) illegal as a means to keep survivors quiet. Some advocates are starting with at least making NDAs illegal for minors in their state; Texas and Missouri passed Trey's Law in 2025, but again, more states need to follow suit.

- There are advocacy groups and resources to help give survivors the therapy they need to recognize and heal from what happened to them. This includes support for survivors during the initial pushback attempt to destroy their reputation in order to protect the reputation of an institution.

- There are new organizations and resources to help churches and ministries prevent abuse. Evangelical Council for Abuse Prevention (ECAP) is an example, as well as the book *Safe Church* by Dr. Andrew Bauman, and the Safe Church Pledge by the Spiritual Abuse Institute and Jeff Cochran.

Change Is in the Air

In short, THE GIG IS UP, even though word hasn't reached everyone and it will take many more years to dismantle the system that is breeding abusers. It is a messy process, but I believe God is using it to purify the church. Historically, it was felt that the church needs to keep its dirty laundry hidden or people will not come to Christ. Victims have been told that it will hurt the name of Jesus and literally send people to hell if they make it public that a "man of God" is a hypocrite, and they have been told they are in sin if they "touch the Lord's anointed." Now people are recognizing that the church needs to be purified because people can smell the stench from a mile away. Here are some factors contributing to change.

- Millennials and Gen Z are less impressed by celebrity preachers. They appreciate authenticity and are less enamored than previous generations with a preacher who struts around a platform, even if dressed down in jeans and cool shoes. People are beginning to see the pitfalls of megachurches and celebrity pastors. Millennials and Gen Z are educated about narcissism and can spot it more easily. Gen Z is experiencing revival through avenues outside organized, denominational church walls. They are running with para-church organizations such as TPUSA and UniteUsMovement.com. When groups like the latter plan a revival at a college campus in a city, sadly, they don't get much cooperation from area churches because churches want their name on things they are involved in. So, churches just make themselves irrelevant to Gen Z.

- Success in building a big crowd is no longer the instant pass for an entitlement attitude. Well, unless there is major support from an organization which knows what is needed to "launch big" so sets up an insulating structure. However, some of these organizations (i.e.

Acts 29, ARC, Upper Room, and ACTS[56]) are beginning to be held accountable for who they platform and support and for not having accountability structures in place for individual churches. (This accountability can't happen without investigative reporters.)

- Abusers are being disqualified. There's some good news/bad news about this one. A Lifeway Research (division of LifeWay Christian Resources, publishing arm of the SBC) survey found that 83% of Protestant pastors believe that sexual abuse of a minor should permanently disqualify a pastor from ministry, and 74% believe that sexual abuse of an adult should permanently disqualify a pastor.[57] Rather than feeling relief that "most" pastors believe that offending pastors should permanently step down, I feel the emphasis should be flipped and there should be horror that almost one in five pastors do not understand the gross perversion and betrayal involved in molesting a child, and over one in four do not understand the gross betrayal in taking sexual advantage of an adult. There is a huge difference in restoring someone to fellowship and restoring them to a position of leadership and trust. People who don't understand such a grievous trespass of trust don't deserve trust themselves. There is work to be done until 100% of pastors believe in permanent disqualification. I appreciate that Lifeway did the survey and is bringing attention to the issue.

A huge factor in breaking all this open was the late brave Jennifer Lyell who exposed gross sexual abuse by her SBC Lifeway publishing mentor and SBC seminary professor. The abuse was exponentially

56 Antioch Center for Training and Sending (ACTS), a training center for church planters based in Colorado Springs. julieroys.com/denver-pastor-with-ties-to-ihopkc-accused-of-bullying-spiritual abuse/?mc_cid=3a65e3fe9a&mc_eid=b3e198f0a9

57 Aaron Earls, "Most Pastors Say Sexually Abusive Ministers Should Step Down Permanently," LifeWay Research, June 22, 2021, https://research.lifeway.com/2021/06/22/most-pastors-say-sexually-abusive-ministers-should-step-down-permanently/.

more painful because of how she was treated by the institutions that should have protected her.

The Lifeway survey might have been paving the way for an SBC 2024 conference resolution that any sexual abuse should result in permanent withdrawal from public ministry. This was a great move (though long overdue) and seems only to have happened because SBC churches were still platforming disgraced former SBC president, Johnny Hunt, to the convention's embarrassment. Even secular entities are recognizing what constitutes abuse of parishioners by clergy; sexual involvement is not an "affair" because of the power and influence differential.

(Hunt sued the SBC and the independent investigator hired by the SBC, Guidepost Solutions, for finding that he acted inappropriately. Two others who were found to have committed sexual abuse (including Lyell's abuser) also sued the SBC for disclosing their conduct after they took jobs in other ministries. The suits cost the SBC millions of dollars and I believe it effectively frightened them regarding exposing more predators. This fear led to siding (via amicus brief) with those who don't want accountability for the people who fail to report abuse. In 2023, four major SBC entities sided against a Kentucky victim's attempt to gain retroactive accountability for anyone who knew but didn't report the abuse of a child. Then-SBC President Barber apologized when the amicus brief was reported in the news, but there was no remedial action taken and Plaintiff Killary lost her case. https://www.christianitytoday.com/2023/10/southern-baptist-betrayal-amicus-brief-kentucky-abuse/)

- There is more recognition of sexism in the church. Founder & Director of the Christian Counseling Center: For Sexual Health & Trauma (CCC), Dr. Andrew J. Bauman, is a therapist with a Doctorate from Northeastern University. His dissertation was a study of the impact of sexism and abuse on women in the Protestant

Church. Andrew is the author of seven books, and his newest book is titled *Safe Church: How to Guard Against Sexism & Abuse in Christian Communities* (2025). Bauman's research found that 82% of women say sexism shaped their church experience, and 35% report sexual harassment.

Bully Pulpit: Confronting the Problem of Spiritual Abuse in the Church by Michael Kruger (2022) explores how authoritarian leadership, manipulation, and coercion can harm congregations and distort biblical teachings. Kruger argues that some churches prioritize charisma and authority over humility and servant leadership, leading to environments where abuse is tolerated or even encouraged. He provides biblical insights, case studies, and practical solutions to help churches recognize and address spiritual abuse.

- There are more people talking about the biblical basis for women leaders in the church. I don't believe that current, national, complementarian leaders will ever change their minds because they have a high personal stake in being "right," but I trust that as more of us talk about it, those leaders will eventually find their followings dwindle. Besides the biblical basis for female leaders in the church, the problems listed in this chapter are reasons that women should have access to leadership in the church and provide true complementary balance. It is "not good for man to be alone" in any area, including leadership.

- The church attendance of women is declining faster than men, causing people to ask questions about what is happening with women instead of taking women for granted.

A Pew Research study came out in February of 2025 showing that the rate at which women are becoming less religious exceeds that of men. It reported that women are still more religious, but the gap is closing due to younger women. Generation Z is the first generation ever to have more men attending church than women. Due to this report, there is much commentary in conservative circles on "What's wrong with today's women?" Many conclude that young women are too selfish and independent, not wanting to marry, have children, and go to church.

Social media is flooded with responses to questions like "Why don't women want to get married?"—ranging from critiques of traditional gender roles to reflections on inequitable emotional labor, financial independence, indoctrination by liberal universities, and generational trauma. There are many factors, but I think the better question than "What's wrong with women that they don't want to go to church and get married?" is, "What's wrong with the church that younger women aren't attracted to it?" When historically, women tend to be more spiritually, morally, and family attuned, why are they not finding what they're looking for in church? I believe if they found the doctrinal and community depth they were looking for, they would want to be there and marry someone there. Who wants to go to church where they feel disconnected, treated as second class, or sucked into an abusive system? Yes, women have realized they can survive financially without men. I believe they still desire relationship, but now that marriage isn't required for survival, men must offer more than economic security.

For some good news, there seems to be a Gen Z Revival with those born after 1997 attending church more than any other generation. https://www.barna.com/research/young-adults-lead-resurgence-in-church-attendance/ However, even though the Barna Report says these young adults are more faithful in church attendance than older generations, they still attend barely half the time. The Barna report did not research gender difference so I'm still leaning on the Pew report and anecdotal reports, that young women are less interested in church than men. I suspect they are more involved in para-church organizations where they can lead.

I have personally sat with women of all ages who tearfully said they can't see themselves in the Bible. They see that Jesus was kind to women, but they don't see themselves in the larger book full of men. They don't hear women talked about as heroes of the faith in church. Especially for women who have been abused by men, a God who prefers men is alienating. Evangelicals who are so confident about following God's supposed hierarchy have closed their hearts to the harm done by it. A pastor told me in a personal conversation (and I have heard it preached), "God loves authority (he described hierarchy)—that is how he has chosen to work." I don't think we're reading the same Bible and I don't think these men understand God's heart (more on that in Part Four).

Dr. Scot McKnight challenges common misconceptions about deconstruction, often mislabeled as "rebellion" or "exvangelical angst." Using survey data conducted for his 2024 book, *Invisible Jesus* (co-author Tommy Preson Phillips), McKnight highlights the real reasons people begin deconstructing. These reasons include spiritual abuse, political partisanship, hypocritical leadership, injustice, silencing of women, and science-faith conflicts. I see gender-related aspects in at least three of those reasons. Just because women are exiting the church doesn't mean they have completely given up on God/Jesus, it means they have given up on organized religion.

- People are recognizing the manipulation of an insidious "Christian" system that has copied the world and doesn't look at all like Jesus. Author, pastor, and church planter Lance Ford, who's worked inside pastor training networks for decades, answers the question about the reason for rampant power abuse with a line reminiscent of Bill Clinton's first presidential campaign motto. Ford says, "It's the system, stupid." I believe there are four aspects to the system which contribute the most:

1) The system of leadership that's been imported into the church from corporate America. This system has been wholesale embraced by Christians, but there's nothing biblical about it. It's the hierarchical system which Jesus called "the way of the Gentiles." And unless we start to dismantle this godless system and replace it with a godly one, the church will continue to be plagued by scandals and spiritual abuse.

   Over decades, Ford has identified the toxic leadership models that have been imported into the church and he's sought a different path. As one who has designed unique training systems being used by networks, seminaries, and leaders throughout the world, he is speaking from a heart of love for pastors and the church. He has written several books including *The UnLeader, The Missional Quest, The Starfish and the Spirit* and *The Atlas Factor* (LanceFordbooks.com).

2) The hierarchical system of patriarchy with its shiny, new, deceptive name, "complementarianism." The problems with complementarianism are discussed throughout this book.

3) Theological constructs that teach there is a hierarchy in the Trinity and that God is sovereignly unjust. According to them, the supposed hierarchy in the Trinity shows that God loves hierarchy. Also, God created billions of people to supposedly bring glory to himself by damning them to hell without them having an opportunity to turn to him. So it is not hard to believe that this unjust God created half of humanity to be subservient to the other half while hypocritically telling humans to be just and impartial. When those who have a coherent theological construct try to offer different explanations for the proof texts used by this theology, they are shut down with slams such as, "You just don't believe the Bible."

4) Meanwhile, millions of dollars support what Skye Jethani described in 2011 as the Evangelical Industrial Complex (based on Eisenhower's warning about the Military Industrial Complex). Jethani described how, in the same way the military industrial complex would need to influence society and promote war in order to stay in business and power, the Evangelical Industrial Complex (EIC) needs to influence what happens within evangelical circles in order to stay in business. It raises billions of dollars from books, music, and conferences, primarily by choosing and placing good-looking and talented people in high-visibility positions and marketing them well. Anyone who threatens to call out these chosen are quickly maligned and sidelined. This insidious "Christian" complex is explained well by several whistleblowers in the Love Thy Neighborhood podcast episode #39 found here: https://lovethyneighborhood.org/39-where-the-gospel-meets-evangelical-industrial-complex/. A recent example (2025) is when the National Religious Broadcasters convention leadership threw lowly podcasters out of the Dallas convention for daring to expose the powerful Daystar TV Network leadership.

A patriarchal author/speaker who benefitted greatly from the EIC was John MacArthur. He was credibly accused of not writing many of the books with his name on them and of plagiarism. These are long-standing accusations (with plenty of testimony) which have not been addressed. Book publishers swept it under the rug to sell more books by having an endorsement from MacArthur. The number of books published under his name gave everything he said tremendous authoritative weight. He misspoke so much toward the end that finally, no one would publish his book on children in 2024.

Part 3 Closing Thoughts

It is reasonable to believe that first-century women were church teachers and leaders due to:

- The sheer numbers and logistics (1/3 of population—women, made up 2/3 of the church) and the secular witness that the movement was made up of women and slaves
- Churches were held in homes which were considered the woman's domain, whereas if they were led by men, they would have been held out in community buildings
- Women named by Paul with the same "co-worker," "laborer with me," and "deacon" titles as men
- The naming of women and their home churches (Chloe, Lydia, Nympha)
- Paul referring to both sexes as receiving the inheritance of sons
- Paul's commendation of a female teacher of a highly recognized male teacher
- Paul's commendation of a female teacher with her being listed before her husband whenever the context was teaching
- Paul's mention of a woman and her husband as being highly regarded among the apostles and both having spent time with him in prison
- Paul's teaching in Galatians 3:28 that God doesn't see ethnicity, social status, or gender
- Paul's list of women in Romans 16 with commendation of their ministries that exceeds the commendation of men and their ministries

- Paul's mentions of women praying and prophesying in public worship (prophecy having the same goals as teaching and a mention that prophecy is more highly regarded)
- Paul's rebuke of men trying to silence women
- Paul's gender inclusivity when telling all believers who come together to bring things such as "a teaching"
- Examples of women throughout the Bible whose teachings are recorded: Rebekah, Ruth, King Lemuel's mother, Elizabeth, Mary
- Female prophets throughout the Bible, and a judge which is the civil and spiritual leader
- Women receiving the same Holy Spirit and evidentiary speaking in tongues (that no doubt taught people) at Pentecost
- Peter's teaching that Joel's prophecy about the last days began with Pentecost (therefore we are in the last days) and Joel described the same gifts for men and women

Housecleaning and Healing Before Harvest

The authoritarian and sexist culture of religious organizations makes them breeding grounds for various kinds of spiritual abuse. This fact has been verified many times over by professionals such as Boz Tchividjian (founder of GRACE - Godly Response to Abuse in the Christian Environment), Diane Langberg (leading psychologist who specialized in trauma), Victor Vieth (previously headed the Gundersen National Child Protection Training Center) and Wade Mullen (author of *Something's Not Right)*. The prioritization of the SBC to double down on the restriction of women instead of repenting for sexual abuse and coverup of abuse is a harbinger of the denomination's eventual fall.

Some people reading the above paragraph, especially the first sentence, will feel very defensive. Here's what needs to happen for that sentence to not be true: good Christian men need to police the bad men who claim to be Christian. Not just in their own church, but nationally. When a big-name preacher gets national attention for saying that women are for making babies and sandwiches (a certain man in Idaho who also valued a "repentant" pedophile over a woman and married them), good men in his vicinity and with any platform elsewhere need to make it clear to the nation that he does not represent Christianity. When a preacher gets national attention for saying that if a woman calls the police because her husband is beating her, she is evil (founder of the New Independent Fundamental Baptists), good men in his vicinity and with any platform need to make it their mission to see him prosecuted for beating his wife and children and that everyone knows he does not represent Christianity. When a Christian leader is caught in abusive sin, good men don't let anyone "restore" him to ministry! But "good" men stay silent. Why? Respected Christian men say things like, "See those Iranian women who are willing to be beaten and raped for their faith? You (American women) should be like them" in response to protest regarding Christian brothers who misbehave.

Are good men afraid of misspeaking and getting cancelled? If they have the humility to apologize and admit they have some things to learn, misspeaking would be forgiven. But saying things like, "It was a joke" and gaslighting the listeners is not acceptable. Don't downplay it, cover it up, play power games, and protect the institution over the sheep. How about church leaders do these things to clean house before worrying about whether a woman is "preaching" the Word?

I closed Part Two with this thought: Jewish women in Pharisaic and Rabbinic circles (not the broader Jewish world) were more oppressed in the first century than in previous Israelite history. Jesus, God in the flesh, chose to arrive during this time, and his response to what was happening among his people who sincerely desired to follow God is one we should carefully study and emulate. Something parallel is happening today; conservative religious leaders are becoming more oppressive of the women in their midst. Is history repeating itself? Perhaps something big is going to happen on the redemptive timeline?

In the last few decades, the church has experienced the following attacks on women:

- The largest Protestant denomination (the SBC) brought us the "Conservative Resurgence" which has largely revealed itself to be about purging women from leadership under the guise of protecting the inerrancy of the Word.
- The homeschool movement brought us much good but also some extremes including purity culture, the courtship movement, and the stay-at-home-daughter movement (championed by figures like the late Reformed Baptist Voddie Baucham, Jr.).
- The Council for Biblical Manhood and Womanhood (CBMW) brought us complementarianism, which among other things, brought us a glut of harmful books in the 1990s and 2000s.
- Arguably the most influential individual on young pastors for over 50 years, John MacArthur was extreme in his anti-women teaching, claiming women "don't want equality…they want the power of the pulpit."[58] (Interesting revelation of his view on the pulpit).

If the reader feels the list is incomplete, I agree, but am withholding some factors that can't be adequately explored within the limits of this book.

58 Emily McFarlan Miller, "John MacArthur tells Beth Moore to 'go home,'" Religion News Service, October 21, 2019, https://religionnews.com/2019/10/21/john-macarthur-tells-beth-moore-to-go-home/.

Now, on top of the above attacks on women, rampant abuse in churches has come to light. Also, people are seeing the pitfalls of the church "growth" movement where small churches were decimated as people flocked to the megachurches that offered better entertainment, conveniences, and celebrity hierarchical or even dictatorial leadership (after the world's business model). People are lonelier than ever in spite of big churches and a thousand social media followers.

Could it be that God is about to free women to humbly lead countless microchurches but there needed to be some housecleaning first? Christ *will* purify his church, even if it means public exposure of wrongdoing whether it be moral or structural.

Chapter 15 was heavy, but be encouraged there are ways of being the church (instead of "doing church") with respect for both genders and with elder leaders that have safeguards in a group and help individuals check their heart attitude.

Rob Wegner has an amazing testimony of how God took him on a journey of spiritual renewal from a megachurch leader to microchurch pioneer. One of the first experiences that significantly moved him was seeing a humble woman in India lead several microchurches, then realizing that back home in America, he was contributing to the crippling of women leaders. Wegner explained that too many people look at charismatic, beautiful, capable leaders in our churches and say, "I couldn't do that." But people look at the woman in India and say, "I could do that." Wegner is now one of the founding leaders of the Kansas City Underground, a mission agency that supports decentralized networks of microchurches and missional leaders. He and others that lead the support aspect are very careful not to exercise authority over the microchurches. The Tampa Underground and Canvas Network microchurch networks are also intentionally both mutual (encouraging to both men and women) and non-hierarchical. (See The KC Underground Podcast.)

PART FOUR

WOMEN IN THE HOME

The three passages most frequently used to support hierarchy in the home are:

- 1 Peter 3:1-6 (wives submit to own husband and Sarah called Abraham "lord")
- Ephesians 5:22-24 and Colossians 3:18 (wives submit to own husband as to the Lord and husband is the head of the wife)
- 1 Corinthians 11:3 (the head of the woman/wife is man/husband)

In chapter 16, we will examine Jesus's prohibition of lording and exercising authority in Matthew 20, Mark 10, and John 15 and then use his words to interpret the epistolic passages. We are assuming that Peter and Paul are disciples of Jesus, not the other way around. I list the uses of "authority" and what that authority is exercised over. First Peter 3 and its instructions for wives makes its debut.

In chapter 17, I compare the Greek words for "submit" and "obey" and show where and how they are used in the epistles. Readers will encounter more translator choices that are misleading, considering Ephesians 5:22-24 and 1 Peter 3.

In chapter 18, we engage with the concept of marital "headship" in Ephesians 5 and 1 Corinthians 11. The revelation in this chapter regarding the use of the Greek word *kephalē* for "head" and the understanding of it in Paul's time is stunning in its implications for our daily Christian walk.

The chapter clears out the remaining troublesome passages by addressing head coverings in 1 Corinthians 11, the "weaker vessel" phrase in 1 Peter 3:7, and the idea of washing wives with the Word in Ephesians 5.

Chapter 19 wraps things up by identifying how the church contributes to difficulties in the home even if husbands don't intend to dominate. We consider the concept of godly resistance.

Chapter 16:

AUTHORITY ACCORDING TO JESUS

"Not so with you."

A "lord" wields authority, control, and power. When James and John tried to secure ruling positions in Jesus's kingdom, he said this (identical in Matthew 20:25-28 and Mark 10:42-45):

> *You know that those who are regarded as rulers of the Gentiles lord it over them, and their high officials exercise authority over them. Not so with you. Instead, whoever wants to become great among you must be your servant, and whoever wants to be first must be a slave of all. For even the Son of Man did not come to be served, but to serve, and to give his life as a ransom for many.*

I've often heard that "lording" is a bad attitude, so exercise authority, but don't be a jerk. But Jesus also forbids exercising authority. Before diving into what's forbidden, what is directed?

"You are my friends if. . ."

Possibly the most astounding and overlooked verse in the Bible is John 15:15. We tend to stop at verse 14, which reads:

You are my friends if you do what I command.

That verse taken alone distorts our thinking about our privileged relationship with Jesus. How would you feel if someone said to you, "You're my friend if you do what I tell you to do"? You would feel like, "Wow, that's really controlling! Doing whatever you tell me to do is not a price I'm willing to pay to be your friend!" Even Jesus, whom we love, revere, and are greatly indebted to, would be displaying a very authoritarian attitude if the passage stopped with verse 14. Even though he, as our creator and lord of the universe, has every right to be authoritarian, labeling that statement as "friendship" does not make sense. When we hear that verse quoted by itself, it should rub us the wrong way. It's a real shame that verse 14 was separated from verse 15 which begins to give the context:

I no longer call you servants, because a servant does not know his master's business. Instead, I have called you friends, for everything that I learned from my Father I have made known to you.

So, actually, this is not "If you want to be my friend, just do what I say," it's "I'm letting you partner with me in this business, letting you in on the big plan, so now, you get to do as I say because you understand the business plan and get to execute the plan with me." Big difference!

Verse 16 goes on to basically say we get full access to the credit card and the management part of the plan, so we are true partners, not just privy to what's happening.

You did not choose me, but I chose you and appointed you so that you might go and bear fruit—fruit that will last—and so that whatever you ask in my name the Father will give you.

What is the command he wants us to obey?

Jesus then gives the important command which refers back to verse 14 when he said "You are my friend if you do as I command":

This is my command: love each other.

So, we are his friends if we love our co-workers in this business. It's not, "You're my friend if you serve ME." If verse 14 is taken by itself, all kinds of commands from a "lord" come to mind, but not friendship and love for our co-workers in this Kingdom of Heaven business.

Many times, I have heard verse 14 quoted by itself with the application that we need to be following all the commands of the NT if we think we are real Christians. Although it is true that if we are genuine Christians, we will want to learn and obey all that God commands, *that is not the context of John chapter 15, and especially not verse 14.* The context is Jesus saying that we are his true friends if we learn his business, join his mission, use the authority of Jesus to make Kingdom requests of the Father, and most importantly, love our co-workers. (Remember, "co-laborer" was Paul's favorite title for his fellow ministers.)

No human could make a blanket statement to another, "If you love me, you'll do as I say" because every human would abuse that privilege. The Lord of the universe has every right to boss us like a lord, but instead, he raises our status up to friend and business partner! He says we can know what God is up to, we can make requests and direct affairs with his authority, and we can claim his promises. Let that sink in for a minute.

Jesus's command in this passage was to serve him by loving *others.* He is not benefitting from being our lord—our fellow believers are benefitting. That is a huge difference from someone who is receiving benefit by acting authoritarian. If Jesus brings us up in status and position like this passage describes, how much more should we bring our fellow believers up to mutual status?

> "You are my friends if you do as I command" has been taken out of context as if God is exercising authoritarianism. The command is to love others.
> Misleading Tactic #16

(As a side note, I want to make the point here that we evangelicals too often take one verse in isolation, like verse 14, and run with it, quoting it all by itself over and over until it has a life and meaning of its own outside of context. Those uninspired verse, paragraph, and chapter divisions often hinder us from understanding things in context and then we exacerbate the problem with isolated quotations. I have decided to be more careful about that.)

A Friend Has More Responsibility Than a Servant

I have never balked at the word "servant" when it comes to serving Jesus. It is a privilege to be his servant. (It's harder to serve others!) But the more I think about the difference between "servant" and "friend," the more I realize that there is an even higher responsibility for me as his friend. Here's why:

If I have a master (say, my employer), when I have fulfilled my duties, I am finished. I go home and that master has nothing to say about how I spend the rest of my time that day. But if my friend has a problem, it doesn't matter what time of the day or night, I don't just feel obligated, I desire to rush to help. When I talk with my employer, I try to understand what is required of me so I can please this "lord" to whom I have indentured myself for an economic transaction. I have a sense of loyalty, but there's a limit.

However, when I talk with a friend, I make much more effort to understand this person because I want to know this friend so well that I can deeply relate and minister to them in a meaningful way. I am actively, voluntarily seeking to perform a deep, relational, loyal, committed service. There is a great difference between duty and friendship—that was Jesus's point.

Jesus Forbade Exercising Authority over Each Other

We know it's wrong to have a "lording" attitude, but did you know that after James and John asked for seats on Jesus's right and left in the kingdom, Jesus not only forbade "lording," but also forbade "exercising authority?"

> *You know that those who are regarded as rulers of the Gentiles lord it over them, and their high officials exercise authority over them. Not so with you. Instead, whoever wants to become great among you must be your servant, and whoever wants to be first must be a slave of all. For even the Son of Man did not come to be served, but to serve, and to give his life as a ransom for many. (Mark 10:42-45, emphasis mine)*

As stated, Jesus wanted things to be different in his kingdom than in the world. Some say that his word for exercising authority, *katakurieuo* (G2634), is harsh because it includes the preposition "over," thus, we should exercise authority, just don't be harsh about it. The only place in the epistles where this word is used is in 1 Peter 5:3 where it is forbidden again. Therefore, I set out to find when the exercise of authority is permissible in God's kingdom.

Exousia (and its closely related words) is a normal Greek word for "authority" (with nuanced meaning sometimes of power or rights). We discussed this word (Chapter 9 related to 1 Timothy 2) as meaning a normal exercise of authority in contrast to the *authentein* which Paul forbade of a woman in Ephesus.

A concordance search through the NT for *exousia* finds it around 110 times (depending on whether you count the same word twice in one verse). I grouped them into categories of who had authority and for what.

—Most mentions were about Jesus, that he taught with authority, has the authority to forgive sins, has authority to cast people into hell, has authority over demons, sickness and disease, nature, worldly authorities both visible and invisible, and all of mankind—in short, Jesus has authority over everyone, everything, spiritual and material, everywhere, for all time.

—The second most mentions were that Jesus gave authority to his disciples in the following areas:

- Authority over the physical world, sickness and disease
- Authority over all the power of the spiritual enemy: seen throughout the Gospels, Ephesians chapters 3 and 6, and all the "in Christ" phrases
- Authority over the physical world's authority structure at some point in the future per the parable in Luke 19:17 and Revelation 2:26
- Delegated authority from Jesus for making disciples (In Matthew 28:29 Jesus said all authority was given to him; therefore, all his disciples should go and make disciples, baptize them and teach them.)
- Authority over self with the following diverse examples:
    - John 1:12 "Yet to all who did receive him, to those who believed in his name, he gave the right [power or authority] to become children of God."
    - Acts 5:4 The personal property was under the power or authority of Annanias and Saphira before they sold it and lied about it.
    - 1 Corinthians 7:37 A man has power over his own self will and can choose whether to control his passions or to marry.
    - 1 Corinthians chapters 8 and 9, Paul mentions that apostles have human rights or authority to have food and drink, right to marry a believer, and right to be paid for ministry work.

- 1 Corinthians 11:10 the woman has authority over her own head.
- 1 Corinthians 7:4 "The wife does not have authority (*exousiazō*) over her own body, but yields it to her husband. In the same way, the husband does not have authority (*exousiazō*) over his own body, but yields it to his wife." (This doesn't fit neatly under "Authority over self" but is mutual with one-flesh partner.)
- 1 Corinthians 6:12 (context is addiction to selfish living) All things are lawful unto me, but all things are not expedient: all things are lawful for me, but I will not be brought under the power (*exousiazō*) of any.

—There are several mentions of secular human authorities such as the following:

• The Roman centurion mentions his military/political authority.

• Various mentions of religious and civil authorities in the synagogue, magistrates, etc.

• Mentions of secular governmental authority such as in Romans 13 and 1 Peter 2.

—There are a few mentions of beings of authority in the spiritual realm:

• Ephesians 2:2 refers to the prince of the authority of the air.

• Ephesians 3:10 [God's] intent was that now, through the church, the manifold wisdom of God should be made known to the rulers and authorities in the heavenly realms.

• Ephesians 6:12 "For our struggle is not against flesh and blood, but against the rulers, against the authorities, against the powers of this dark world and against the spiritual forces of evil in the heavenly realms."

> *Interpreters have taught that it is wrong to have a lording attitude instead of teaching that it is wrong to be a lord or to exercise authority over others in the Kingdom of God.*
> Misleading Tactic #16

NOTABLY ABSENT is any mention of authority as it relates to men over women, husbands over wives, or even church leaders over church members. There are only two mentions of authority regarding church leaders—the authority to build up but not to tear down:

> *So even if I boast somewhat freely about the authority the Lord gave us for building you up rather than tearing you down, I will not be ashamed of it. (2 Corinthians 10:8)*

> *We are glad whenever we are weak but you are strong; and our prayer is that you may be fully restored. This is why I write these things when I am absent, that when I come I may not have to be harsh in my use of authority—the authority the Lord gave me for building you up, not for tearing you down. (2 Corinthians 13:9-10)*

So, if the only mentions of church leader authority have to do with building up, why is it that exercising authority (often disguised as "leadership") is a favorite topic in Christendom, especially when Jesus specifically forbids it? I believe the Bible sees spiritual leadership or authority not as a "role" or position, but as an opportunity for caretaking and serving. If that is done well to where people desire to follow one's example, they will. Because this is far different than a secular structure, we get confused. Jesus delegated his authority (to all of us believers) but of all the delegated authority mentioned, none had to do with exercising authority over other people.

The delegated authority was to teach people (with God's Word having the authority) and to dominate nature and the spiritual realm.

This is a reflection of the "Dominion Mandate" in the Garden of Eden. There was a mandate to have dominion over the physical realm, but *not over each other.*

We all know what an authoritarian, entitled tone (voice and action) is, compared to a caring and serving tone that makes optional requests. We know the kind of life-draining attitude that doesn't give or share credit, doesn't build up, encourage, empower, speak life into others, or seek collaboration, and has double standards for what is appropriate behavior. We know when words are spoken with expectation of obedience.

We all know the top-down hierarchy that the world uses in business as a matter of efficiency. The world often needs a strict, vertical authority structure. (However, studies have shown that since women entered the marketplace on the managerial level, it began a radical shift to more of a team atmosphere in the workplace.[59])

God gives the authority of the "sword" to the government—to punish evildoers. We cannot expect the world to act like Spirit-filled believers, so there is hierarchy in the world as a necessary evil. God tells us to cooperate with it (in the world's sphere) in Romans 13 and 1 Peter 2. These are "the Gentiles" of the world as opposed to "among you." There is a myriad of ways that the kingdom of Jesus Christ is an up-side down kingdom. The Sermon on the Mount has inspired entire books on the upside-down kingdom. What about the way Christians do life is clearly upside-down to the world? Is hierarchical authority upside-down?

When an unbeliever comes into our church gatherings, ministries, homes, and businesses, they should see a stark difference that is a witness of Jesus. They should see a radically different way of living that

---

59 A, H, Eagly, M.G. Makhijani, & B. G. Klonsky, "Gender and the evaluation of leaders: A meta-analysis," APA PsycNet, 1992, https://psycnet.apa.org/doiLanding?-doi=10.1037%2F0033-2909.111.1.3.

helps everyone involved to flourish. There should be mutual submission and respect even when there is perceived or established authority or leadership (like a business owner or church elders who exercise authority as a group, not individuals, and like someone with more experience guiding others).

A Christian business owner should not exist simply to earn a profit. He or she should exist to bless others by employing people who need work, rewarding their diligent work, and providing a valuable service or product to those who need it. Even as "the boss" of the business, the owner must put the needs of those he or she is responsible for ahead of him/herself. (Not in a way that encourages bad behavior or hurts the business and others who are employed.)

In every other realm besides government and business, the words of Jesus, "not so among you" (related to lording and to exercising authority) should mean exactly that. Why do we ignore Jesus's words in this matter in every aspect of life, from the most simple (home life) to the more complex ministry? If we can't figure it out at home, how are we going to figure it out elsewhere? Creating a practical and spiritual authority with two people in a marriage is contrary to the teaching of Jesus. It is unnecessary, harmful, and a poor witness. If Christians cannot display mutual submission between just two people in a marriage, they are unlikely to be able to serve well elsewhere in Christendom.

It would be interesting to poll how many complementarian marriage wives have been told, "This is MY house, and you're MY wife, so, I can have/do what I want." Or, there is a double standard for what she is "allowed" to do (such as make plans without consultation) or "get away with" (speaking disrespectfully or other misbehaviors) compared to what he can do. In 2024, a clip went viral on Tik Tok of popular preacher Joel Webbon stating that his wife was not allowed to read theological books until he vetted them. He said that he refused to let his wife have any sort of knowledge that he may not have quite yet because, "God forbid she be able to teach him anything." She was not allowed to "outpace" him. Webbon's podcast has around 10k listeners per episode. I wonder how many complementarians would not say these things out loud, but they conduct themselves with this underlying belief. If they don't conduct themselves this way, they are either egalitarian or complegalitarian (which could mean they believe one thing but behave in a better way because their conscience doesn't line up with stated beliefs).

The real leader is the one whom others willingly follow out of earned trust, not position, coercion, or intimidation. No one has to tell people to follow this trustworthy person and they don't have to "exercise" authority because they have moral authority from their servant-like, humble actions. They can teach or provide guidance, but they can also learn from anyone. Sadly, we too easily follow anyone who has achieved "success" by getting a number of other people to follow them. We seem to have a need to idolize people.

These few pages cannot adequately cover the topic of leadership and authority. Lance Ford has done an excellent job with the topic of Christ-like leadership in several books including *UnLeader – Reimagining Leadership and Why We Must*, and *The Atlas Factor* which explores shifting leadership onto the shoulders of Jesus rather than relying on hierarchical systems that often lead to power struggles and lack of accountability. He is recognized as an author, mentor, and advisor, particularly for developing innovative training systems utilized globally by various organizations, seminaries, and leaders.

There are many excellent resources coming out that re-imagine leadership in a way that's more closely aligned with Jesus's teaching. The microchurch movement is intentionally non-hierarchical and has a growing body of podcasts and resources that describe and illustrate leaders who are "catalytic." These leaders pour into others to help them replicate the same thing rather than making themselves essential. At this writing, there are over 30 networks in North America and many have affiliate microchurches in other countries. This church model frees women to lead.

Finally, America needs a different kind of leadership to address the mental health crisis in America. Christy Boulware, founder of Fearless Unite, offers biblical help for mental health. She moved away from large events to small, "Walk With Me" groups, because God told her the mental health crisis is due to lack of discipleship. As explained by the microchurch movement, growth happens best in dialogic interactions, not in settings where everyone watches a speaker. This method is as old as Socrates and Jesus, but somehow, Americans thought we need to watch great orators and celebrities in church.

Boulware's organization (FearlessUnite.com) trains people to lead groups and ministers to a significant number of people suffering from church hurt. These include many women who suffered due to teaching in complementarian churches. As the name implies, women are taught to become fearless in their identity and calling.

This chapter was titled, "Authority According to Jesus." The Bible exhorts God's people to not fear over a hundred times. When women and the men around them don't fear the sound of her voice, women can exercise the authority to build others up—the only kind of authority endorsed in the New Testament.

Chapter 17:

SUBMISSION VS. OBEDIENCE

In this chapter and the next, it will be important to remember that how the original author and reader would have understood a particular word should determine how we interpret a biblical word, and that might differ from how we understand that word today. Secular literature from the first century provides invaluable insight into how people in that culture would have used and understood a word.

A good example of a word changing in connotative meaning is the word "charity" used in English translations in 1 Corinthians 13. It retained its definition and connotation as an act of love and graciousness for centuries and then changed within the span of a hundred years to connote more of a financial act of benevolence. Hence, translators updated "charity" to "love." This is an example of nuance, where today's charity is still an act of love, but now with the connotative distinction of material gifts. Since 1 Corinthians 13 was not about material gifts, but about loving characteristics such as patience, it would lead to misunderstanding if translators didn't make the change.

For your quick reference as you read the sections below on the words "submit" and "obey," I've provided some passages which include either or both of those words. (Because they are edited down to the relevant phrases which include those two words and to the motive for their use (underlined), they are not full quotes.)

Ephesians 5: Submit to one another, and the wife to her own husband. Now as the church submits to Christ, so also wives to their husbands in everything.

Ephesians 6: Children obey your parents in the Lord, for this is right. … Slaves, obey your earthly masters with respect and fear, and with sincerity of heart, just as you would obey Christ. Obey them not only to win their favor when their eye is on you, but as slaves of Christ, doing the will of God from your heart. Serve wholeheartedly, as if you were serving the Lord, not people, because you know that the Lord will reward each one for whatever good they do, whether they are slave or free. And masters, treat your slaves in the same way. Do not threaten them, since you know that he who is both their Master and yours is in heaven, and there is no favoritism with him.

Colossians 3: Wives, submit yourselves to your husbands, as is fitting in the Lord. Husbands, love your wives and do not be harsh with them. Children, obey your parents in everything, for this pleases the Lord. Slaves, obey your earthly masters in everything.

1 Peter 2: Submit yourselves for the Lord's sake to every human authority: … Show proper respect to everyone... Slaves, in reverent fear of God submit yourselves to your masters...

Romans 13: Therefore, it is necessary to submit to the authorities, not only because of possible punishment but also as a matter of conscience.

Titus 2: Urge the younger women to love…and to be subject to their husbands, so that no one will malign the word of God. Young men … [list of good conduct] so those who oppose have nothing bad to say] … Teach slaves to be subject to their masters in everything…

so that in every way they will make the teaching about God our Savior attractive.

Greek Word for "Submit"

All the words for "submit" above are the Greek word *hypotassō* (G5293). The definition in the *New American Standard Greek Lexicon* has a military usage and a non-military usage. Obviously, Scripture is a non-military context.

> *(hupo, "under," tassō, "to arrange") A Greek military term meaning "to arrange [troop divisions] in a military fashion under the command of a leader." In non-military use, it was "a voluntary attitude of giving in, cooperating, assuming responsibility, and carrying a burden."*[60]

> *(The NAS New Testament Greek Lexicon is based on Thayer's and Smith's Bible Dictionary, plus others. It is keyed to the large Kittel and the "Theological Dictionary of the New Testament." These files are public domain.)*

> *Paul never used the word "obey" with wives, despite vocabulary options to do so. Interpreters and teachers have erroneously used "submit" and "obey" interchangeably.*
> Misleading Tactic #16

Greek Word for "Obey"

The Greek word for "obey" used above in Ephesians 6 and Colossians 3 for children and slaves is *hypakouō* (G5219). It is one of six Greek words used in the NT for obey. Although the word for "submit" isn't completely separate from any meaning of obedience, if Paul wanted to put

60 Hupotasso, Bible Study Tools, Accessed September 16, 2025, https://www.biblestudytools.com/lexicons/greek/nas/hupotasso.html.

across the idea of obedience, he had plenty of choices. He did not use the word "obey" with wives. Nowhere. There are some versions which inaccurately translate *hypotassō* to "obey" instead of "submit" (i.e. the Worldwide English Version).

I learned another point of nuance from my Blue Letter Bible study. The word *hypakouō* for "obey" had the idea of "listening" (like hearing a knock on the door and responding appropriately by going to the door), from very ancient Greek times of authors Homer, Plato, and Plutarch. However, by the time of the writer Herodotus, much closer to the time of Paul, the word "obey" meant "absolute obedience," what we would call "blind obedience." "Submit" in a non-military setting, hypotassō ("a voluntary attitude of giving in, cooperating, assuming responsibility, and carrying a burden") has a different nuance than the listening and the absolute obedience word, *hypakouō*.

> *Translators could recognize that the word "submit" (hypotassò) has been synonymous with "obey" (hypakouò) for hundreds of years, so it's past time to choose an English word such as "cooperate" for hypotassò.*
> Misleading Tactic #18

For the last 500 years, people have conflated "submit" and "obey." This is why "obey" was put in standard marriage vows for the wife (rather than "submit") in 1549 in the Church of England's *Book of Common Prayer*. In my upbringing, they used the word "submit" to sound nicer, but they clearly meant "immediate and absolute obedience." All of my life, I have mistakenly thought "obey" every time I see "submit" in the Bible. Now that my mind reads "willingly cooperate" when I see the word "submit," it helps me tremendously. Some of my readers will be saying "Well, of course," but other women will experience great relief, knowing that God is not contradicting himself by commanding non-association with a fool (Proverbs 13:20) while commanding blind obedience even to a fool.

When a wife (or husband) chooses to submit, that is voluntary and cooperative. A good measurement for whether obedience is demanded is whether there is a clear request with the very real option to decline. Even then, women will often feel an obligation or coercion to agree to do what's been "asked" because of training. They need much reassurance that they truly have the option to decline without consequence.

Translator Dr. Marlon Winedt testifies about how significant it is that the word *hypotassō* is in all the passages listed above with "submit." When conducting a translation training, he heard women in the country of Guyana pointing at Titus 2:5 and saying, "This is why our husbands beat us." When he explained to the men that the word for "submit" in this passage is the same as the word used in 1 Peter 2:13 and Romans 13:1, they understood that they were interpreting the passages about wives too harshly. Their understanding of the Titus and Romans passages was that citizens submit to the government according to conscience, cooperating with those who are doing the will of God.[61] (Note that the apostles were thrown into jail for disobeying government, because they submitted to government according to conscience, not with obedience, so sometimes that meant they did not submit.)

Dr. Winedt also emphasized in this interview that we need to have a hermeneutic that pays close attention to exceptions to the rule. Jesus showed us what is different about his kingdom. When something in scripture is vastly different than the culture, that is something that should turn our heads because it's important. Paul advocating for mutual submission, kindness, and respect for wives was astounding in that time, as was the fact that he said "in the same way" for both husbands (1 Peter 3:7) and masters (Ephesians 6:9). This progressive

61 Ibid, Winedt

> *The same passages that were used to progress the equal dignity of women in the first century are now used to digress the church on the equal dignity of women.*
> Misleading Tactic #16

(forward-moving) view of human rights and dignity was highly subversive to the culture in that time. Today, a segment of the church reads the same passage as justification for moving backwards to the very same affronts on human rights and dignity that Paul was preaching against.

If the apostles encouraged rebellion, Christianity would become known as a slave and woman uprising. Instead, they called Christian men to live by conscience and do what they could to help individuals to flourish. The apostles reminded Christians that they all had the same master in heaven and therefore men should be exemplary in how they viewed and treated their wives with a view of cooperation—not obedience, contrary to culture. In this way, they would have a greater influence on the world than women starting a revolt. Notice that the verses which mention submission and obedience include concepts about this behavior being for the Lord's sake, so that no one will malign the Word of God, and so that teaching about the Savior is attractive. Cooperative people (both men and women) are attractive and please the Lord. Contentious people (both men and women) do not attract the world to Christ.

Today, men who don't believe in Jesus know that if they don't treat their wives as equals, they will likely lose them. But many Christian men take their wives for granted and use the Bible as reason not to treat their wives equitably. They know their wives can be guilted into obedience or at least into silence about the husband's bad behavior. They use spiritual coercion phrases like, "We were made into one flesh, so you can't leave without breaking covenant with God." Christian marriage authors point at the similar divorce rate between Christians and non-Christians and blame "a lack of commitment." However, if a marriage is satisfying to both people, no one has to fall back on enduring it only due to commitment. These authors aren't identifying the real problem (a lack of mutuality), just shaming Christians into "hanging in there" in spite of misery. How does that bring glory to God? Oh, I know, they say that marriage is meant to make you holy, not happy, as if it can't be both. As if it's acceptable for this picture of Christ and the church to be anything but wonderful. Will it be easy? No, but it doesn't have to be miserable due to lack of mutual respect.

Because our culture today assumes greater equality between the sexes, we look back on these inequitable Bible passages and don't see how they are actually radical and forward moving for their time. Combine that with our missing the first-century need *not to promote equality too strongly at the expense of the gospel* message, and you have a recipe for a misunderstanding that leads to inequality and misery in today's Christian home. Today we have the opposite problem, where we are *failing to promote equality at the expense of the gospel.* I think Christianity initiated the subversion of inequality but then let the world pass us up and promote equality for different reasons and often in the wrong way. Again, I appreciate the distinction Kate Wallace Nunneley makes in her blog post, *Why I am a Feminist and an Egalitarian (And Why They Aren't the Same Thing):*

> *Both feminism and egalitarianism resist patriarchy as a corrupt and abusive system, but they do so in different ways and for different purposes: where feminism fights for equal rights, egalitarianism advocates for "equal access to servanthood." We need feminism outside the Church to fight for women's rights. We need egalitarianism inside the Church to advocate for mutual servanthood.*[62]

---

62 Kate Wallace Nunneley, "Why I am a Feminist and an Egalitarian (And Why They Aren't the Same Thing), The Junia Project, October 4, 2013, https://juniaproject.com/feminist-and-egalitarian-not-the-same/.

Mutual Submission in Ephesians and 1 Peter

Translators have employed misleading tactics in Ephesians chapter five. There are some considerations that individually might be inconsequential, but the cumulation of all of them creates a significant issue.

First, a word was added which shifts the emphasis. That shift not only pointed in one direction, but distracts from what could be the author's true intention. Then, choices were made for a pericope (a break which isolates several verses to be focused on together, separate from surrounding verses). Finally, a heading was inserted in the break, making it even more pronounced. All of this influences the reader's perception of the passage. Let's look at each of these problems one at a time.

A word is added which changes the emphasis.

> *[21]"Submit to one another out of reverence for Christ. [22]Wives, submit yourselves to your own husbands as you do to the Lord."*

In the oldest Greek manuscripts, there is no verb "submit" in verse 22. There is actually no verb at all. In Greek, the verb isn't always repeated but the sense carries over from a previous mention of the verb. A more accurate translation of verses 21-22 would read thus:

> *"Submit to one another out of reverence for Christ, wives, to your own husbands as to the Lord."*

The kind of submission that a wife should have for her husband is the same kind of submission the husband should have for his wife. However, due to separating those two verses and repeating the verb to wives, the resulting (incorrect) interpretation is more like this: "All you people out there submit to each other, but wives, you especially have extra submission for your husband, more than he has for you, or a different kind of submission than he has for you." However, the verb "submit" cannot mean one thing in verse 21 and something different in verse 22, because the verb isn't even in verse 22 in the Greek since it's relying on the verb in verse 21.

The NASB italicizes the words "subject yourselves" to indicate that the words are added. However, I don't believe it was necessary to add them, and instead of adding clarity it muddies the water. (And how many people know that italicized words were added?)

> *Since one word for "submit" is used for everyone, the command is not different for wives. Translators adding the word "submit" again for wives implies more emphasis.*
> Misleading Tactic #7

To be fair, translators didn't add a word that wasn't meant by the author. They can get away with this subtle change, even though it changes the emphasis (and therefore the meaning) of verse 22. Below we will see what I believe the author's true intent was.

One can see why this tactic is important for the ESV which specifically supports complementarian theology in their Study Bible commentary. To be clear, there are later Greek manuscripts with the word "submit" repeated. This means a copyist decided it should be added before translators decided it should be there. However, translators know there are many variants introduced in later manuscripts, and could have chosen to use the older manuscripts, but did not. It seems likely that their choices were influenced by their theology rather than letting their theology be influenced by accurate translation of the older manuscript.

A limiting clarification could be the author's true intention.

I believe the reason for additional clarification for wives is because they should submit to their *own* husbands, and not to all men. It's a limiting clarification, rather than an extra emphasis. The problem is that the instruction to everyone to submit to each other could cause

> *Adding the word "submit" again for the wife obfuscated the emphasis on a protective, limiting qualifier.*
> Misleading Tactic #16

more vulnerable people (women) to find themselves in difficult situations because they feel obliged to submit. It still happens today. Everyone (including men) is vulnerable to being taken advantage of (especially by someone viewed as more spiritual) but women more so because they can be especially giving, empathetic, and targeted by men. Therefore, Paul was protecting women by clarifying and limiting their submission to their own husbands and not every male.

There are Christian men who teach that all women should submit to all men. I had the misfortune of reading some of them while studying for this book and it is truly disturbing. I won't take any more space than this paragraph to address something so wrong and dysfunctional. Even for those complementarians who do not hold to "all women should submit to all men," there is teaching (from the CBMW crowd) that a woman should recognize that her life role is to support men in their endeavors, so she should constantly be on the lookout to affirm men in their endeavors. Even the postman (real example from these teachers) should receive her affirmation. First, I make it my goal to affirm everyone, because they are human beings, not because of their gender. Second, that kind of teaching can cause trouble. If a man is receiving special affirmation from a woman, it can touch on his vulnerabilities and encourage him to pursue her, making her more vulnerable. It's hard to believe men teach this but it underscores why Paul needed to clarify.

Paul also instructs that the submission (which is already happening out of compulsion) be with a different motive. Rather than submitting reluctantly, because the culture is set up for subjugation, wives should submit in the same willing and reverent way they submit to the

Lord. It is a shorter repetition of the previous phrase where everyone is instructed to submit to each other out of reverence to Christ.

Men were not typically submitting to their wives, therefore, the instruction in verse 21 for everyone to submit to one another is the more startling phrase, but it became less emphasized than the idea that there is extra submission for wives.

Space is added to break up verses which belong together, and a heading is inserted.

The first 14 verses of Ephesians 5 are about living in the light. Then beginning with verse 15, there is a list of instructions for practical actions which demonstrate walking in the light by the Spirit and living with wisdom. Each instruction was assigned its own verse in AD 1551 by a French printer who assigned verses to the entire Bible.

> 15*Be very careful, then, how you live—not as unwise but as wise,*
>
> 16*making the most of every opportunity, because the days are evil.*
>
> 17*Therefore do not be foolish, but understand what the Lord's will is.*
>
> 18*Do not get drunk on wine, which leads to debauchery. Instead, be filled with the Spirit,*
>
> 19*speaking to one another with psalms, hymns, and songs from the Spirit. Sing and make music from your heart to the Lord,*
>
> 20*always giving thanks to God the Father for everything, in the name of our Lord Jesus Christ.*
>
> 21*Submit to one another out of reverence for Christ.*
>
> 22*Wives, submit yourselves to your own husbands as you do to the Lord.*

The ESV leaves verse 21 about submitting to one another up with the previous section (list of instructions), creates a pericope (thought break), and inserts a section heading between verses 21 and 22. This is how it should be:

"Submit to one another out of reverence for Christ, wives, to your own husbands as to the Lord."

This is how the ESV has it:

21 submitting to one another out of reverence for Christ.

Wives and Husbands

22 Wives, submit to your own husbands, as to the Lord.

So, not only are the two sentences divided by an uninspired verse number, they are also divided by a period, break, and section heading which give the impression these are two separate thoughts. The average person doesn't know that the original Greek language writings do not have verse, paragraph, and chapter divisions. And even for those of us who do know, the divisions still have a subliminal effect.

The NIV also has a pericope and section heading, but they put verse 21 down after the section heading along with verse 22 rather than dividing the two verses about submission. The journal article (Conspectus) makes a scholarly case for why there should not be a pericope even before verse 21, as done with the NIV. Grammatically, verse 21 belongs with the verses before it.[63]

It really wasn't necessary to put a pericope and section heading anywhere around here, either before or after verse 21, and it does more

63 Kevin G. Smith and Jose de Carvalho, "The Pericope Boundary in Ephesians 5:18–24: Discourse Markers Favor the Break Being at Verse 22," Conspectus: Vol. 30, October 2020, https://sats.ac.za/wpcontent/uploads/2021/01/Conspectus30-05-Smith-deCarvalho.pdf.

harm than good. This is a passage about conduct that shows we are walking in the light and behaving in a way that edifies fellow believers. Inserting the heading "Instructions for Christian Households" interrupts the flow of thought and changes the topic instead of letting household members be an example of what has just been taught.

People seem to think that there must be a break to indicate a slight change in topic. Household codes of conduct were common in ancient times so it was probably intriguing for scholars to see one in the Bible and identify it as such. Paul loves run-on sentences, run-on paragraphs, and run-on connected thoughts. These thoughts need to stay connected or what makes this code of conduct special (mutual submission) loses what makes it special. Many of us believe translators should put the whole controversy to rest and have no break until later, thus avoiding the misunderstanding of this passage.

Translators know why the division of these verses is grammatically problematic in the Greek, but they obfuscated the meaning of the passage by inserting a pericope and section heading.
Misleading Tactic #19

First Peter 5:1-6 is another broad command to everyone to be humble and submit to each other with an attitude of service. If everyone endeavors to submit to each other, there will be no need to exercise authority.

> *To the elders among you, I appeal as a fellow elder and a witness of Christ's sufferings who also will share in the glory to be revealed: Be shepherds of God's flock that is under your care, watching over them—not because you must, but because you are willing, as God wants you to be; not pursuing dishonest gain, but eager to serve; not lording it over those entrusted to you, but being*

examples to the flock. And when the Chief Shepherd appears, you will receive the crown of glory that will never fade away. In the same way, you who are younger, submit yourselves to your elders. All of you, clothe yourselves with humility toward one another, because, "God opposes the proud but shows favor to the humble." [Proverbs 3:34] Humble yourselves, therefore, under God's mighty hand, that he may lift you up in due time.

Sarah Called Abraham "lord"

How does all this fit with Sarah calling Abraham "lord"? 1 Peter 3:3-7

Your beauty should not come from outward adornment, such as elaborate hairstyles and the wearing of gold jewelry or fine clothes. Rather, it should be that of your inner self, the unfading beauty of a gentle and quiet spirit, which is of great worth in God's sight. For this is the way the holy women of the past who put their hope in God used to adorn themselves. They submitted themselves to their own husbands, like Sarah, who obeyed Abraham and called him her lord. You are her daughters if you do what is right and do not give way to fear. Husbands, in the same way be considerate as you live with your wives, and treat them with respect as the weaker partner and as heirs with you of the gracious gift of life, so that nothing will hinder your prayers.

Without the context of Jesus' teaching in John 15, it would be easy to look at this passage and get the idea that a husband should be the lord or "king of his castle" and the wife his obedient queen/servant. Does God's Word contradict itself? Does Jesus say "don't lord over others" and then Peter commends a husband and wife doing that? The clear teaching of Jesus should be the yardstick by which other passages are understood, because Peter is following Jesus, not the other way around.

Let's get the big-picture context established first. Based on John 15, this is what the husband would say to his wife "Although the world would put me above you, you're not my servant, you're my friend. We discuss things. You get to know everything that I know. When you ask for something, it is as if I am asking for it. We submit (*hypotassō* = cooperate) in order to honor and respect each other ("husbands, in the same way"). Then, you take all that I can bless you with and use it to love others." If the Lord of the universe takes that attitude with us, how dare a husband take a more authoritative attitude with his wife? How unChrist-like if he considers his own desires first.

One more textual caveat: As with English words, Greek words have nuances. Some scholars feel *katakurieuo* (for lording) in Mark 10:42 is more harsh because of a preposition in it (*kata*) lending to "over." *Kyrios* used with Sarah and Abraham seemed to be more of a common term of respect, such as "sir" or even a term of endearment. So, it's possible we have imposed far too much of our own understanding of the English word "lord" when reading this passage. However, I will treat it going forward as "lord."

A heart attitude, not a requirement

So why would Peter commend Sarah for calling Abraham her lord and obeying him when elsewhere Jesus says to not lord over each other and not even call another "father"? Because the passage is about a beautiful, gentle spirit and heart attitude. It is recognition of the fact that Sarah was willing to offer that respect, even if it wasn't required. This is the only way I can reconcile seemingly opposite concepts. Then, I appreciate that God recognizes that it takes courage to do right in this matter. It's easy to fear that if she surrenders her will to a selfish man, he will continually take advantage.

As Peter goes on, the same heart attitude is being taught to husbands as wives. Husbands, "in the same way," are to be considerate, understanding, show honor, respect, and mutual submission (1 Peter 3:7, Eph. 5:21).

> *Husbands, in the same way be considerate as you live with your wives, and treat them with respect as the weaker partner and as heirs with you of the gracious gift of life, so that nothing will hinder your prayers.*

God feels so strongly about this kind of consideration by husbands that a severe consequence is attached, that the offending husband's prayers will not be heard. When Jesus said we are not to "lord" or "exercise authority," he is speaking of a heart attitude and also the action. As soon as we start demanding submission, or say one partner should show more submission than the other, we have crossed a line which Jesus said not to cross. Willingly offering mutual submission, respect, and honor is what Jesus is demonstrating for us and asking us to follow in the spirit of humility and love.

At one point, God told Abraham to listen to Sarah (Genesis 21:12). Does that indicate one-sided listening/submission at all times? No, and neither would Sarah's submission be one-sided at all times.

Sarah went above and beyond what was required by God, and God was pleased with her attitude. She was like Jesus, who though he was God, did not grasp at the honor and recognition of being equal with God (Philippians 2). He showed a humble attitude beyond what was required, not only by not grasping up, but by inviting us up to share in his glory. It was Sarah's willing offering. Therefore, a husband should never point at this

> *"Sarah called Abraham 'lord'" has been cherry-picked by teachers over Jesus's command to not act like a lord and over God telling Abraham to listen to Sarah.*
> Misleading Tactic #5

passage as if his wife should do likewise. If a woman is told she *should* submit, that is subjugation, not submission. If anything, the husband could look at himself and wonder what he could do to inspire such a willing response. (The answer to what he could do is spelled out in verse 7 of 1 Peter 3.)

I believe that if Abraham and Sarah had valued Sarah as much as God did, they would not have twice let her be taken by another man and they would not have thought it a good idea to have Abraham impregnate her maid. God had said Sarah would be the mother of Abraham's chosen son, showing God valued Sarah's partnership with Abraham. God changed Sarah's name when he changed Abraham's name, and God insistently stood by Sarah when Abraham didn't value her.

A lording or superior attitude by a husband is basically acting in any way that would not be considered appropriate for a wife to act likewise. The Christian life would be far easier if we had a big book of rules to follow for every situation, or if there was just one rule (the wife should always submit to the husband who is always the leader). But those would be shortcuts which would not require the fruit of the Holy Spirit, such as humility, gentleness, and patience, in order to determine what course of action to take. This fruit brings glory to God. Galatians 5:22-23 does not say the fruit of the Spirit is leadership.

Imagine a husband and wife in a contest of sorts to see who can willingly submit, honor and respect best, rather than expecting it of the other or even hoping for it from the other! I had friends who bought a new car and they were "arguing" because they each wanted the other spouse to have the privilege of it being their primary car. Such honor is a delight to those who observe as well as to God.

****

Biblical submission is not about who makes decisions, authority, office, or position. It's about considering the needs and interests of others, and then submitting our own needs and interests as a lesser priority. It has everything to do with kindness and showing greater honor to others, regardless of any kind of perceived status. It is not about enabling the bad behavior of fellow believers. (Just some of the Scriptures which advocate godly resistance are Galatians 6:1, 1 Corinthians 5:1–13, 2 Thessalonians 3:14–15, 1 Timothy 5:20, Titus 3:10–11, James 5:19–20, Ephesians 5:11, Romans 16:17.)

I need to give a personal testimony of the harm of a father who truly believed in patriarchal hierarchy. I surmise that many who think they are complementarian don't actually believe or practice hierarchy, but this is about my father, who was a true believer.

When I was a teen, my sister who was 13 months older than me, ran away from home because of the violence and psychological/spiritual abuse we were experiencing from our father. The court ordered family counseling. Our father was greatly humiliated to be compelled to go to someone for counseling. He owned a book for preachers titled *Competent to Counsel* and told us that his position made him competent to counsel and everything would be fine if we just obeyed and kept our sassy mouths shut. When my parents, sister, and I sat down in the counselor's office, my father said to the man, "Here's how this is going to go. You will start out by affirming to these women that God set up the household with me in charge and they are to obey God by submitting to me, or we will leave." The man tried to ask my sister a question and she was too terrified to speak (as were my mother and I). Because the man was not complying, my father announced the man was not a biblical counselor and marched us out of there.

Of course, nothing changed. All through the years, church people saw the bruises and signs of trauma on our family (six kids) and said nothing (as far as I know). I applied myself to my studies so I could graduate a year early and leave for college at age 17 (clueless about how unprepared for life I was). My father abused my mother until her death at 88. There was no escape for her because she believed she had to obey according to the twisted Bible interpretations she was taught. The violence was actually not as bad as the spiritual abuse which wreaked havoc on all of us psychologically.

Christian men have told me to praise my mother for her faithfulness to my father. So, they would call it "faithfulness" to enable a man's sin, to not protect children in her care, to live a lie that everything is fine, to behave in dysfunctional ways in attempts to not set off his rage since she was supposedly responsible for his behavior, and to dissociate emotionally and have no genuine relationships because it was the only way to deal with the incongruencies of life. That is not praiseworthy (although I understand her choices and the limited options she felt she had). Children who grow up in abusive homes take away a myriad of consequences, probably different for each child. For me, of all the harms in my life, missing out on a relationship with my mother was the most harmful, causing me to seek mother figures all of my life. I couldn't mourn her death—it was finally an escape—I mourned her life. I resolved that I wouldn't be like her.

I understand that including these aspects of my life story will cause some readers to believe I just have an ax to grind, and therefore I'm unable to impartially consider the biblical issues presented here. However, I've come to believe that those who have never experienced spiritual abuse, or at least never attempted to deeply empathize with what the misrepresentation of God's heart does to a soul—it is they who are unable to rightly evaluate these issues. Especially those who have enjoyed the privileged position of "authority" and righteously look down on "the rebellious," are unable to be God's instrument of healing and bind up the broken hearted. They are not motivated to say, "Something is not right with this picture of God" and search for a better answer rather than to claim "complementarianism" isn't being done well enough and we need to double down on it. Because I deeply believe the Bible is the only light for this dark world, I chose to wield a light rather than an ax, and study the Bible better rather than abandon my faith due to a "biblical" system that produced evil. I trust it's evident that I have done my homework and I'm committed to continue. God called me to do something positive with the pain I have experienced and I've had countless affirmations during my search, so I'm joyfully advocating for the truth about God's heart.

Chapter 18:

THE HEAD

Ephesians 5:23-25, 31-32

The "headship" issue is possibly the biggest obstacle to advocates of hierarchy/complementarians changing their minds about husbands having a superior position. The current, western, *English*, perception of the word "head" as a top-tier leader (like a CEO) causes a tremendous amount of confusion. However, that metaphorical understanding is not true of all western languages, such as French.

Let's take a fresh look at Ephesians. There are three pieces to the puzzle. Each one is strong enough on its own, but together they complete a beautiful picture. All three pieces are from Ephesians because context within a particular epistle is key to a coherent interpretation. (We should not cherry pick one verse here and there.)

The use of the Greek word *kephalē* for "head," and the understanding of the head/body metaphor in Paul's time is first fascinating, and then mind-blowing in its theological implications for the church's position in Christ. As I attempted to write this, I was wrecked. I went to sleep and woke up thinking and praying about it. I have yet to grasp the full implications. It's no wonder that our spiritual enemy has done so much to obfuscate the meaning of these passages. It's as if the enemy put a lid on a deep well of transformational truth and labeled it, "This is simply about husbands having authority over wives, nothing else to see here."

The first puzzle piece is related to the first-century understanding of the word "head."

We already looked at Ephesians 5:21-22 related to mutual submission and how those verses should not be separated as two separate thoughts with a word added. Now let's move on to verse 23:

> *For the husband is the head of the wife as Christ is the head of the church, his body, of which he is the Savior.*

I read and listened to many hours of teaching by complementarians and egalitarians about the word which Paul used for head. Once again, the egalitarians have by far the most scholarly work. Marg Mowczko, Cynthia Long Westfall, and Bruce Fleming all have excellent content. In Terran Williams' book, *How God Sees Women, his Appendix 3: What kephalē Means* is an excellent summary of the issue. For more detail, he has a series of YouTube videos where he and Andrew Bartlett counter Mike Winger's teaching. https://terranwilliams.com/what-winger-presently-gets-wrong-male-headship-is-it-really-biblical/. [Andrew Bartlett is a Barrister (legal counsel and arbitrator) and Bible scholar from the UK, not to be confused with a politician by the same name in Australia.]

I further summarized Williams' *Appendix 3*, organized his reasons into a numbered list, and quoted three paragraphs.[64] I recommend my reader to his full explanation and footnotes.

64 Terran Williams, *How God Sees Women: The End of Patriarchy*, Cape Town, The Spiritual Bakery Publications, 333-336.

Today, the metaphor "head" means the top authority, such as a CEO who gives orders. Is that what Paul meant when he used *kephalē* and what did his audience think he meant? Wayne Grudem argues that the word almost always means authority over, but other scholars argue that it *seldom if ever* means that in Paul's time. Williams determined that it rarely meant authority. Typical of metaphors, it can have a different sense in different contexts, so in some, the idea of authority is included, but rare. **Life-source is the better understanding of *kephalē* for four reasons.**

1. For centuries up through Paul's time, the physical head was sometimes used as a **metaphor for the life-source of the body.** Aristotle and many medical writers believed this, including Pythagoras, who taught that the head even generated the male semen. Philo, a Greek-speaking Jewish teachers claimed the head had a life-force for the body from heaven. So, when Greeks spoke of a person as the head, it was a reference as a life-source or progenitor. Paul would have been well-versed in Greek idiom and thought. He writes his epistles to Greek-speaking people.

2. **There were better metaphorical words for an authority figure**. The Hebrew word for the human head is *rosh* and when used metaphorically, it meant authority. When the Hebrew Scriptures were translated into Greek (called the Septuagint or LXX), Cynthia Westfall studied 171 places where rosh is reliably confirmed to mean authority but the Greek translators only translated rosh into *kephalē* four times, almost always opting for other Greek words that more clearly denote authority. That's a 97.7% rate of other Greek words over *kephalē*.

3. The LSJ Greek-English Lexicon, the most exhaustive ancient Greek lexicon in existence, lists **48 possible metaphoric mean-**

ings for *kephalē*, and not a single one of them is authority. The more recent Cambridge Greek Lexicon agrees. [These lexicons catalog the uses of words by many ancient Greek authors.]

4. **Paul's mentions of Jesus as *kephalē* fit well with life-source for the body.** He mostly uses *kephalē* as a head-body analogy, in which Jesus is the life-source to which the church, by salvation and the Spirit, is organically connected. (See verses below.) Today, with our understanding of the executive function of the brain, we would assume that Paul would also make some reference to Jesus' provision of leadership, direction and dominion. However, Paul with his understanding of a head does not.

"Grudem, though admitting the head-body metaphor may imply the idea of "source," (*Evangelical Feminism and Biblical Truth,* p. 567) pushes back on the idea that *kephalē* seldom meant authority, and collects an impressive list of examples in literature of military generals and kings being the *kephalē* of the army or people. But, for that, he turns primarily to later literature. Besides, the ancient Greeks probably understood their leader to also be their life-source.

"What about the two places where Paul does seem to conflate the meanings—Ephesians 1:22 and Colossians 2:10? Even in those passages, Paul may closely hold side-by-side ideas of Jesus as being authoritative with Jesus as *kephalē*, but he does not necessarily fuse them. (Help from Cynthia Westfall, The IVP Dictionary of Paul and His Letters.)

"Ephesians 1:22 has the phrase "*kephalē* over everything." It is part of a spatial image of Jesus on a throne above all things. The surprise, when we read this verse in the context of 1:18-2:6, is that it is not just Jesus-as-the-head, but Jesus-*and-the-church,* or the-head-and-the-body seated on a throne. Paul says that Jesus as *kephalē* above all things is "for the church, *which is his body*." All things are "under his feet"—but we are his feet. All that to say, Jesus being *kephalē* here does not specifically mean he has authority over us, even all things (which of course he does)—it rather explains how Jesus who is the rightful Lord over all things, shares that authority with us; after all, a king's entire body, not just his head, is in charge."

Before I read Williams's assessment, I had listened to hours of tedious listings of the use and context of *kephalē* by church fathers. I was not impressed, primarily because of the length of time between Paul and the examples from various authors (100-500 years). Remember, language changes over time. Remember how the word "charity" changed in connotative meaning roughly over a hundred years? The usage of head as a metaphor is another example. To understand the passages, we must focus on how Paul and his readers understood it in their time (life-source of the body). I'm surprised that Grudem appealed to later literature instead of the Bible and first century.

> *There are at least four good reasons that "head" in the first century was understood as the "source" or "beginning," not an authority figure.*
> Misleading Tactic #18

The second puzzle piece is Paul's other uses of the head/body metaphor.

Following are excerpts from "Paul's Main Point in Ephesians 5:22-23" by Marg Mowczko:

Paul also uses a head-body metaphor in Ephesians 1 when he speaks about how amazingly God has endowed the church. For example, "the riches of his glorious inheritance in his holy people, and his incomparably great power for us who believe" (Eph 1:18-

19). As his body, we the church, are "the fullness of him who fills everything in every way" (Eph 1:23).

We need to understand Paul's wonderful view of the church if we are to understand Paul's use of the church in his illustration in Ephesians 5 and his instructions to wives and husbands. Ephesians 5 needs to be read with Ephesians 1 in mind and with the knowledge that we are raised and seated with Christ! (Eph. 2:6)[65]

And this from a message to me from Marg in answer to a question (she is Australian, hence the spelling):

Christ did condescend, lower himself, to become our Saviour. He gave himself for his church (Eph. 5:25 cf. Eph. 5:2). But this is only half of the story. As "Saviour of the body" (Eph. 5:23), Christ also elevates and glorifies the church (Eph. 5:26-27).

There are many New Testament verses that indicate our salvation means that we become like Jesus. We will resemble him physically and spiritually. See, for example, Rom. 8:29-30, 1 Cor. 15:49, 2 Cor. 3:18, Eph 1:22-23, Phil. 3:21-22, Col 1:28-29, 1 John 3:2, and 2 Pet. 1:3-11.

Paul saw the end goal of ministry as us "attaining to the whole measure of the fullness of Christ" (Eph. 4:13). And Paul took this ministry seriously (Gal. 4:19).

The astonishing message of the gospel is that there is a levelling of status between Christ and his redeemed people.

In the Greco-Roman world, husbands usually had a higher status and more social power than their wives. In other words, husbands

65 Mowczko, "Paul's Main Point in Ephesians 5:22-23," April 30, 2012, https://margmowczko.com/pauls-main-point-in-eph-5_22-33/.

were typically considered superior to their wives. Paul, however, wanted these first-century husbands to lower themselves and give themselves for their wives (Eph. 5:25 cf. Eph. 5:2). And he wanted husbands to elevate their wives by treating them as their own (male) bodies which, at that time, had a higher status than women's bodies (Eph. 5:28-30). Paul wanted a levelling of status between husband and wife. This would foster true "one-flesh" unity.[66]

I remember from my own Greco-Roman studies that the male body was held in higher esteem during that time (just remember Aristotle's teaching and look at Michaelangelo's art during the Renaissance), whereas in modern times, the female body has been more highly esteemed.

Let's look closer at these same passages where Jesus is called the head.

Ephesians 4:15-16: "[W]e will grow to become in every respect the mature body of him who is the head, that is, Christ. From him the whole body ... grows and builds itself up in love.

We are the body and he is the head and from him the body grows and is built up. This is a head/body metaphor with the head providing what is needed for growth.

Colossians 1:18 And he is the head of the body, the church; he is the beginning and the firstborn from among the dead, so that in everything he might have the supremacy.

Christ is the life-source of the body (church), Christ is the beginning (creator of all), and Christ is the firstborn among the dead, so

66 Personal email from Marg Mowczko to author.

that in everything (all those things put together as conclusive proof) he has the supremacy.

> *Colossians 2:10 In Christ you have been brought to fullness. He is the head over every power and authority.*

> *Translators added the English word "over" to Colossians 2:10 even though it is not in the Greek. This gives the impression that "head" means superiority instead of source.*
> Misleading Tactic #7

In this verse, the English word "over" was added because translators thought it would read better. They could have just as easily decided to add the word "of." It could be translated as, "He is the source of every power and authority" but there's nothing wrong with keeping "head" if only people understood the metaphor. Adding "over" strengthened the idea that "head" means superiority, which added ideology to the translation. The English translation should have italicized "over" since it was added. Even in those versions where it is italicized, many readers don't know that italics mean a word was added.

> *Colossians 2:19 They have lost connection with the head, from whom the whole body, supported and held together by its ligaments and sinews, grows as God causes it to grow.*

This verse says that the head is the source of the rest of the body. In fact, the English word "supported" is the Greek word *epichorēgeō* (G2023) with the idea of "*being supplied.*" Commas are rendered at the discretion of translators as well, adding to the meaning and thus the interpretation. A reasonable translation of this verse is, "They have lost connection with the head, from whom the whole body is supplied, held together by its ligaments and sinews, growing as God causes it to grow." The head/body metaphor is clear here, with the head being the source.

> *Colossians 2:19 says the head supplies the body, causing it to grow. It does not say the head exercises authority over the body.*
> Misleading Tactic #16

Similarly, the context of the book of Ephesians is our position "in Christ" and all the blessings and provisions we have from him. Entire books have been written on this glorious concept. Interpretation of chapter five needs to take larger context into consideration. So, verse 5:23 needs to be viewed in that context, "For the husband is the source/provision of the wife as Christ is the source/provision of the church, his body, of which he is the Savior." Paul would have been very familiar with the traditional *Ketubah*, a traditional Jewish marriage contract. It outlines the husband's obligations to his wife—such as providing food, clothing, and marital relations—and includes financial provisions in case of divorce or his death.

The third puzzle piece is related to "one flesh" and the "mystery" of Christ and the church.

> *"For this reason a man will leave his father and mother and be united to his wife, and the two will become one flesh." This is a profound mystery—but I am talking about Christ and the church. (Ephesians 5:31-32)*

Following are excerpts from "A Note on the Mystery in Ephesians 5:31-32" by Marg Mowczko:

> *In Ephesians, Paul mostly uses "mystery" in the context of unity: unity between the heavenly realms and earth, between Jewish and Gentile believers, between Christ and the Church. The mystery in Ephesians 5:31-32 is that the bond between Christ and the*

Church, between the Messiah and his people, is close in a way that was previously unimaginable.

In Ephesians 5:22-30, Paul had been using the words "head" and "body" in a head-body metaphor to convey the unity between Christ and the Church and between husbands and wives. In verses 31-32, however, the picture isn't of a head and body (two parts joined together) but "one flesh." The "one flesh" image even more vividly highlights a union where there is no distinction of body parts; there is no head, there is no body, but one flesh.[67]

I'm not advocating for changing the word "head" to "source" in the NT because there is a head/body metaphor that is essential. But there needs to be acknowledgement of what it meant then versus now and more education for average people, just like Christian teachers have to be diligent on teaching many complex topics.

Besides what we saw of the head/body metaphor in Colossians chapters one and two, let's review the metaphor in Ephesians:

- Head/body metaphor in chapter 1 = The context in verses 18-23 describes how the church is the fullness of Christ and in him, having the same power that raised Christ from the dead, and in him is over all the powers of darkness (cf. Ephesian 6:12). The church is on the throne with him, not under his feet.

And God placed all things under his feet and appointed him to be head over everything for the church, which is his body, the fullness of him who fills everything in every way. (Ephesians 1:22-23)

67 Marg Mowczko, "A Note on the Mystery in Ephesians 5:31-32," Exploring the biblical theology of Christian egalitarianism, March 3, 2024, https://margmowczko.com/mystery-ephesians-531-32/.

- Head/body metaphor in chapter 4 = We grow to become the mature body of him who is the head. From him (the source of life) the whole body grows and builds itself up in love.

- Head metaphor in chapter 5 = Christ is our source (provider and protector) like a husband is the source for the wife.

- Mystery in chapter 5 = Christ and the church are one flesh like husband and wife are one flesh, referring back to Genesis. There is no distinction between head and body.

See the amazing way that Christ teaches unity and brings the church as his body to sit on the throne with him! Both a wrong impression of the word "submit" and missing the unity that Christ has given to the church with him cause us to imagine a hierarchy in the statement that "as the church submits to Christ, so also wives should submit to their husbands in everything." **Christ has elevated the church to do his work on earth with his full authority. Does complementarian teaching elevate wives to minister in every way with full authority? Or do they say, "I do the important work, and you do the lesser work and support me?"** Christ actually removed himself from the world and made us the physical "doers" while he is the source of our life, our power, our strength, and our wisdom. He provides for us so that we can "do"—an amazing partnership.

The church becomes "the fullness of Christ," seated with him on the throne, and ministering to the world as the body Jesus. This is a contrast to complementarian teaching where the man is leader and does the important work with the woman's support.
Misleading Tactic #16

At this point, someone might think I'm trying to diminish the deity and authority of Christ. I am not. Metaphors (and analogies)

> *The metaphor for marriage is not a hierarchical Trinity; it is Christ and the church on the throne together with "one flesh." "One flesh" doesn't mean one person gives up their personhood to support the other. It means there is no distinction between the head and body.*
> Misleading Tactic #16

simply make one point about how two things are alike. Aside from the fact that Christ is the supreme authority in the universe, he uses a metaphor when he says that the way he invites the church to receive his blessings and participate in the affairs of the world is the way husbands provide for wives while inviting them to participate in unity and partnership. That is the extent of the metaphor. If taken any further, it falls apart, because husbands are not rulers of the universe (or even the world) like Christ is. So, the metaphor for marriage is not a hierarchical Trinity, it is Christ and the church with marital "one flesh." I can see why hierarchalists would superficially see superiority between Christ and the church and put that on marriage. But that's not what Christ and Paul were doing with the head/body metaphor.

It was especially true in historical cultures that the wife was physically dependent on the man for her protection and provision. Due to cultural patriarchy, a woman couldn't even sign a contract, so the husband was her practical, physical provider or source of sustenance. (If a father or husband wasn't available, a "tutor" was provided to oversee her affairs.) I already mentioned the *Ketubah* marriage provision. Even today, when a woman carries and gives birth to children, nurses and nurtures them, she is dependent on a husband or someone else to be her physical protector and provider. This puts her in a vulnerable position. She needs to be able to trust that a man will take care of her sacrificially and not take advantage of her vulnerability. If she doesn't cooperate (submit), she will face a crisis of survival. Sacrificial care on his part means submission of his needs and interests, placing her and the children's needs and interests above his own.

This is what makes him like Christ: they both have the means and power to take advantage, but Christ does not take advantage and tells men they shouldn't either. In fact, related to the free will of individuals, Christ steps back unless invited. He allows us full agency. Mutual, cooperative submission makes the ideal unity and oneness possible. Introducing hierarchy into this ideal does not lend to trust or unity. Hierarchy is unnecessary and paves the way for men to take advantage.

Notice the correlation between these verses in Ephesians 5 and Colossians 3:15-25.

Colossians 3:15-25

> *15 Let the peace of Christ rule in your hearts, since as members of one body you were called to peace. And be thankful. 16 Let the message of Christ dwell among you richly as you teach and admonish one another with all wisdom through psalms, hymns, and songs from the Spirit, singing to God with gratitude in your hearts. 17 And whatever you do, whether in word or deed, do it all in the name of the Lord Jesus, giving thanks to God the Father through him.*
>
> *Instructions for Christian Households*
>
> *18 Wives, submit yourselves to your husbands, as is fitting in the Lord.*
>
> *19 Husbands, love your wives and do not be harsh with them.*
>
> *20 Children, obey your parents in everything, for this pleases the Lord.*

21 Fathers, do not embitter your children, or they will become discouraged.

22 Slaves, obey your earthly masters in everything; and do it, not only when their eye is on you and to curry their favor, but with sincerity of heart and reverence for the Lord. 23 Whatever you do, work at it with all your heart, as working for the Lord, not for human masters, 24 since you know that you will receive an inheritance from the Lord as a reward. It is the Lord Christ you are serving. 25 Anyone who does wrong will be repaid for their wrongs, and there is no favoritism.

> *Today, the church agrees that this command to slaves was due to the culture of that day, yet, there is disagreement that the inequal submission of wives was cultural.*
> Misleading Tactic #1

Once again, the general topic is how to be peaceable within the body of Christ. There is instruction for *everyone* to admonish one another. Then again there is an (unnecessary) editorial decision to put in a break and the title of "Households." Included in these codes are instructions to slaves to obey their earthly masters with reverence for the Lord. Why is it that today, the church agrees that this command to slaves was due to the culture of that day and that today no one should have slaves, yet there is disagreement that the *inequal* submission of wives was cultural? Paul finishes with the statement that we are actually serving the Lord Christ, not masters, that anyone who does wrong will be repaid for their wrongs, and with God, there is no favoritism (Romans 2:11). This should bring great comfort for those in a situation where they are constrained to inequal submission, and it should bring terror to those who think they have superiority. God is just!

I hope it is obvious that these passages on their own are not a strong case for one-sided submission today. (Are there roles? Yes, but one role is not meant to be the authority over the other.) We've already seen why other passages are also weak on their own, so they can't be used to support these. The ESV Study Bible commentary for Genesis 3:16 refers to Ephesians 5 as proof that God put hierarchy in the marriage relationship. No doubt some use Genesis as proof to read hierarchy into Ephesians 5. I suspect circular proof texting. The truth is, hierarchy is not clear in either one. Ephesians 5 is about living in sacrificial service to each other, not about who's in charge and who must submit more than the other.

All About Unity

I am overwhelmed with astonishment that Christ would elevate us, the church, to the status that Mowczko points out. In pondering this teaching, I believe that our unity with each other, making up the church (the body of Christ) is key to this principle. How are we "one in Christ Jesus" (Galatians 3:28) unless we have spiritual equality and functional equality?

> *There is neither Jew nor Gentile, neither slave nor free, nor is there male and female, for you are all one in Christ Jesus.*

In Chapter 1, under "Creation Order" we saw how creating man first and bringing woman out of him equalized the sexes according to 1 Corinthians 11:11-12 which talks about how woman came from man and how man also comes from woman. Ephesians 5 also reflects this by referring back to the one flesh in Genesis.

We have seen how "source" is about provision rather than authority. We can see in Ephesians 5:23 the concept of man being the source of woman and then Christ being the source of the whole church whom He sacrificially saved, which then correlates to the husband being told to sacrificially love and value the wife as himself.

If Ephesians 5:23-24 was talking about hierarchy, it would be in contradiction to the words of Jesus which forbade the exercise of authority "among you" (not the world).

Jesus's Prayer for Unity

Remember Jesus's prayer for unity before he went to the cross.

> *My prayer is not for them alone. I pray also for those who will believe in me through their message,* [21] *that all of them may be one, Father, just as you are in me and I am in you. May they also be in us so that the world may believe that you have sent me.* [22] *I have given them the glory that you gave me, that they may be one as we are one—* [23] *I in them and you in me—so that they may be brought to complete unity. Then the world will know that you sent me and have loved them even as you have loved me. (John 17:20-23)*

Jesus prayed that we would be one with each other just as he and the Father are one (equal in the Trinity). When husband and wife are believers, how can the two be equal in all ways with the other in the Body of Christ yet also have a hierarchy in the marriage? Those are not compatible. Then with Jesus in all of us, we are brought to "complete unity." Then the world will know that Jesus was sent from the Father, and we are all loved by the Father. In other words, our unity is a testimony to the world. How will the world see that testimony if we don't understand and practice oneness instead of hierarchy?

Philippians has been nicknamed "the joy book" but if one looks closer, it has a theme of unity. If Paul was endorsing one-way submission, then the humble example of Jesus in Philippians chapter 2 should have been directed only to women or wives. But it is directed to everyone for every situation, as are many other Scriptures that apply to all believers. As we saw earlier, 1 Corinthians has a major theme to stop selfishness and be in unity. Romans was written to Jewish and

Gentile believers who were experiencing racial tension. The first half of the book was primarily to Jews, explaining that they don't have the corner on the gospel, and that it was Abraham's faith, not possession of the law, that saved him and everyone after him, including Gentiles. Then he explained to the Gentiles that they are grafted into the covenant. Paul is exhorting everyone to stop with competition and superior attitudes and embrace mutuality. Revelation emphasizes every nation at the throne. I could go on, but the entire NT teaches that the new life in Christ does away with the world's system of hierarchy.

> *Ephesians 5 is about living in sacrificial service to each other, not about who's in charge and who must submit more. Jesus said our oneness will testify to the world about him.*
> Misleading Tactic #16

A better way to interpret or paraphrase Ephesians 5:23 is as follows: For the husband is the source and provider (physical savior) for the wife who is one with him as his very own body, like Christ is the source and provider of the church, which is his body, of which he is the Savior. Therefore, as the church cooperates in every way with Christ, fully representing Christ and acting on his behalf, the wife should cooperate in every way with the husband as they are also one flesh.

1 Corinthians 11:1-16

This is a complicated passage, so the number of interpretations is too many to go into, and I don't believe anyone can have it completely figured out. There are seeming contradictions and bizarre statements. For example, it seems to say that a woman dishonors her head by praying and prophesying uncovered, but then later says her long hair is her covering. Then it says long hair on a man is disgraceful, but plenty of godly people have had long hair and Paul possibly had long hair when he was with them. Then there's talk of angels and contradictory thoughts about who came first and from where.

I'm going to offer the interpretation that makes sense to me and is consistent with the rest of the interpretations in this book. I also believe this interpretation is pretty simple—and simple can be good!

The abrupt topic change at the beginning of Chapter 11 indicates Paul is moving to another of the Corinthians' questions. We don't know whether the question is assumed (so not stated) or if Paul quotes them at some point(s) in the chapter and then refutes their errant thinking. My vote is the latter, because otherwise, the passage doesn't make sense, and Paul is rambling and contradicting himself. Remember, 1 Corinthians contains many quotes from errant people which Paul refutes.

In the Head Covering section in Chapter 9, we saw that head covering for women was a secular cultural practice, as a symbol of marriage, before the church was born. So, I have a hard time seeing how a secular practice could suddenly become a spiritual practice or a spiritual symbol. I suspect that the same thing is happening here that happened in 1 Corinthians chapter 14, where men tried to apply a secular law (banning women speaking in public) to church gatherings, and Paul corrected them. In the chapter where we looked at that issue, I listed seven clues that Paul was quoting their errant thinking in verses 34-35. I believe those two verses should be inside quotation marks. Some who promote the quotation idea for this passage in 1 Corinthians 11 go back and forth with a quick dialogue between Paul and the Corinthians, like the dialogue in chapter 10. Just one block of verses being the Corinthian quotation makes far more sense to me.

Let's start with verse 3:

> *But I want you to realize that the head of every man is Christ, and the head of the woman is man, and the head of Christ is God.*

Because Paul starts with "I want you to realize/understand..." I think this truly is a statement from Paul and not an erroneous idea that he is going to refute. The Greek word for "head" here is *kephalē* which we covered in the section on Ephesians 5 to mean that the physical head is a metaphor for "source" for the rest of the body. To be consistent, we would read this to mean that the source of men is Christ, and the source of women is men, and the source of Christ is God. Read that way, there is no reason to view the verse as hierarchical. We already discussed the physical source that men can be for women and as men provide for women, they need to look to Christ for provision. When Christ operated as a human, he certainly looked to God the Father for provision. If we looked at it as a hierarchical list, we would be back to the EFS Trinitarian problem described in Chapter 1.

There are plenty of verses that direct all believers (includes women) to look directly to God as their source, so there is no reason to interpret this verse as meaning that men stand between women and God. I think Paul is teaching his favorite head/body metaphor (it's not found in anyone else's letters) before answering some practical questions about the physical head and its physical covering. Some might believe the metaphor and the physical practice are connected, but I think he could have been making a contrast, otherwise he would be contradicting himself and other Scripture.

Now comes verses 4 through 9 which I suspect should be in quotes. This is where I believe that the Corinthians were wrongly trying to spiritualize physical head coverings, a long-standing cultural tradition. I believe these verses contain error, which is the clue that they should be in quotes. Then Paul refutes the thinking, and everything makes sense.

> *Every man who prays or prophesies with his head covered dishonors his head.*

But every woman who prays or prophesies with her head uncovered dishonors her head—it is the same as having her head shaved.

For if a woman does not cover her head, she might as well have her hair cut off; but if it is a disgrace for a woman to have her hair cut off or her head shaved, then she should cover her head.

A man ought not to cover his head, since he is the image and glory of God; but woman is the glory of man.

For man did not come from woman, but woman from man; neither was man created for woman, but woman for man.

The first clue that verses 4-9 are errant is this statement: "A man ought not to cover his head, since he is the image and glory of God; but woman is the glory of man." Genesis 1:27 and 5:1 say both man and woman were created in the image of God, but this statement says that only man was created in God's image and reflects God's glory, and woman is a step down from that, the glory of man, not God. Which are we going to believe, the statements in Genesis, or this very confusing passage? A rule of hermeneutics is to use clear passages to interpret unclear passages. Since this passage contradicts Genesis, I believe it is a quote from errant men who were trying to retain power for themselves in the church where there were so many women being used by God.

The remaining verses would be Paul's refutation, pointing out even more errant thinking above. Let's start with verse 10 (bold is my emphasis).

It is for this reason that a woman ought to have authority over her own head, because of the angels. (NIV)

That is why a wife ought to have a symbol of authority on her head, because of the angels. (ESV)

This verse has been interpreted to say that a woman should wear a head covering to demonstrate that she is under her husband's hierarchical, spiritual "headship." And now that head coverings are no longer culturally practiced, women should still recognize that this passage teaches spiritual headship. Following are three translation problems which have led to this errant teaching:

> *Three of our four Bible versions added the words "a symbol of" to give the impression that the verse is talking about head covering being a symbol of a husband's authority.*
> Misleading Tactic #7

1) The NKJV, ESV, and NASB added the words "a symbol of" (authority) to this verse, to make this idea appear reasonable, even though those words or any idea of them absolutely cannot be found in the original Greek, nor is there mention of husbands (or man) connected to the word authority. In fact, the word "authority" (*exousia*) is active, meaning the woman is exercising authority. But when translators added the extra words, it made exousia passive as if the woman is submitting to the authority of others. In his *New International Commentary on the NT, 1 Corinthians, Gordon D. Fee* explains on pages 511-514 why the active sense is grammatically and contextually stronger, and that the passive reading is a theological imposition rather than a linguistic necessity.

2) Those who rendered the translation to have a symbol of authority on her head also ignored the intensive modifier to "her" which would make it "her own" head.

The NIV corrected these two errors by leaving out the added words ("a symbol of") and showing ownership of her own head in their 2011 edition, but they kept the erroneous translation in a footnote which still gives it legitimacy as if it was a reasonable alternative.

The same Bible versions give the impression that someone else's authority is on her head rather than she has authority over her own head.
Misleading Tactic #2

Out of the three versions that added words, the NKJV is the most honest by italicizing the words "a symbol of" to show they have been added.

The addition of the words "a symbol of" is a desperate attempt to impose man's own interpretation onto the text (eisegesis) rather than extracting the actual meaning of the text (exegesis). Then they take the reference to angels and say angels would look on in embarrassed horror if a woman didn't have her head covered to show her submission. That is a lot of conjecture! This is what I was taught growing up. I heard it countless times, but now I see that it's a blatant addition to God's Word. Other translation teams also disagreed with the rendering that Paul was saying that a head covering is a symbol of a husband's authority.

3) The ESV alone made an editorial choice to translate the female word to "wife" rather than "woman" in verses 3, 5, 6 and 10. The choice upset those who believe that all women should be subordinate to all men (again, what I read by these angry men made me ill). Verse 3 in the ESV has a footnote that it could be "woman" but does not mention the other verses in the chapter like it does with the first-mention footnoting in Ephesians chapter five (yet another inconsistency). The editorial choice to translate "wife" instead of "woman" is a poor choice because the passage is not about marriage.

I believe the issue here is simply an attempt to make a cultural practice a spiritual practice and exercise more control on other people. Remember, head coverings were a cultural norm prior to Christianity. Yes, a woman would cover her head as a cultural show of being married, but that doesn't transfer to spiritual authority. The passage is actually about whether it is appropriate for women and men to worship with head coverings and whether any length of hair causes anyone dishonor. Today's church also struggles with appearance issues.

> *The editorial choice to translate to "wife" instead of "woman" is a poor choice because the passage is about the appearance of people when they pray, not marriage.*
> Misleading Tactic #4

The phrase about angels has puzzled many people who give all sorts of explanations. I think the best one is that earlier in chapter 6, Paul stated that believers would someday judge angels, so they should be capable of settling disputes among themselves. Since he just talked about that, this brief reference back to it would make sense. Since women are going to judge angels, they should be able to judge which occasion is appropriate for a head covering. Do they not know their culture and all the nuances of what is appropriate in various situations? Of course they do, so leave them alone to have authority (a reasonable *exousia*) over their own heads.

Now, remember above in the verses which I believe should be inside quotation marks from the Corinthians, they said, "For man did not come from woman, but woman from man; neither was man created for woman, but woman for man." So, the next refutation points are in verses 11-12:

> *Nevertheless, in the Lord woman is not independent of man, nor is man independent of woman.*
>
> *For as woman came from man, so also man is born of woman. But everything comes from God.*

So now, either Paul is contradicting himself, or those words were from errant men and he's refuting them. As a refutation, he is saying, just because a woman can make up her own mind about when to cover her head, that doesn't mean she's totally independent of man and shouldn't consider who she might dishonor by her choices. But then again, neither is man independent of her. And it's not important that woman came from man and that woman was made for man. He's correcting their male superior attitude by saying that man is also born of woman, that "in the Lord" (spiritually), neither is independent of the other (so I think that means he was made for her too), and after all, everything ultimately comes from God—so stop making a big deal about who comes from whom, when, and why.

Paul's final refutation points on this topic are in verses 13-16:

> *Judge for yourselves: Is it proper for a woman to pray to God with her head uncovered? Does not the very nature of things teach you that if a man has long hair, it is a disgrace to him, but that if a woman has long hair, it is her glory? For long hair is given to her as a covering. If anyone wants to be contentious about this, we have no other practice—nor do the churches of God.*

Acts 18:18 says that when Paul left Corinth for Syria, he had his hair cut (possibly shaved) in Cenchrea (a short ways east of Corinth where Phoebe was from), due to a vow he had taken. (This could have been a Nazarite vow, where men didn't cut their hair until after their vow was fulfilled.) We don't know how long he had let his hair grow, but it would be strange if Paul was being dogmatic about the length of hair in this letter to the Corinthians while having different lengths himself. In addition, many godly men in Scripture had long hair. A consistent interpretation would be that Paul is basically repeating what he said above about women being able to judge for themselves and have authority over their own heads. Now he is saying they should further judge for themselves whether it's proper for a woman to pray with her head uncovered, and whether men should have long hair—but consider this; if a man has long hair (in their time) something is wrong, like he's in distress (possibly taken a vow because of the distress) perhaps he looks unkempt, and perhaps he would be considered socially unacceptable in some circles at that time when the short Roman cut was the most accepted style (all of these ideas have some sense of "disgrace"). However, a woman's long hair is glorious—her glory, not a man's.

Pointing out that her hair is *her* glory is another refutation to what was said about the woman being the man's glory. Also, her hair doubles as a covering, therefore, additional covering may not be necessary, contrary to the statement about how being uncovered is a disgrace. Again, if these statements were not a refutation of what was said above by the Corinthians, then it would seem Paul is contradicting himself.

Paul wraps it up by saying it's pointless to be contentious because 1) there's no consistent practice among the churches or 2) all the churches are practicing covering during prayer. I lean toward the first idea because he just said hair doubles as a covering and I highly doubt everyone was doing the same thing or there wouldn't be controversy. Again, it shouldn't have mattered to them and perhaps he's not giving them a rule, more like throwing out possibilities and saying they could judge for themselves, because it was a cultural practice, not a Christian practice. But I think some men were trying to make it a Christian practice. Again today, some men are trying to make it a spiritual authority/submission symbol by adding words to Scripture. Even if they aren't trying to make us wear a head covering, they point to a supposed symbol and make us feel like something is over our heads.

What matters to us now is 1) the principle that women should have authority over their own heads while both men and women should think about what is appropriate and not dishonor anyone else, and 2) the principle that we both come from each other, so don't try to attain leverage over the other.

I feel this interpretation avoids contradiction with other Scripture and avoids contradiction within the passage itself. But I could be wrong. Many theologians have tackled this passage with very little consensus, so it doesn't make sense for anyone to be dogmatic or to form a significant doctrine on it. I'm dismayed at how it has been used to dominate women when it is not at all clear. I offer these ideas to show there could be other possibilities that have a coherent interpretation.

Husbands Washing or Sanctifying Wives

There is the idea that a husband should "wash his wife in the Word" and be responsible for her spiritual life so he can present the wife to himself and to God as holy and blameless. It comes from these verses in Ephesians 5:25-33:

> *Husbands, love your wives, just as Christ loved the church and gave himself up for her to make her holy, cleansing her by the washing with water through the word, and to present her to himself as a radiant church, without stain or wrinkle or any other blemish, but holy and blameless. In this same way, husbands ought to love their wives as their own bodies. He who loves his wife loves himself. After all, no one ever hated their own body, but they feed and care for their body, just as Christ does the church—for we are members of his body. "For this reason a man will leave his father and mother and be united to his wife, and the two will become one flesh." This is a profound mystery—but I am talking about Christ and the church. However, each one of you also must love his wife as he loves himself, and the wife must respect her husband.*

I believe the part about Jesus doing the washing is a parenthetical phrase about what Jesus does, and not what husbands do. There is no other passage that indicates husbands should wash their wives in the Word or be spiritually responsible for them; in fact, there's plenty of evidence for women being responsible to God for themselves. Sanctification happens for women in the same way it happens for men. Not everything Christ did for the church is something husbands can do for wives. Therefore, we should be extremely cautious about building such an important doctrine from one passage, especially when there is an alternate interpretation. I believe it's possible that after "Husbands, love your wives, just as Christ loved the church and gave himself up for her," the rest of the sentence should be in parenthesis, specifically elaborating on what Christ did for the church, not expectations for husbands. Paul's sentences often take off on a bit of a rabbit trail.

> *Jesus washes the church, and the Holy Spirit cleanses through the Word. It is not the husband's job to try to wash the wife spiritually. Those who teach this are making an interpretive overreach.*
> Misleading Tactic #19

The cleansing happens to *both the men and women of the church by Jesus,* as Jesus loves and provides for the church. Paul tells men to love their wives, tells how Jesus loves the church (with the washing etc.), and then says, "In the same way" so now here comes the specific command to husbands to love wives as much as themselves and their own body. They don't do all the same things that Jesus did, they just love and sacrifice themselves like Jesus did, feeding and caring for her body to the same level as his own body—which is a high enough calling without having to do spiritual "washing" as well. Only Jesus can do it.

I've never forgotten after a homeschool conference one year, one of my friends whom I really looked up to, said, "I'm never going to another one of these homeschool conferences again! My husband will never be the great patriarch they glamorize, and it just makes me dissatisfied!" A year later (2013), the man who most famously taught patriarchy (founder of Vision Forum) was found to be sexually abusing the young family nanny. He had walked up to me in 1999 at a political conference in St. Louis and told me I didn't belong there and should be at home. He bragged about how he had convinced his wife to leave law school and how happy she was at home with their eight children, and I should be like her. I can't say I envy her.

A man who tries to exercise spiritual authority over his wife/partner and to the point of thinking he can "cleanse her with the Word" is grasping for an audacious level of the Holy Spirit's domain. Bad teaching has led to men overstepping in their wives' spiritual lives and to thinking that they should influence their wives, but their wives shouldn't influence them. Both should be in the Word and open to the Spirit's work.

The Weaker Vessel

Let's take a closer look at 1 Peter 3:7:

> *Husbands, in the same way be considerate as you live with your wives, and treat them with respect as the weaker partner and as heirs with you of the gracious gift of life, so that nothing will hinder your prayers.*

(The KJV and ESV use "vessel" instead of "partner" and the NASB uses "as with someone weaker.")

I've heard this used to generally portray the woman as weaker in every way possible—mentally, emotionally, spiritually, abilities including leadership, etc.

The word "weaker" in Greek is truly a comparative adjective, which means that the man is also weak, but the woman is weaker yet. It's not like "she's the weak vessel." Humility acknowledges we are all weak and need help, and we also need to help those who are (at times or in some ways) even weaker. And again, we have no reason to think this word is referring to anything other than physical weakness, which historically led to social and economic weakness. Pregnancy, childbirth, and nursing babies also leaves the woman physically vulnerable and thus weaker. Intellectual and emotional weaknesses can be induced by denying education to people (which leads to a lack of ability and confidence) and by expecting emotional frailty. People live up (or down) to the expectations of parents and community. We saw in Chapters 5 and 6 that Jesus expected much of women intellectually, spiritually, and even economically (they financially supported him) despite their culture and community.

> *A "vessel" is a metaphor for the body. In 1 Peter 3:7, Paul forbids domination based on a woman's physical weakness. Expanding the meaning of the "weaker vessel" to include intellect, emotions and spirituality has been harmful.*
> Misleading Tactic #19

The word "vessel" *skeuos* (G4632) indicates a physical implement or piece of equipment. It is a metaphor for a person's physical body. If God wanted to indicate something spiritual, emotional, or intellectual, there are plenty of other word choices. First Thessalonians 4:4 says:

> *...that each of you know how to possess his own vessel [skeuos] in sanctification and honor.*

This verse is about keeping one's body set apart and clean, not related to the strength of it. Likewise, in 2 Timothy 2:20-21 where the vessel/body can be used for wickedness, so must be "cleaned" for a higher purpose. Pots were a common implement in the first century, used for many things and easily used for metaphors. Today we have far more choices for more precise metaphors. First Peter 3:7 has to do with the strength of the body, and the other two passages have to do with the holiness of the body.

Even if the reader is not convinced that "weaker" vessel in 1 Peter 3:7 is simply physical, 2 Corinthians 12 has much to say about the value of weakness and the power of God through various weaknesses, therefore, it shouldn't be used to support the notion that God condones the dominance of one gender based on strength.

Chapter 18 covered some complicated and ambiguous passages. They should be interpreted using clear passages such as Galatians 3:28 where God does not want us to see race, status, or gender, but to consider ourselves "one in Christ."

Chapter 19:

THE CHURCH'S INFLUENCE ON HOMES

What People See at Church

If a man sees that women never speak in church on Sunday morning, are not included when decisions are made, serve in the menial tasks while men do the "important" jobs, he will get the idea that women should not have a meaningful voice in the home either. He will start to believe that the woman's contribution to the home is less important than his. He might also feel that he should not lower himself to those things but focus on the "important" things. These conclusions may not be overt or conscious, but subliminal. They will feel "right" because the spiritual leaders of the church have set the example.

If men and women see and hear frequent teaching on the authority of people when at church, they are both being conditioned to ignore abuse of power and just submit/cooperate with whatever those in power instruct. They will not ask good questions to make sure things are being run in an accountable way in their church. Following are some spiritual-sounding platitudes given to women in church which (intentionally or not) coerce them into accepting mistreatment in the home:

"Just follow your husband without fear, trust God, and God will take care of everything." (You are not responsible for speaking up if your husband is doing something foolish.)

"If your husband is doing wrong, just duck so God can smack him. If you don't duck, you'll be in God's way." (Stay quiet, submit more, and wait for God to discipline your husband even if it means you endure abuse or ruin for your family.)

"Your husband is your umbrella of protection. If you step out from under it, you are in danger of judgment, but if you stay under it, all God's judgment goes on him if he is doing wrong." (You will get zapped by God's judgment if you follow your conscience. Obedience to a sinner or a fool is more important than your God-given conscience. Two examples of Bible wives who didn't stay under their husband's "umbrella" were Abigail, wife of the fool Nabal, and Jael who killed an enemy general to whom her husband was loyal.)

"Marriage does not exist to make you happy; it exists to make you holy." (Don't hope for happiness or to be treated well, just be a martyr. The more you suffer, the more holy you will be and the more you will please God. Commands to hold a believing brother accountable are not for married women, just all other believers.)

"If you love your husband well, you will not fear him or fear submitting to him because perfect love casts out fear." (However, 1 John 4:18 is about our relationship with God. His perfect love drives out our fear of him even though he could judge us harshly. An overbearing husband does not have the kind of love which drives fear out of his wife.)

I could go on with more examples of warped advice, but I trust you get the picture. Rebecca Davis has a wonderful series of books called *Untwisting Scripture* which are a must-read. Book #2 is on Patriarchy and Authority so it's the most relevant to this topic. For more information, visit her website "Here's the Joy" at heresthejoy.com.

The Role of the Church

The church can help in three ways—example, education, and intervention.

Example

First Peter 5:1-4 says this to church leaders:

> *To the elders among you, I appeal as a fellow elder and a witness of Christ's sufferings who also will share in the glory to be revealed: Be shepherds of God's flock that is under your care, watching over them—not because you must, but because you are willing, as God wants you to be; not pursuing dishonest gain, but eager to serve; not lording it over those entrusted to you, but being examples to the flock. And when the Chief Shepherd appears, you will receive the crown of glory that will never fade away.*

So, church leaders are meant to stand in for God as shepherds and guardians of people, and as examples. Remember, people (not a brand, institution, or denomination) are the church. As such, the church should be the safest place for oppressed people to go for help, not a place which only tells them to be quiet or to do better at submitting, especially to another believer who refuses to mutually submit. Elders should be setting a fantastic example of servanthood and mutuality in their marriages.

Instead, church leaders often send the message that institutions are more important than people by teaching individuals to have no personal boundaries, and if that doesn't work, intimidation does. Allow me just two examples.

In 2023, Bill Shannon, the pastor who oversees the counseling ministry at Grace Community Church (led by John MacArthur), was removed from the list of approved counselors by the Association of Certified Biblical Counselors (ACBC).[68] The ACBC, which is the oldest and largest biblical counseling organization in the world, took this action after credible concerns were raised about GCC's counseling practices. Although GCC remains an approved training center for counseling, ACBC is investigating complaints against the megachurch regarding its counseling practices. Multiple women testified that GCC's counseling protected abusers while harming their victims. There isn't space for examples here but there are lawsuits and documented evidence of MacArthur's involvement in shocking examples at JulieRoys.com.

These tactics aren't only used against victims, but also those who try to advocate for them. Two letters were leaked from Russell Moore who, as President of the SBC Ethics and Religious Liberty Coalition (ERLC), corresponded with the members of the ERLC Board of Directors and to the SBC Convention President. The letters allege tactics of intimidation by the SBC Executive Committee (EC) to silence Moore. He also claimed the EC spewed racist and sexist garbage about victims, while bestowing an award on an SBC seminary president (Patterson) who went to great lengths to "break down" (his words) a sex-abuse victim at the seminary. Moore reluctantly left the SBC in 2021 and has since admitted that he feels he was complicit due to staying quiet in order to "protect the witness of the church." Here's a man who has felt some of the pressure that countless female victims have felt. He described it as "psychological terror."

Covering up abuse is a clear message that institutions should be protected over individuals. The years 2019 and 2020 were especially shocking with the failure of several megachurch celebrity pastors, and the revelation that the largest evangelical denomination (SBC)

68 Michael Gryboski, "Christian counseling group removes Grace Community Church pastor from approved counselors list," The Christian Post, November 1, 2023, https://www.christianpost.com/news/acbc-removes-grace-community-church-pastor-from-approved-list.html.

had covered up knowledge of the sexual abuse of over 700 women for decades. They had a secret database (which they denied) of over 500 credibly accused men in ministry, many of whom were merely transferred away from the place where they committed the abuse with no further accountability. Some of the abusers and other men involved in the coverups were former presidents, former vice presidents, and former seminary presidents and leaders.[69]

I listened to the available recordings from the ERLC during the 2019 hearings (led by Russell Moore) on the abuse coverup and it restored my faith in the SBC because the speakers were not censored. But then the outraged Executive Committee pushed Moore out. I don't think the SBC leadership is coming even close to realizing the extent of the underlying, systemic, cultural, and theological problems.

More actions in 2022, 2023, and 2024 show their real heart. For example, the aforementioned amicus brief in Kentucky. Next, they failed to fund the entity recommended by the abuse task force to maintain a database of abusers and take care of other abuse issues. Then they put great effort into forbidding women from holding the title of pastor for any ministry in local churches. I do believe that if Jesus were here, he'd be calling them whitewashed tombs. Expressed intentions can be good, but it's the attention to sincere and repentant follow-through that shows what's on the inside.

Evangelicals have an unreasonable fear of female leadership while churches collapse all over the place due to actual abusive male leadership. It's time to admit failures and truly work for restoration of those who were hurt, regardless of the fallout. Doing the right thing and trusting God with the results would set an amazing example.

69 Yonat Shimron, "Southern Baptist pastor: Minister accused of abusing a dozen boys never investigated," Religion News Service, June 15, 2021, https://religionnews.com/2021/06/15/southern-baptist-pastor-says-minister-accused-of-sexually-abusing-as-many-as-13-never-investigated/.

Education

This is an area where many churches fail (even though their intentions are good). Churches usually follow the advice found in resources of long-term organizations and best-selling authors of books that are harmful. Churches hold marriage seminars and small groups with those materials and are getting the same poor, or even more harmful, results. Churches need to become better informed about which materials are helpful and harmful. Thankfully, there are some research-based resources now which identify exactly why specific materials are harmful.

The most prolific of these new resources is the website of Shelia Wray Gregoire, sheilawraygregoire.com, which offers one-sheets on specific popular materials, identifying harmful content. Sheila and Keith (pediatrician) Gregoire authored an excellent book, *The Marriage You Want: Moving beyond Stereotypes for a Relationship Built on Scripture, New Data, and Emotional Health.* Sheila teamed up with her daughter, psychology graduate Rebecca Gregoire Lindenbach, and epidemiologist and statistician Joanna Sawatsky, to research the claims in many conservative marriage books from the last several decades. They reveal shocking delinquency by those authors for making statements that are not supported by actual studies, let alone scientific studies, instead using made-up statistics based on anecdotes or horribly unscientific surveys. Gregoire's team has had at least one of their research studies peer-reviewed and published in the journal Sociology of Religion, demonstrating the quality of their work.

Another great resource for churches and for women and children who have experienced abuse is Sarah McDugal's website at WildernesstoWild.com.

When a church decides that it will become mutualistic, education for its members on the topic is crucial. I appreciate the midweek lecture series taught by Tyler Staton to Bridgetown Church. It can be heard on two episodes of the Bridgetown Audio Podcast posted in August of 2023.

Because I've quoted Calvin several times in this book, I should add one curious clarification. Jane Dempsey Douglass has done extensive research on Calvin's writings about women. In the peer-reviewed journal, Church History[70], Douglass cites that Calvin acknowledged that Phoebe was a church leader and probably delivered the book of Romans with explanation, he acknowledged that Pricilla taught Apollos significant doctrine (not just a quick side commentary), and he acknowledged that Deborah was a spiritual leader. However, Calvin's commentaries include negative opinions such as that when God used women, it was only to shame men, and the creation order was confused in these instances.

This idea could come from Isaiah 3:12 where it says Israel will be cursed by having women and children rule over them. The metaphor is that due to their sin, they will have weak and unqualified leaders. Also, in Judges 4 when Barak asked Deborah to accompany the army and she said that if she did, the credit for the victory would go to a woman. He was fine with that, and the woman Jael put a spike into the opposing general's head. As I explained in the section on Roles in Chapter 1, men and women do have specific roles, such as men providing protection. This should not translate into men deserving shame because of a female civic or spiritual leader. The Bible does not teach that. Deborah and Jael were not weak and unqualified, nor were the other women we have mentioned. Judges 5:31 says that under Deborah the land had peace for 40 years—that's an endorsement!

Here's what I find especially curious: Douglass explains how Calvin wrote that whether women spoke in church or had public ministry was "indifferent," meaning neither necessary *nor forbidden.* Due to

---

70 Jane Dempsey Douglass, "Christian Freedom: What Calvin Learned at the School of Women," Church History 53, no. 2 (June 1984): 155–173.

societal beliefs about women, it seems this issue was not one he felt needed much attention because the probability of a women being allowed to exercise any kind of leadership was *unlikely due to cultural inequalities.*

Fast forward to the 21st century. As egalitarian views flourished in general society, the church could no longer be "indifferent," and addressing the female issue became more necessary than Calvin anticipated. Because biblical scholars agree that the Bible is very clear that both male and female are created in the image of God, it became harder for the church to defend hierarchy. In Calvin's day, hierarchy could be easily accepted by the church because society believed that women were inferior to men. Now that society knows women are not intrinsically inferior, the church's position has come under question and hierarchalists need more support from somewhere, hence the new "complementarian" construct which ironically forbids women more than Calvin did. Our Neo-Calvinist Reformed brothers need education on the fact that Calvin actually didn't believe women were forbidden by God; he believed women to be inferior so when God had to resort to using them, men should be ashamed. Perhaps it's time to try "power under" to lift others up to the level of capable partners rather than "power over."

Intervention

This one is very difficult. Church leaders don't know whether to believe the husband or wife when hearing different accounts of what is happening. They don't have experience in dealing with emotional and spiritual abuse or with psychological disorders. They have trouble calling out sin without "sin levelling" to make everyone equally responsible. An easy recourse for them (especially if the husband won't give any ground) is to fall back on more submission by wives.

Resistance to bad behavior (rather than enabling or complying) is a biblical principle. However, there are ungodly, sinful ways of resistance such as retaliating in kind with similar bad behaviors. There are godly, non-sinful ways to resist such as correctly practicing boundaries including removing oneself from the offender's presence. Matthew 5:39 is poorly translated in several versions, portraying Jesus as saying, "Do not resist an evil person." The context and correct translation are, "Do not *retaliate*" which means, "don't behave badly likewise." That is far different from not resisting evil, which implies that if you see someone committing a wrong, you shouldn't even get in their way, let alone attempt to stop them by nonviolent means. Many Bible passages teach resisting the bad behavior of a fellow believer. Scripture also teaches advocacy (nonviolent) for those who are helpless. This article by a Hebrew scholar explains why the translation "do not resist" is poor, and "do not retaliate" is better: jerusalemperspective.com/2699/.

> *A poor translation of Matthew 5:39 portrays Jesus as saying "Do not resist an evil person" rather than "Do not retaliate against an evil person." Godly resistance against bad behavior is a biblical principle.*
> Misleading Tactic #2

The term "Biblical Counseling" is frequently misused to employ various forms of spiritual abuse using the inaccurate interpretations which are called out in this book. It is often used to disparage even Christian, professionally trained counselors as being "unbiblical" if they don't employ the same inaccurate interpretations. It is usually not helpful to confront dysfunctional marital behavior with a pastor who is untrained in professional counseling. If a pastor feels inadequate or the couple doesn't feel that meeting with the pastor is helpful, the pastor should refer them to a professional Christian counselor and receive permission from the couple to get updates from the counselor so that appropriate church action can take place. Counseling privacy is a hindrance to the church being able to understand the truth of a situation and to respond in a helpful way.

Jesus described vulnerable sheep as being harassed (Matthew 9:36) without a shepherd to beat the wolf away. This is a good illustration of emotional abuse. Just because there aren't physical signs of abuse doesn't mean intervention isn't necessary. When there is frequent, toxic strife, then separation with the goal of restoration could be helpful, could save a life, or save the marriage. When Paul says "a woman should not leave her husband, but if she does..." (1 Corinthians 7:11) he is acknowledging that sometimes it's necessary. Church leaders are often in too big of a hurry for reunification before there is adequate healing and growth.

Parents are shepherds to their children. I've heard praise for women who never left their husbands in spite of abuse. Sadly, that meant they kept their children in an environment of verbal and physical abuse, so failed to protect them. Were they too afraid for their own financial security? Were they not able to trust God to take care of them and their children by leaving the abuser? What does it mean to "do what is right and do not give way to fear"? Were they afraid of the church excommunicating them and losing any supportive community, perhaps even losing the approval and support of God? That is not praiseworthy or good shepherding by the mothers or the church.

Too many pastors have such an emphasis on "saving the marriage" that it communicates the marriage must be saved at all costs, even the sanity and safety of the wife. They feel that if they just get the couple reunited, they are successful. That is not caring well for the sheep. Although every pastor would love to help with reconciliation, they need to be careful to not get in over their head and cause more damage. Something else to remember is Jesus's words in Mark 2:27 about how the Sabbath was made for mankind, not mankind made for the Sabbath. In the same way, I believe marriage was made for people, not people made for marriage. The elevation of the institution of marriage regardless of how dysfunctional it is, can be idolatrous.

The church has great influence on homes and needs to take care that there are not unintended, harmful consequences to its teaching on marriage.

CONCLUSION

What to Do Next

Now that you know what you were never told before, what is next?

- Be free. If you are a woman who has felt inhibited by complementarianism, who has felt confused by why God would give you or another woman leadership abilities but then tell her to be quiet, who longs for partnerships, who has felt that somehow God loves you less than men – be free! Be free to say what God puts on your heart, with graciousness of course, but with the same courage and conviction that any man would say it. Be free to dream and let God use you in big and small ways that you didn't feel free to dream about before. Be free to embrace the role of "pastor," to recognize you are a shepherd of those whom God has given to you to disciple.

- Take a hermeneutics course to blow open your personal reading of the Word. Seminaries like Bethel in St. Paul, Minnesota have a program called "Seminary for Everyone" where you can take online courses with or without credit, but everyone needs to take Hermeneutics to gain the curiosity and tools to look deeper in the text.

- If you are a man who has not understood the gender issue well, ask God to show you what to do with this information. Consider how complementarian teaching may have harmed you, your relationships, and your church. Consider asking the women in your life if there's anything you can do to advocate for them. Most people don't understand how spiritual abuse harms us to our very core, affects our spiritual formation, affect our view of God, and interfere with a woman's belief that God values her. Affirmation from men is very helpful.

- Emphasize unity. There are people who believe that talking about this issue is divisive. Be clear that you are not trying to cause division, you are advocating for more unity. Mutual respect and partnership promote unity by eliminating the awkwardness and reasons to divide that were illustrated in the stories at the very beginning of this book. Andrew Bartlett, author of *Men and Women in Christ: Fresh Light from the Biblical Texts*, says that teaching "manhood" and "womanhood" is a distraction – just teach Christhood! All these gender-divided classes and Bible studies in the church may be good for same-gender fellowship, but we might be taking it too far if we want healthy unity and recognition of our similarities more than our differences. Aimee Byrd's book, *Why Can't We Be Friends?: Avoidance Is Not Purity,* discusses the fear in our relationships as we treat each other primarily as threats to our purity, rather than as brothers and sisters in Christ.

- Learn what the Bible has to say about women well enough to be able to defend the mutualist position. Read and reread until you know it well enough to speak knowledgeably to others. Always speak graciously and don't waste your time arguing with people who are hostile about the subject. If it starts feeling like an uncomfortable debate with interruptions or dismissive statements, say something like, "I sense that you are uncomfortable with this topic. I'd be glad to talk with you about the biblical support for mutualism if ever you feel like we can do it without getting upset."

- Support authors and speakers who are developing good research and materials. Promote their materials and attend their events. They have invested valuable time and resources and are in need of your support. A good place to find excellent resources is CBE International (Christians for Biblical Equality) cbeinternational.org.

- Find advocates. Ask friends to read mutualist materials and discuss it with you. Be on the lookout for women who could present the evidence to their husbands without suffering consequences. Find men who are willing to consider the mutualism position. Ask them to be an advocate.

- Find a church or fellowship in your area which is of your particular faith practice persuasion and is also mutualist and consider attending there. If there are none, investigate other denominations and consider changing. (See my website for information.)

- Before leaving your current church, provide your leadership with biblically supported mutualist materials and request that they read it. If after a reasonable amount of time, they don't take you seriously, give everyone in your leadership a friendly and respectful farewell with the reason for your departure.

- Beware of ministries that say they give equal opportunities to women but those in charge are personally complementarian, because there will still be a glass ceiling. Many ministries have been changing their 501c3 status to become a "church" because they are afraid of being told they must hire people who don't agree with them doctrinally. (Some also do it because churches are not required to file an annual Form 990 with the IRS so there is less financial accountability.) Then, because they are a "church," they practice the prohibitions that the complementarian leaders believe are in 1 Timothy chapters 2 and 3. For example, they hold regular church or chapel "services" and only invite men to speak, exclude women in certain activities or spiritual decision making, act superior in meetings, make department titles for women nonequivalent to the men in other departments, etc.

- Consider leading a microchurch. The last several years have been rough for the church with all the exposure of corruption and abuse. Could it be that God is about to free women to humbly lead countless microchurches but there needed to be some housecleaning first? Perhaps you cannot find a church in your area that is evangelical and mutualist, so perhaps God would lead you to start one. (Disclaimer: I believe megachurches are a bad idea, but mid-size and small churches have their place as well as microchurches—my favorite. Diversity is good!)

In Closing

I'm dismayed that I was under the teaching of seminary graduates all my life and never heard 98% of the points in this book. The two points I did hear were told to me privately and not spoken from the pulpit. There is great resistance to this truth. Why else would men study everything else in Scripture so diligently, with libraries of books covering every possible nuance of every conceivable biblical topic, but most of them have never studied the role of women any further than accepting the superficial appearance of a few odd passages? I do not doubt this book will need some edits in the future—corrections and additions, but I've seen enough evidence of misleading tactics to be convinced that the enemy has been sidelining women as a way to attack the effectiveness of the church and marriages. This tactic also maligns the character of God, making it appear that "authority" is more important to God than servanthood, and causes people to miss God's amazing example.

I want to say that I am impressed with and grateful for the men I know who are affirming advocates for women, some at great personal cost. It takes great strength to be humble and I have been deeply moved by the men who display such strength, even to ask their wives, "How am I doing?"

If there is only one thing you remember from this book, let it be that the Lord of the universe has every right to boss us like a lord, but instead, God raises our status to friend, business partner, and co-ruler! (John 15:9-17; Ephesians 2:6; and Revelation 3:21) That is the example we must follow. We love and serve God by loving, serving, and elevating our sisters and brothers in Christ. Blessings on you, dear reader, as you experience God's love, grace and truth. Pass it on!

SPECIAL ENDORSEMENT

I wish to give special endorsement to Margaret Mowczko's articles at https://margmowczko.com. The benefit of a blog website is that one can continue to add new information based on one's own research and on new discoveries and scholarship by others. A book like mine isn't infinitely editable. The quality of the scholarship on this website is impressive. I could not have written this book without her resources. Marg would probably not agree with everything I've written and I still have much to learn from her work. Also, her writing is less confrontational. Her stated purpose is to stimulate conversation, but her work has allowed me to discern where discrepancies lie in the English translations and commentaries we read today. That discernment helped me to more clearly state misleading tactics.